Reading Drills

Jamestown's Reading Improvement

Edward B. Fry Ph.D.

JAMESTOWN PUBLISHERS

a division of NTC/CONTEMPORARY PUBLISHING GROUP
Lincolnwood, Illinois USA

Cover Design: Lightbourne

ISBN: 0-8092-0360-X
Published by Jamestown Publishers,
a division of NTC/Contemporary Publishing Group, Inc.,
4255 West Touhy Avenue,
Lincolnwood (Chicago), Illinois 60712-1975 U.S.A.
© 2000 by NTC/Contemporary Publishing Group, Inc.

Manufactured in the United States of America.

9 10 11 12 13 14 15 021 09 08 07 06 05

Acknowledgments

Acknowledgment is gratefully made to the following publishers, authors, and agents for permission to reprint these works. Every effort has been made to determine copyright owners. In the case of any omissions, the Publisher will be pleased to make suitable acknowledgments in future editions.

"A Day's Wait" reprinted with the permission of Scribner, a division of Simon & Schuster, Inc. from *The Short Stories of Ernest Hemingway* by Ernest Hemingway. Copyright © 1933 by Charles Scribner's Sons. Copyright renewed 1961 by Mary Hemingway.

"Mines in the Sky" from "Mines in the Sky Promise Riches, a Greener Earth" by William K. Hartmann. Published in *Smithsonian* magazine, September 1982. Reprinted by permission of the author.

"Letter to Susan" by Margaret Culkin Banning. Copyright 1934 by Margaret Culkin Banning. Copyright renewed © 1962 by Margaret Culkin Banning. Reprinted by permission of Brandt & Brandt Literary Agents, Inc.

"All Creatures Great and Small" from *All Creatures Great and Small* by James Herriot. Published by St. Martin's Press, New York. Additional rights granted by Harold Ober Associates, Inc.

"Battle Tactics" from *The Dog Who Wouldn't Be* by Farley Mowat. Copyright (c) 1957 by Farley Mowat, Ltd; copyright © renewed 1985 by Farley Mowat Ltd. By permission of Little, Brown and Company (Inc.) and McClelland & Stewart, Inc. The Canadian Publishers.

"Watership Down." Reprinted with the permission of Scribner, a Division of Simon & Schuster, Inc. from *Watership Down* by Richard Adams. Copyright © 1972 by Richard Adams.

"How the Weather Works," by Ron Kotulak, *Chicago Tribune*, November 30, 1980. © Copyrighted Chicago Tribune Company. All rights reserved. Used with permission.

"The Martínez Family" from *Five Families: Mexican Case Studies in the Culture of Poverty* by Oscar Lewis. Copyright © 1959 by Basic Books, Inc. Copyright renewed 1987 by Ruth Lewis. Reprinted by permission of Basic Books, a member of Perseus Books, L.L.C.

"The Yellow Emperor" reprinted from *Dragons, Gods & Spirits from Chinese Mythology* by Tao Tao Liu Sanders. © 1980 by Eurobook Limited. Used with permission of Peter Bedrick Books.

"Ishi, the Last Yahi" from *A Proud Nation* by Ernest R. May. Copyright © 1989 by McDougal, Littell, Inc. All rights reserved. Reprinted by permission of McDougal, Littell, Inc.

"Just Like Bernard Shaw" from *The Lord God Made Them All* by James Herriot. Copyright © 1981 by James Herriot. Published by St. Martin's Press, New York.

"The Medieval Castle" reprinted from *A Medieval Castle* by Fiona Macdonald. © 1990 by The Salariva Book Co. Used with permission of Peter Bedrick Books.

"A Dying Art" reprinted from *More Six-Minute Mysteries* by Don Wulffson. © 1995 by RGA Publishing Group, Inc. Used with permission of NTC/Contemporary Publishing Group, Inc.

"Days of Valor" reprinted with the permission of Simon & Schuster, Inc. from *Pioneer Women* by Joanna L. Stratton. Copyright © 1981 by Joanna L. Stratton.

"The Pigman" from *The Pigman* by Paul Zindel. Copyright © 1968 by Paul Zindel. Used by permission of HarperCollins Publishers.

"The Wall" from "The Wall: A Memorial Brings Americans Together" by Scott C. Ingram. Special permission granted, *Read* magazine, copyright 1987, published by Weekly Reader Corporation. All rights reserved.

"University Days" from *My Life and Hard Times* by James Thurber. Copyright © 1933, 1961 by James Thurber. Published by Harper & Row, Publishers, Inc. Reprinted by permission of Rosemary A. Thurber.

"My Family and Other Animals" from *My Family and Other Animals* by Gerald Durrell. Copyright © 1957, renewed © 1985 by Gerald Durrell. Published by Viking Penguin, Inc.

"Points of Origin" by Michael Olmert. Published in *Smithsonian* magazine, January 1983.

"The World of the Gods" reprinted from *Gods, Men & Monsters from the Greek Myths* by Michael Gibson. © 1977 by Eurobook Limited. Used with permission of Peter Bedrick Books.

Contents

To the Student

You probably talk at an average rate of 150 words a minute. But if you are a reader of average ability, you read at the rate of 250 words a minute. So your reading speed is already nearly twice as fast as your speaking or listening speed. This example shows that reading is one of the fastest ways to put verbal information into your mind.

The following chart illustrates what an increase in reading speed can do for you. It shows the number of books read over a period of 10 years by various types of readers. Compare the number of books read by a slow reader and the number read by a fast reader.

Reading Drills is for students who want to read faster and with greater understanding. By completing the 30 lessons—reading the selections and doing the exercises—you will certainly increase your reading speed, improve your reading comprehension, and sharpen your critical-thinking skills.

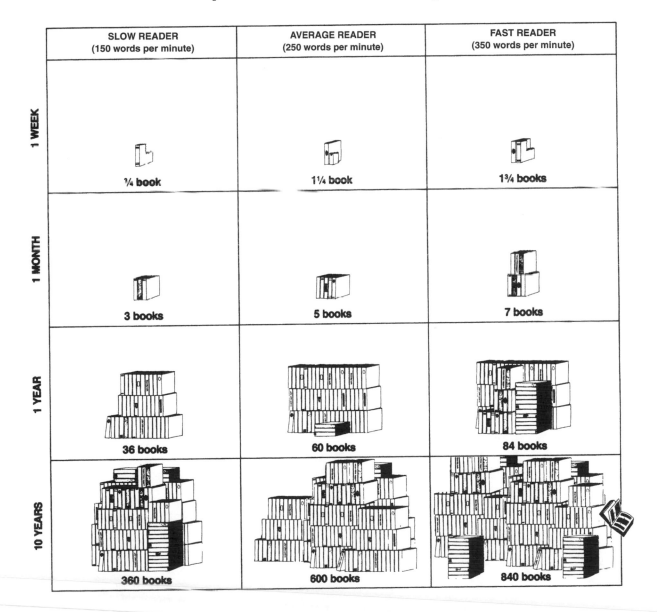

	SLOW READER (150 words per minute)	AVERAGE READER (250 words per minute)	FAST READER (350 words per minute)
1 WEEK	¾ book	1¼ book	1¾ books
1 MONTH	3 books	5 books	7 books
1 YEAR	36 books	60 books	84 books
10 YEARS	360 books	600 books	840 books

How to Use This Book

About the Book

Reading Drills, Advanced Level contains 30 lessons. Each lesson begins with a fiction or nonfiction reading selection. The lesson also includes exercises in reading comprehension, critical thinking, and vocabulary, as well as personal response questions. The reading comprehension and vocabulary exercises help you understand the selection. The critical-thinking exercises help you reflect on what you have read and how the material relates to your own experience. At the end of the lesson, the personal response questions give you the opportunity to respond to various aspects of the story or article.

The Sample Lesson

The first lesson in the book is a sample lesson that your class or group will work through together. It helps you understand how the lessons are organized. The sample lesson explains how to complete the exercises and score your answers. Sample answers and scores are printed in lighter type. If you have any questions about completing the exercises or scoring them, this is the time to get the answers.

Working Through Each Lesson

1. Begin each lesson by reading the introduction. It prepares you to read the selection. As you read the selection itself, you are timed. Either you or your teacher will set a timer when you begin reading the selection. When you finish reading, record your time on the Reading Time line in the box at the end of the selection. Then find your reading speed on the Words-per-Minute table on pages 162–163 and record it on the Reading Speed line in the box. Finally, record your speed on the Reading Speed graph at the end of the book. Keeping track of your reading speed will help you monitor your progress.

2. Next complete the exercises. The directions for each exercise tell you how to mark your answers. When you have completed all four exercises, use the answer key provided by your teacher to check your work. Record your scores after each exercise. Then fill in your scores on the appropriate progress graphs at the back of the book. Your teacher will help you interpret your progress on the graphs.

3. Check your progress. To get the most benefit from working through these lessons, you need to take charge of your own progress in improving your comprehension, critical-thinking, and vocabulary skills. The graphs and charts help you keep track of your progress, but you need to study them from time to time to see whether your progress is satisfactory or whether you need additional work on some skills. The How Am I Doing? questions on pages 168–170 provide guidelines to help you assess your progress and determine what types of exercises you are having difficulty with.

Lessons

Sample Beneath the Rubble

From every disaster one or more stories of great courage and heroism often emerge. One such story came out of the disaster that struck Northridge, California, early one January morning.

In California, people live in fear of the Big One—a massive earthquake along the San Andreas fault that will take thousands, if not tens of thousands, of lives. While they are waiting for the Big One, however, Californians have experienced plenty of Small Ones. Even these small earthquakes have managed to decimate whole regions.

On January 17, 1994, a "small" earthquake, showing 6.8 on the Richter scale, hit Northridge, California. (The Richter scale is used to measure the ground motion during an earthquake. The largest recorded quake hit Japan in 1933. It measured 8.9 on the Richter scale.) The Northridge quake lasted just 30 seconds. It hit in the early morning, when most people were in bed sleeping. At 4:30 A.M. all was peaceful and quiet. Less than a minute later, however, the region around Northridge, a suburb of Los Angeles, looked as if it had just been bombed. Highways had ruptured and split in two. Downed power lines had plunged more than three million people into darkness. Broken gas and oil lines caused countless fires. And a total of 61 people died during the quake or later as a result of injuries caused by the quake.

It was in the wake of this disaster that a heroic rescue took place. The rescue centered around Salvador Pena, who had left his native El Salvador 12 years earlier to escape a civil war and start a new life in the United States. Pena worked two jobs to support his wife and five children. During the day he worked as a janitor at a local college, and at night he ran a street sweeper at the Northridge Fashion Plaza.

At 4:30 A.M. on January 17, Pena was driving his power sweeper on the lower level of the mall's three-story parking garage. When the earthquake struck, the garage began to shake violently, and Pena realized that he had no time to escape. "It happened so fast, I wasn't able to do anything," he said later. "I put myself in God's hands." Within seconds, the parking garage crumbled like a house of cards, trapping Pena—still inside his sweeper—beneath 20 tons of concrete.

The search for survivors began right away. Firefighters and paramedics soon found Pena, but then faced the monumental task of getting him out. Rescuers managed to dig a passageway to him, but this tunnel was unstable at best and was studded with chunks of concrete and twisted ribbons of metal. When firefighter Vincent Jenkins crawled through it the first time, he could see only Pena's upper body. As the rescue work proceeded, Jenkins crawled through the tunnel again and again, bringing encouragement and comfort to the trapped man. Pena, for his part, never lost consciousness or his faith in God. At one point he even asked his rescuers to pray with him. Although he feared death was near, Pena later said he refused to give up the struggle to live because he felt that his family would not survive without his support. "I've always fought to give them food," he said, "give them a little strength to sustain themselves."

The rescuers couldn't just pull Pena out because his legs were pinned beneath the rubble. They had to use jackhammers to clear away the loose debris in the tunnel, and then they had to drill holes into the concrete that was resting on top of the sweeper. These holes allowed the paramedics to pump oxygen in to Pena. The holes also allowed the rescuers to slip four plastic air bags into the space around Pena. Then rescuers inflated the bags, lifting the concrete off Pena's legs. To get him out of the sweeper, the rescuers had to cut off the roof of the vehicle, its door, and its entire dashboard. Only then could the rescuers free him. "He was pinned between two beams," said Jenkins, "and they had to lift in unison to free him."

The whole rescue was covered on television, and a large crowd had gathered at the site. Everyone cheered when, after eight hours, Salvador Pena at last appeared on a stretcher from beneath the rubble. His body was broken and bloodied, but he was still alive. Pena was quickly placed on a rescue helicopter and rushed to the UCLA Medical Center.

But Pena was not out of danger yet. He had suffered a partially dislocated spine. Also, doctors feared that they might have to amputate his crushed right hand, as well as both his legs. Five surgeons labored for five hours on Pena's injured limbs, making almost a dozen inch-long incisions to relieve swelling and reduce pressure. Luckily, they were successful and Pena was soon on the mend.

Despite his painful ordeal, Pena remained optimistic, even sunny, as his body healed. He poured out praise for the many people who had played a role in saving his life. Doctor Michael J. Zinner said, "He's just remarkable—bright and responsive. He's a wonderfully courageous man who is extremely lucky to be alive."

In another sense, the whole Northridge region was lucky. The earthquake happened so early in the day that most people were home rather than in vulnerable places such as the Northridge Fashion Plaza. "If this had happened during daylight hours," said Doctor Zinner, "there would have been hundreds of Mr. Penas and not much we could do for them." And keep in mind, the Northridge earthquake was just a "Small One." What if the next earthquake to strike is the Big One? ■

✔ Enter your reading time below. Then look up your reading speed on the Words-per-Minute table on page 162.

Reading Time _____

Reading Speed _____

Enter your reading speed on the Reading Speed graph on page 164.

Comprehension

Put an ✗ in the box next to the correct answer for each question or statement. Do not look back at the selection.

1. Northridge is a suburb of
   - ☐ a. San Francisco.
   - ☒ b. Los Angeles.
   - ☐ c. San Diego.
   - ☐ d. Oakland.

2. The Richter scale is used to measure the
   - ☒ a. ground motion during an earthquake.
   - ☐ b. number of aftershocks following an earthquake.
   - ☐ c. amount of damage caused by an earthquake.
   - ☐ d. temperature changes during an earthquake.

3. The largest recorded earthquake took place in
   - ☐ a. Mexico.
   - ☐ b. Hawaii.
   - ☒ c. Japan.
   - ☐ d. Oregon.

4. Salvador Pena moved to the United States from
   - ☐ a. Guatemala.
   - ☐ b. Mexico.
   - ☒ c. El Salvador.
   - ☐ d. Puerto Rico.

5. At what time did the earthquake strike Northridge?
- [ ] a. 4:30 P.M.
- [ ] b. 12:00 A.M.
- [ ] c. 12:00 P.M.
- [x] d. 4:30 A.M.

6. At the time the earthquake struck, Salvador Pena was working at his job as a
- [x] a. street sweeper.
- [ ] b. janitor.
- [ ] c. night watchman.
- [ ] d. bus driver.

7. How long did it take to rescue Pena?
- [ ] a. 1 hour
- [x] b. 8 hours
- [ ] c. 12 hours
- [ ] d. 24 hours

8. After his rescue, Pena was rushed to the
- [ ] a. Northridge Medical Clinic.
- [ ] b. Los Angeles General Hospital.
- [ ] c. U.S. Army Base Hospital.
- [x] d. UCLA Medical Center.

9. At first, doctors feared they might have to amputate Pena's
- [x] a. right hand.
- [ ] b. right leg.
- [ ] c. left leg.
- [ ] d. right foot.

10. The Northridge earthquake was considered to be
- [ ] a. the Big One.
- [x] b. a small one.
- [ ] c. a large one.
- [ ] d. an unusual one.

✎ ____10____ **Number of correct answers**
Enter this number on the Comprehension graph on page 165.

Critical Thinking

Put an **X** in the box next to the best answer for each question or statement. You may look back at the selection if you'd like.

1. The main purpose of the first paragraph of the selection is to
- [ ] a. inform you that people in California are afraid of earthquakes.
- [ ] b. warn people that a massive earthquake along the San Andreas fault could take many thousands of lives.
- [ ] c. point out that even small earthquakes can cause great damage.
- [x] d. identify the setting and the topic of the selection.

2. Which of the following statements best expresses the main idea of the selection?
- [ ] a. When an earthquake strikes, the efficiency of emergency crews is put to the test.
- [ ] b. Salvador Pena was running a street sweeper in the parking garage of the Northridge Fashion Plaza when an earthquake that measured 6.8 on the Richter scale struck.
- [x] c. Showing persistence and courage, workers rescued a man who had been pinned under the rubble of an earthquake in Northridge, California.
- [ ] d. A small earthquake demolished a shopping plaza in Northridge, California, pinning a man under the plaza's rubble.

3. Based on the selection, you can conclude that
- [ ] a. Californians are needlessly worried about earthquakes.
- [x] b. most people feel happy and relieved when someone, even a stranger, is rescued.
- [ ] c. small earthquakes seldom if ever cause very serious damage.
- [ ] d. large earthquakes generally occur only in California.

4. Based on what you've read, you can predict that
   - ☒ a. more earthquakes will occur in California.
   - ☐ b. only small earthquakes will occur in California.
   - ☐ c. having had one earthquake, Northridge, California, will not likely have another.
   - ☐ d. thousands of people will move away from California because of fear of earthquakes.

5. As a result of the earthquake striking Northridge at 4:30 A.M.,
   - ☐ a. rescue crews were slow to respond.
   - ☐ b. darkness greatly hindered rescue efforts.
   - ☐ c. there was little damage to buildings there.
   - ☒ d. hundreds of lives were saved.

6. Which of the following is a statement of opinion rather than fact?
   - ☒ a. "He's a wonderfully courageous man who is extremely lucky to be alive."
   - ☐ b. The whole rescue was covered on television, and a large crowd gathered at the site.
   - ☐ c. Broken gas and oil lines caused countless fires.
   - ☐ d. Pena was quickly placed on a rescue helicopter and rushed to the UCLA Medical Center.

7. Which event happened first?
   - ☒ a. The largest recorded earthquake hit Japan.
   - ☐ b. An earthquake hit Northridge, California.
   - ☐ c. Salvador Pena left his native El Salvador.
   - ☐ d. Salvador Pena was rescued from the rubble of the Northridge Fashion Plaza.

8. Which of the following does *not* fit with the other three?
   - ☐ a. Doctor Zinner
   - ☐ b. Vincent Jenkins
   - ☒ c. Richter scale
   - ☐ d. Salvador Pena

9. Compared to the earthquake in Japan in 1933, the earthquake in Northridge, California was
   - ☒ a. less severe.
   - ☐ b. more severe.
   - ☐ c. of about equal severity.
   - ☐ d. of longer duration.

10. Choose the best one-sentence paraphrase for the following sentence from the selection: "Downed power lines had plunged more than three million people into darkness."
   - ☐ a. More than three million people could not see the downed power lines because of the darkness.
   - ☒ b. More than three million people were affected by a power outage caused by downed power lines.
   - ☐ c. More than three million people reported that the downed power lines created a strange darkness on the day of the earthquake.
   - ☐ d. More than three million people complained to the power company that they had no electric power because of downed power lines.

✎ _____10_____ **Number of correct answers**
Enter this number on the Critical Thinking graph on page 166.

Vocabulary

Each numbered sentence contains an underlined word or phrase from the selection. Following are four definitions. Put an ✘ in the box next to the best meaning of the word or phrase as it is used in the sentence.

1. Even these small earthquakes have managed to <u>decimate</u> whole regions.
   - ☒ a. destroy
   - ☐ b. rebuild
   - ☐ c. disturb
   - ☐ d. surprise

2. Downed power lines had <u>plunged</u> more than three million people into darkness.
   - ☐ a. dived into
   - ☐ b. forcibly thrown
   - ☒ c. brought suddenly
   - ☐ d. rushed forward

3. Firefighters and paramedics faced the <u>monumental</u> task of getting him out.
   - ☐ a. insignificant
   - ☒ b. extremely difficult
   - ☐ c. impossible
   - ☐ d. annoying

4. Rescuers managed to dig a passageway to him, but this tunnel was <u>unstable</u> at best.
   - ☐ a. not complete
   - ☐ b. steady
   - ☐ c. unbroken
   - ☒ d. not firm

5. "I've always fought to give them food, give them a little strength to <u>sustain</u> themselves."
   - ☐ a. improve
   - ☐ b. understand
   - ☐ c. slow down
   - ☒ d. keep going

6. Then rescuers <u>inflated</u> the bags.
   - ☐ a. properly placed
   - ☐ b. laid out
   - ☐ c. released
   - ☒ d. filled with air

7. "He was pinned between two beams, and they had to lift <u>in unison</u> to free him."
   - ☐ a. energetically
   - ☐ b. one after the other
   - ☒ c. all together
   - ☐ d. straight up

8. He had suffered a partially <u>dislocated</u> spine.
   - ☒ a. put out of place
   - ☐ b. separated
   - ☐ c. cracked
   - ☐ d. immovable

9. Despite his painful ordeal, Pena remained <u>optimistic</u>, even sunny, as his body healed.
   - ☐ a. continually depressed
   - ☐ b. childlike
   - ☒ c. always cheerful
   - ☐ d. comfortable

10. The earthquake happened so early in the day that most people were home rather than in <u>vulnerable</u> places.
    - ☐ a. popular
    - ☐ b. abandoned
    - ☒ c. unprotected
    - ☐ d. safe

✎ ____10____ **Number of correct answers**
Enter this number on the Vocabulary graph on page 167.

Personal Response

What do you want to know about earthquakes that you don't already know?

[Explain what information you would like to learn about earthquakes.]

1 | The Tomb of King Tut

by Henry and Melissa Billings

This selection tells about one of the greatest archaeological discoveries in history. But was this great discovery cursed, as some people have believed?

On November 4, 1922, archaeologist Howard Carter dragged himself out of bed. Would it be another day of failure in the choking dust and searing heat of Egypt's Valley of the Kings? For 15 years Carter had been searching for the tomb of King Tutankhamen, often called simply King Tut. If he didn't find it soon, he might have to give up.

Luckily, however, this day would be different. The workers, who had begun digging earlier that morning, had found something. It was a stone step about six feet long. Carter knew almost immediately that it was part of a sunken staircase. Did it lead to King Tut's tomb? Carter took that day and the next to dig—carefully and slowly—down to the 12th step. There he found a doorway. The seals on the outer door, made 3,000 years earlier, proved it was a royal tomb and that its contents were intact.

Excitedly, Carter sent an urgent telegram to his financial backer and partner, Lord Carnarvon, who was in England. "At last have made wonderful discovery in Valley. Congratulations," he wrote. Carter knew that Carnarvon would want to share in the thrill of opening and entering the tomb. So he covered the stairway with dirt again to protect the tomb from thieves and waited for Lord Carnarvon's arrival.

Eighteen days later Lord Carnarvon arrived from England. The two men began uncovering the stairway once more. On November 25, they reached the outer door of the tomb. The next day they arrived at the inner door. "Feverishly," Carter later wrote, "we cleared away the remaining last scraps of rubbish on the floor of the passage before the doorway." They then saw the royal seal of Tutankhamen pressed into the plaster. There was no mistake—this was it! Carter's years of toil and failure had turned into triumph. "The day of days," were the words Carter used to describe this moment, "the most wonderful that I have ever lived through."

Fighting to control his excitement, Carter used a knife to make a small hole in the top of the door. He took a lighted candle and peered inside. "At first I could see nothing . . . , but presently, as my eyes grew accustomed to the light, details of the room emerged slowly from the mist, strange animals, statues and gold—everywhere the glint of gold."

Carter stood in awed silence. "For the moment—an eternity it must have seemed to the others standing by—I was struck dumb with amazement."

Lord Carnarvon, unable to stand the suspense any longer, called out from behind Carter, "Can you see anything?"

"Yes, it is wonderful," was all Carter could say. Howard Carter had unearthed the greatest treasure ever found in Egypt. The four rock-hewn rooms held more than 5,000 objects. It took Carter two months to reach the highlight of his discovery—the burial room. There he found a solid 22-carat gold coffin weighing 2,448 pounds. He also found what is now the most famous item in the tomb—the extraordinary golden mask which covered King Tut's mummified head.

As was the custom in his day, King Tutankhamen had been buried with everything he might need to make him happy in the afterlife. His tomb was crammed with games, lamps, boats, jars of honey, flowers, statues of gods and goddesses, bows and arrows, baskets, jewels, clothes, and chairs. The tomb also contained two golden chariots which were so large they had to be taken apart to fit into the tomb. He was even buried with a lock of his grandmother's hair. Carter wrote, "So crowded [was the tomb] that it was a matter of extreme difficulty to move one [precious item] without running serious risk of damaging others." Searchers worked patiently and carefully for 10 years to excavate the entire tomb. The contents of the tomb are now on display at the Egyptian Museum in Cairo.

While other pharaohs had similar tombs, these other resting places had all been robbed eons ago. King Tut's was the only tomb that was left almost completely untouched.

Why was this tomb left alone? One theory is that King Tutankhamen was only a minor figure in Egyptian history. He came to the throne in 1352 B.C. and died nine years later at the age of 18. Perhaps big-time grave robbers passed over his tomb for the riches of more tempting targets. Or perhaps his underground tomb was too well covered to be noticed. After all, the tomb of another pharaoh, Ramses VI, was built right next door just 200 years later. During the building of Ramses's tomb, workers lived in huts erected over King Tut's tomb. The huts later fell to rubble, obscuring King Tut's burial site. In addition, much of the dirt for Ramses's tomb was dumped on the entrance to Tut's tomb.

When Carter began his excavation of Tut's tomb, some people proclaimed that breaking into it would bring bad luck. Dire inscriptions etched on the tomb warned that anyone who disturbed the king's tomb would be punished. The newspapers in London dubbed the warning "The Curse of the Pharaoh." And in fact, barely six weeks after the discovery of Tutankhamen's tomb, Lord Carnarvon died. He died from a mosquito bite which caused a blood infection. There's more. During the night Carnarvon lay dying in Cairo, the city went black from a mysterious power failure. At the same time, back in London, Carnarvon's dog gave a weird howl and then rolled over dead. Over the years, there were other deaths and suicides among people linked to the tomb.

Still, Howard Carter himself said that the "curse" was nonsense. If anyone was going to be

cursed, he figured, it should have been him. But the great archaeologist died of natural causes at the age of 64 at his home in London on March 2, 1939. ■

✔ Enter your reading time below. Then look up your reading speed on the Words-per-Minute table on page 162.

Reading Time   _____

Reading Speed   _____

Enter your reading speed on the Reading Speed graph on page 164.

Comprehension

Put an **X** in the box next to the correct answer for each question or statement. Do not look back at the selection.

1. Howard Carter had searched for the tomb of King Tutankhamen for
   - ☐ a. 6 years.
   - ☐ b. 10 years.
   - ☐ c. 15 years.
   - ☐ d. 21 years.

2. Who was Lord Carnarvon?
   - ☐ a. an official of the British government
   - ☐ b. an English archaeologist
   - ☐ c. Howard Carter's supervisor
   - ☐ d. Howard Carter's financial backer

3. The door of Tut's tomb was decorated with
   - ☐ a. pictures of gods and goddesses.
   - ☐ b. jewels.
   - ☐ c. the royal seal.
   - ☐ d. gold letters.

4. What was the most famous item in the tomb?
   - ☐ a. a golden chariot
   - ☐ b. the pharaoh's boat
   - ☐ c. a golden mask
   - ☐ d. a lock of King Tut's grandmother's hair

5. How long did it take to excavate the tomb?
   - ☐ a. 6 months
   - ☐ b. 2 years
   - ☐ c. 5 years
   - ☐ d. 10 years

6. Where are most items from the tomb on display ?
   - ☐ a. Egyptian Museum in Cairo.
   - ☐ b. British Museum in London.
   - ☐ c. Field Museum of Natural History in Chicago.
   - ☐ d. Smithsonian Institution in Washington, D.C.

7. Why was King Tut's tomb left untouched by grave robbers?
   - ☐ a. Thieves were probably frightened away.
   - ☐ b. Thieves could not find the tomb.
   - ☐ c. The tomb was heavily guarded.
   - ☐ d. "The Curse of the Pharaoh" killed all those that tried to rob it.

8. King Tut died at the age of
   - ☐ a. 9.
   - ☐ b. 18.
   - ☐ c. 31.
   - ☐ d. 64.

9. The tomb of the pharaoh Ramses VI was built
   - ☐ a. 200 years after King Tut's tomb.
   - ☐ b. 200 years before King Tut's tomb.
   - ☐ c. at the same time as King Tut's tomb.
   - ☐ d. 3,000 years before King Tut's tomb.

10. Lord Carnarvon died of
    - ☐ a. injuries he received in a fall in the tomb.
    - ☐ b. an infection caused by a mosquito bite.
    - ☐ c. a virus he picked up from the stale air in the tomb.
    - ☐ d. natural causes from old age.

✎ _____ **Number of correct answers**
Enter this number on the Comprehension graph on page 165.

Critical Thinking

Put an ✖ in the box next to the best answer for each question or statement. You may look back at the selection if you'd like.

1. What was the authors' main purpose in writing *The Tomb of King Tut*?
   - ☐ a. to interest you in the "Curse of the Pharaoh"
   - ☐ b. to inform you about a historic discovery
   - ☐ c. to persuade you to visit Egypt
   - ☐ d. to describe the work of archaeologists

2. Which of the following statements best expresses the main idea of the selection?
   - ☐ a. After entering the tomb of King Tut, Carter was so amazed by its splendor he could not speak.
   - ☐ b. King Tut's tomb was the only pharaoh's tomb that was left almost completely untouched by grave robbers.
   - ☐ c. The 1922 discovery of the tomb of King Tut yielded the greatest treasure ever found in Egypt.
   - ☐ d. While King Tut's tomb contained great treasures, he was only a minor figure in Egyptian history.

3. Based on the information in this selection, you can conclude that
   - ☐ a. King Tut was one of the most powerful of the Egyptian rulers.
   - ☐ b. Lord Carnarvon was as excited about the discovery as was Howard Carter.
   - ☐ c. Lord Carnarvon always resented that Carter entered the tomb before him.
   - ☐ d. Carter and Lord Carnarvon continued the long search for King Tut's tomb because they wanted to get rich.

4. Which word best describes Howard Carter?
   - ☐ a. dedicated
   - ☐ b. disloyal
   - ☐ c. scholarly
   - ☐ d. greedy

5. Howard Carter was able to continue his expensive search because
   - ☐ a. Carter was independently wealthy.
   - ☐ b. the Egyptian government was financing the search.
   - ☐ c. Lord Carnarvon was financing the search.
   - ☐ d. Carter borrowed the money, hoping to pay it back if he found King Tut's treasures.

6. Which of the following is a statement of opinion rather than fact?
   - ☐ a. Howard Carter had been searching for King Tut's tomb for 15 years when he finally found it.
   - ☐ b. Howard Carter had unearthed the greatest treasure ever found in Egypt.
   - ☐ c. The contents of King Tut's tomb are on display at the Egyptian Museum in Cairo.
   - ☐ d. It was inappropriate that English, not Egyptian, archaeologists were the first people to enter King Tut's tomb after 3,000 years.

7. Based on what you've read, you can conclude that the authors want you to think that
   - ☐ a. the fact that Howard Carter died of natural causes at the age of 64 proves that there is no curse attached to King Tut's tomb.
   - ☐ b. the mosquito that bit Lord Carnarvon came from King Tut's tomb.
   - ☐ c. Lord Carnarvon's death was caused by the "Curse of the Pharaoh."
   - ☐ d. the sudden death of Lord Carnarvon was intended as a warning to keep away from the tombs of the Egyptian pharaohs.

8. Which of the following does *not* fit with the other three?
   - ☐ a. tomb of Tutankhamen
   - ☐ b. tomb of Ramses VI
   - ☐ c. Lord Carnarvon
   - ☐ d. Howard Carter

9. In what way was the tomb of Tutankhamen different from the tomb of Ramses VI?
   - ☐ a. It once contained the remains of an Egyptian pharaoh.
   - ☐ b. It was almost completely untouched by grave robbers.
   - ☐ c. It once contained great treasures.
   - ☐ d. It was discovered centuries after it was sealed shut.

10. Which sentence below correctly restates the following sentence from the selection: "The seals on the outer door, made 3,000 years earlier, proved it was a royal tomb and that its contents were intact?"
    - ☐ a. The seals on the door might have suggested that the searchers were about to enter a royal tomb.
    - ☐ b. While the seals on the door proved it was a royal tomb, the searchers worried that the tomb's contents would be damaged when they broke down the door.
    - ☐ c. The searchers hoped that the tomb was still intact, and they were dismayed to find seals on the outer door.
    - ☐ d. Seeing the sealed door, searchers knew that the tomb had belonged to royalty and that its contents had not been touched for 3,000 years.

✎ _____ **Number of correct answers**
Enter this number on the Critical Thinking graph on page 166.

Vocabulary

Each numbered sentence contains an underlined word from the selection. Following are four definitions. Put an **X** in the box next to the best meaning of the word as it is used in the sentence.

1. The seals on the outer door proved it was a royal tomb and that its contents were <u>intact</u>.
   - ☐ a. untouched
   - ☐ b. valuable
   - ☐ c. ancient
   - ☐ d. inside

2. Excitedly, Carter sent an <u>urgent</u> telegram to his partner, Lord Carnarvon.
   - ☐ a. long and detailed
   - ☐ b. unimportant
   - ☐ c. overnight
   - ☐ d. requiring immediate attention

3. "<u>Feverishly</u>," Carter later wrote, "we cleared away the remaining last scraps of rubbish."
   - ☐ a. cautiously
   - ☐ b. excitedly
   - ☐ c. sweating
   - ☐ d. calmly

4. Carter's years of toil and failure had turned into <u>triumph</u>.
   - ☐ a. disappointment
   - ☐ b. opportunity
   - ☐ c. success
   - ☐ d. great wealth

5. "As my eyes grew <u>accustomed to</u> the light, details of the room emerged slowly."
   - ☐ a. blinded by
   - ☐ b. attracted to
   - ☐ c. tired from
   - ☐ d. used to

6. Searchers worked patiently and carefully for 10 years to <u>excavate</u> the entire tomb.
   - ☐ a. learn about
   - ☐ b. clean out
   - ☐ c. bury
   - ☐ d. uncover

7. King Tut was a <u>minor</u> figure in Egyptian history.
   - ☐ a. later
   - ☐ b. young
   - ☐ c. less important
   - ☐ d. very important

8. The huts fell to rubble, <u>obscuring</u> Tut's tomb.
   - ☐ a. hiding
   - ☐ b. revealing
   - ☐ c. damaging
   - ☐ d. blocking

9. Some people <u>proclaimed</u> that breaking into it would bring bad luck.
   - ☐ a. promised
   - ☐ b. declared publicly
   - ☐ c. whispered softly
   - ☐ d. denied

10. <u>Dire</u> inscriptions warned that anyone who disturbed the king's tomb would be punished.
   - ☐ a. cheerful
   - ☐ b. dreadful
   - ☐ c. ancient
   - ☐ d. translated

✎ _____ **Number of correct answers**
Enter this number on the Vocabulary graph on page 167.

Personal Response

Imagine that you are a newspaper reporter covering the remarkable discovery of King Tutankhamen's tomb in 1922. Write your headline and the first 3–4 sentences of your story for tomorrow's paper.

_____

_____

_____

2 | A Day's Wait

by Ernest Hemingway

A young boy's misunderstanding results in great anxiety for him and serious concern for his father.

He came into the room to shut the windows while we were still in bed and I saw he looked ill. He was shivering, his face was white, and he walked slowly as though it ached to move.

"What's the matter, Schatz?"

"I've got a headache."

"You'd better go back to bed."

"No. I'm all right."

"You go to bed. I'll see you when I'm dressed."

But when I came downstairs he was dressed, sitting by the fire, looking a very sick and miserable boy of nine years. When I put my hand on his forehead I knew he had a fever.

"You go up to bed," I said, "you're sick."

"I'm all right," he said.

When the doctor came he took the boy's temperature.

"What is it?" I asked him.

"One hundred and two."

Downstairs, the doctor left three different medicines in different-colored capsules with instructions for giving them. One was to bring down the fever, another a purgative, the third to overcome an acid condition. The germs of influenza can only exist in an acid condition, he explained. He seemed to know all about influenza and said there was nothing to worry about if the fever did not go above one hundred and four degrees. This was a light epidemic of flu and there was no danger if you avoided pneumonia.

Back in the room I wrote the boy's temperature down and made a note of the time to give the various capsules.

"Do you want me to read to you?"

"All right. If you want to," said the boy.

His face was very white and there were dark areas under his eyes. He lay still in the bed and seemed very detached from what was going on.

I read aloud from Howard Pyle's *Book of Pirates;* but I could see he was not following what I was reading.

"How do you feel, Schatz?" I asked him.

"Just the same, so far," he said.

I sat at the foot of the bed and read to myself while I waited for it to be time to give another capsule. It would have been natural for him to go to sleep, but when I looked up he was looking at the foot of the bed, looking very strangely.

"Why don't you try to go to sleep? I'll wake you up for the medicine."

"I'd rather stay awake."

After a while he said to me, "You don't have to stay in here with me, Papa, if it bothers you."

"It doesn't bother me."

"No, I mean you don't have to stay if it's going to bother you."

I thought perhaps he was a little lightheaded and after giving him the prescribed capsules at eleven o'clock I went out for a while.

It was a bright, cold day, the ground covered with a sleet that had frozen so that it seemed as if all the bare trees, the bushes, the cut brush, and all the grass and the bare ground had been varnished with ice. I took the young Irish setter for a little walk up the road and along a frozen creek, but it was difficult to stand or walk on the glassy surface and the red dog slipped and slithered and I fell twice. . . .

At the house they said the boy had refused to let anyone come into the room.

"You can't come in," he said. "You mustn't get what I have."

I went up to him and found him in exactly the position I had left him, white-faced, but with the tops of his cheeks flushed by the fever, staring still, as he had stared, at the foot of the bed.

I took his temperature.

"What is it?"

"Something like a hundred," I said. It was one hundred and two and four tenths.

"It was a hundred and two," he said.

"Who said so?"

"The doctor."

"Your temperature is all right," I said. "It's nothing to worry about."

"I don't worry," he said, "but I can't keep from thinking."

"Don't think," I said. "Just take it easy."

"I'm taking it easy," he said and looked straight ahead. He was evidently holding tight onto himself about something.

"Take this with water."

"Do you think it will do any good?"

"Of course it will."

I sat down and opened the *Pirate* book and commenced to read, but I could see he was not following, so I stopped.

"About what time do you think I'm going to die?" he asked.

"What?"

"About how long will it be before I die?"

"You aren't going to die. What's the matter with you?"

"Oh, yes I am. I heard him say a hundred and two."

"People don't die with a fever of one hundred and two. That's a silly way to talk."

"I know they do. At school in France the boys told me you can't live with forty-four degrees. I've got a hundred and two."

He had been waiting to die all day, ever since nine o'clock in the morning.

"You poor Schatz," I said. "Poor old Schatz. It's like miles and kilometers. You aren't going to die. That's a different thermometer. On that thermometer thirty-seven is normal. On this kind it's ninety-eight."

"Are you sure?"

"Absolutely," I said. "It's like miles and kilometers. You know, like how many kilometers we make when we do seventy miles in the car."

"Oh," he said.

But his gaze at the foot of the bed relaxed slowly. The hold over himself relaxed, too, finally, and the next day it was very slack and he cried very easily at little things that were of no importance. ∎

✔ Enter your reading time below. Then look up your reading speed on the Words-per-Minute table on page 162.

Reading Time _____

Reading Speed _____

Enter your reading speed on the Reading Speed graph on page 164.

Comprehension

Put an **X** in the box next to the correct answer for each question or statement. Do not look back at the selection.

1. When Schatz's father first asked him what was the matter, Schatz complained of having
   ☐ a. a headache.
   ☐ b. a cold.
   ☐ c. an upset stomach.
   ☐ d. the chills.

2. Schatz was
   ☐ a. 14 years old.
   ☐ b. 12 years old.
   ☐ c. 9 years old.
   ☐ d. 7 years old.

3. What was Schatz's temperature?
   ☐ a. 102 degrees
   ☐ b. 98 degrees
   ☐ c. 44 degrees
   ☐ d. 37 degrees

4. What was Schatz's illness?
   ☐ a. pneumonia
   ☐ b. influenza
   ☐ c. a cold
   ☐ d. asthma

5. According to the doctor, Schatz would not be in danger if he avoided
   - ☐ a. having his fever rise to 44 degrees.
   - ☐ b. getting a cold.
   - ☐ c. getting an acid condition.
   - ☐ d. getting pneumonia.

6. When his father read aloud from Howard Pyle's *Book of Pirates*, Schatz
   - ☐ a. seemed uninterested.
   - ☐ b. fell asleep.
   - ☐ c. listened eagerly.
   - ☐ d. wanted him to read from a different book.

7. Schatz's family dog was
   - ☐ a. a Scottish terrier.
   - ☐ b. an English setter.
   - ☐ c. an Irish setter.
   - ☐ d. a German shepherd.

8. Schatz's misunderstanding about his temperature was based on information he learned
   - ☐ a. from his mother.
   - ☐ b. at school in France.
   - ☐ c. at a school in the United States.
   - ☐ d. from a doctor in France.

9. What is a normal temperature on the kind of thermometer the doctor used for Schatz?
   - ☐ a. 102 degrees
   - ☐ b. 98 degrees
   - ☐ c. 44 degrees
   - ☐ d. 37 degrees

10. The next day Schatz
    - ☐ a. laughed often.
    - ☐ b. was feeling much better.
    - ☐ c. cried very easily.
    - ☐ d. was feeling worse.

✎ _____ **Number of correct answers**
Enter this number on the Comprehension graph on page 165.

Critical Thinking

Put an ✗ in the box next to the best answer for each question or statement. You may look back at the selection if you'd like.

1. The author tells this story mainly by
   - ☐ a. using his imagination and creativity.
   - ☐ b. retelling a personal experience.
   - ☐ c. telling two different stories about the same incident.
   - ☐ d. comparing two different incidents.

2. Who is the narrator of this story?
   - ☐ a. Schatz
   - ☐ b. the doctor
   - ☐ c. Schatz's father
   - ☐ d. an outside observer

3. What mood does the author create in this story?
   - ☐ a. anxious
   - ☐ b. relaxed
   - ☐ c. light-hearted
   - ☐ d. depressing

4. Why did the doctor give Schatz pills to overcome an acid condition?
   - ☐ a. Schatz had an upset stomach due to too much acid in his system.
   - ☐ b. Acid helps to kill the germs of influenza.
   - ☐ c. Acid could burn a hole in Schatz's stomach lining.
   - ☐ d. The germs of influenza can only exist in an acid condition.

5. Schatz thought he was going to die because he
   - ☐ a. overheard the doctor say that he had influenza.
   - ☐ b. thought he had pneumonia.
   - ☐ c. suspected his father knew he was going to die but wouldn't tell him.
   - ☐ d. didn't understand that his 102-degree temperature was based on a different kind of thermometer.

6. After this experience, you can predict that Schatz will probably
   - ☐ a. be afraid every time he has an above-normal temperature.
   - ☐ b. not worry about dying whenever he has an above-normal temperature.
   - ☐ c. never again listen to what a doctor says.
   - ☐ d. never get sick again.

7. In what season of the year does this story take place?
   - ☐ a. winter
   - ☐ b. spring
   - ☐ c. summer
   - ☐ d. fall

8. Which word best describes Schatz's mood while he believed he was going to die?
   - ☐ a. sad
   - ☐ b. cheerful
   - ☐ c. resigned
   - ☐ d. stubborn

9. Which of the following does *not* fit with the other three?
   - ☐ a. thermometer
   - ☐ b. influenza
   - ☐ c. pneumonia
   - ☐ d. headache

10. What did Schatz mean when he said, "You don't have to stay in here with me, Papa, if it bothers you"?
    - ☐ a. His father could leave if Schatz's sleeping bothered him.
    - ☐ b. His father could leave if it bothered him that Schatz wasn't paying attention to the story he was reading.
    - ☐ c. His father could leave if it bothered him to watch Schatz dying.
    - ☐ d. His father could leave if it bothered him to see Schatz looking so sick.

✏ _____ Number of correct answers
Enter this number on the Critical Thinking graph on page 166.

Vocabulary

Each numbered sentence contains an underlined word from the selection. Following are four definitions. Put an ✘ in the box next to the best meaning of the word as it is used in the sentence.

1. Downstairs, the doctor left three different medicines in different-colored <u>capsules</u> with instructions for giving them.
   - ☐ a. bottles
   - ☐ b. small boxes
   - ☐ c. small containers
   - ☐ d. bags

2. The germs of influenza can only <u>exist</u> in an acid condition, he explained.
   - ☐ a. be controlled
   - ☐ b. die
   - ☐ c. grow
   - ☐ d. live

3. This was a light <u>epidemic</u> of flu and there was no danger if you avoided pneumonia.
   - ☐ a. treatment
   - ☐ b. type
   - ☐ c. rapid spread of disease
   - ☐ d. container

4. He lay still in the bed and seemed very <u>detached</u> from what was going on.
   - ☐ a. uninterested
   - ☐ b. tired
   - ☐ c. discouraged
   - ☐ d. delighted

5. It seemed as if all the bare trees, the bushes, the cut brush, and all the grass and the bare ground had been <u>varnished</u> with ice.
   - ☐ a. coated
   - ☐ b. frozen
   - ☐ c. cracked
   - ☐ d. brightened

6. I went up to him and found him in exactly the position I had left him, white-faced but with the tops of his cheeks <u>flushed</u> by the fever.
   - [ ] a. spotted
   - [ ] b. dried
   - [ ] c. made wet
   - [ ] d. reddened

7. He was <u>evidently</u> holding tight onto himself about something.
   - [ ] a. understandably
   - [ ] b. tightly
   - [ ] c. secretly
   - [ ] d. plainly

8. I sat down and opened the *Pirate* book and <u>commenced</u> to read, but I could see he was not following, so I stopped.
   - [ ] a. hesitated
   - [ ] b. demanded
   - [ ] c. began
   - [ ] d. desired

9. But his <u>gaze</u> at the foot of the bed relaxed slowly.
   - [ ] a. long, steady look
   - [ ] b. glance
   - [ ] c. firm grasp
   - [ ] d. hesitation

10. The hold over himself relaxed, too, finally, and the next day it was very <u>slack</u>.
   - [ ] a. tight
   - [ ] b. intense
   - [ ] c. loose
   - [ ] d. secure

_____ Number of correct answers

Enter this number on the Vocabulary graph on page 167.

Personal Response

Why did Schatz believe he was going to die?

_____

_____

_____

Do you think Schatz's father handled the situation well, or not? Explain.

_____

_____

_____

_____

3 | Mines in the Sky

by William K. Hartmann

Space explorers, besides seeking knowledge and adventure, are always on the lookout for new sources of basic raw materials. In this selection the author describes a future when we may be mining the vast resources of the solar system to fill our planet's needs.

Sometime in the next few decades, astronomers will discover a small asteroid, only 500 meters across, approaching the earth. It will not hit Earth, of course; asteroids this large hit Earth only about once every 100,000 years. The orbit of this asteroid will take it past Earth's orbit at perhaps 10 times the moon's distance. Planetary astronomers, who have been using spectroscopy to determine the composition of the thousands of already cataloged asteroids, will turn their equipment on this new object. It is stony iron, composed mostly of the pure nickel-iron alloy that composes many meteorites. Meteorites are fragments of such asteroids.

This little asteroid, five football fields across, contains 400 million tons of pure nickel-iron, as well as 50 million tons of rocky material. About 95 percent of the metal is iron and four percent is nickel. At the current price of about $3.50 a pound, the market value of the refined nickel alone would be about $125 billion! The market value of the iron would be similar. The market value of the refined metals from the entire asteroid, counting additional minerals of economic interest, could be a good deal more than $300 billion.

Scientists have awaited this opportunity for some years. An interplanetary reconnaissance ship departs from a space station in orbit around Earth. If the asteroid has an orbit around the sun reasonably close to Earth's, the trip is easy. The total change in velocity that the ship's engines must produce could be less than the change in velocity required in the Apollo program to send astronauts from the surface of the earth to the surface of the moon and back. In other words, the voyage to match orbits with this asteroid is no harder than the voyage to the moon, even though it takes longer. It is made still easier by the fact that no atmospheric passage is required.

The ship takes some weeks to reach the asteroid. It matches orbits, then "parks" close alongside. In this position, the asteroid's gravity will pull the ship toward its surface. The ship will be falling, but it is quite safe. The gravity is so weak that the ship will take about half an hour to fall 250 meters toward the asteroid, even without rocket braking. It can turn its landing legs toward the surface and "hit" with about the impact speed of a pencil dropped from half an inch above a table. The ship lands by falling gently onto the surface.

While the ship is maneuvering to land, the astronauts descend to the asteroid surface. Once the landing has been completed, more astronauts leap from the ship's hatch, undergoing a slow fall, or glide, of several minutes.

Like the moon, the asteroid is covered with a thin layer of powdery dry soil, created during millions of years as micrometeorites pulverized its surface rocks and metal. The soil contains fragments of stone and nickel-iron alloy. Below the soil layer are more coherent rock and metal, shielded by the soil itself, but possibly heavily fractured by ancient collisions between the asteroid and moderate-sized meteorites. The astronauts first sample the surface material, drill to test the depth of the soil, and conduct seismic tests to probe the deep structure of the asteroid.

Now the astronauts begin a strange task. At a selected site, they start assembling a long, spidery tower—part of an assembly called a "mass driver." The mass driver is a magnetic device something like a giant conveyor belt. It accelerates packets of soil along the tower to extreme speed and flings them off into space. The mass driver turns the asteroid into a giant rocket. Instead of expelling flaming fuel, it expels native asteroid dirt, driving the asteroid slowly forward in the other direction. Although the speed is slow, there is a large supply of "fuel" (soil) and a lot of time. The procedure is adequate to change the orbit of the asteroid over a period of many months. Eventually the asteroid can be brought toward Earth's orbit, can match speed with Earth, and then can be maneuvered into orbit around it.

Bringing the asteroid back to Earth could raise political questions. Concerned scientists have pointed out that well before we could put an asteroid into Earth's orbit, we would be able to divert one to make it strike Earth. A half-kilometer asteroid would hit with the explosive force of thousands of megatons, making it a weapon equal to all the nuclear bombs of Earth. Mining asteroids where they are and shipping the metal back to Earth presents no such problems.

As the asteroid mining operation swings into gear, two historically important breakthroughs will have occurred. First, the population of Earth will have acquired a new source of raw materials to replace the supplies that have dwindled during our rapacious mining of the earth's crust. Even as small an asteroid as I have described here would contain most of a year's global consumption of iron and enough nickel to supply the world's demand for 24 years.

Secondly, and just as important, the industrial processing of economic resources will have begun outside Earth's ecosphere. This means that instead of ravaging the earth to obtain materials, and instead of dumping our industrial wastes into the atmosphere, streams, and oceans, we can begin to let the earth relax back to its original, less polluted, more natural state. We will be on our way from being a global society with finite limits to being an interplanetary society with vastly wider horizons.

And there are many more, larger asteroids available for future exploration. Even a modest asteroid, three kilometers across, of which dozens exist in the near-Earth part of the solar system, would supply 36 times as much material as our example. In the asteroid belt, just beyond Mars, there are thousands of still larger asteroids. Some are mostly rock, and others are believed to contain large volumes of metals. Clearly, objects of economic interest exist in space closer to Earth than the nearest planets. ■

✔ Enter your reading time below. Then look up your reading speed on the Words-per-Minute table on page 162.

Reading Time   _____

Reading Speed   _____

Enter your reading speed on the Reading Speed graph on page 164.

Comprehension

Put an **X** in the box next to the correct answer for each question or statement. Do not look back at the selection.

1. According to the selection, large asteroids hit Earth only once every
   □ a. 10,000 years.
   □ b. 50,000 years.
   □ c. 100,000 years.
   □ d. 200,000 years.

2. What does an asteroid contain that would be valuable to human beings on Earth?
   □ a. nickel-iron alloy
   □ b. silver alloy
   □ c. copper
   □ d. gold

3. How large across is the asteroid referred to by the author?
   □ a. five football fields
   □ b. five city blocks
   □ c. five miles
   □ d. five times larger than earth

4. The asteroid has
   - ☐ a. no force of gravity.
   - ☐ b. a weak force of gravity.
   - ☐ c. a strong force of gravity.
   - ☐ d. a force of gravity equal to that of Earth.

5. The asteroid is covered with a thin layer of powdery dry soil like that on
   - ☐ a. Neptune.
   - ☐ b. Earth's moon.
   - ☐ c. Pluto.
   - ☐ d. Earth.

6. The mass driver is a magnetic device similar to
   - ☐ a. a forklift.
   - ☐ b. flexible tubing.
   - ☐ c. a weapon.
   - ☐ d. a giant conveyor belt.

7. The mass driver acts like a
   - ☐ a. rocket engine.
   - ☐ b. meteorite.
   - ☐ c. asteroid.
   - ☐ d. weapon.

8. Bringing an asteroid back to Earth would
   - ☐ a. present many problems.
   - ☐ b. present no problems.
   - ☐ c. be too expensive.
   - ☐ d. be the easiest way to mine its raw materials.

9. A small asteroid contains enough nickel to supply the world's demand for
   - ☐ a. 12 years.
   - ☐ b. several weeks.
   - ☐ c. 24 years.
   - ☐ d. several years.

10. There are thousands of larger asteroids in the asteroid belt just beyond
    - ☐ a. the sun.
    - ☐ b. the moon.
    - ☐ c. Jupiter.
    - ☐ d. Mars.

✎ _____ Number of correct answers
Enter this number on the Comprehension graph on page 165.

Critical Thinking

Put an **X** in the box next to the best answer for each question or statement. You may look back at the selection if you'd like.

1. What was the author's main purpose in writing "Mines in the Sky"?
   - ☐ a. to warn you about the potential danger of asteroids hitting Earth
   - ☐ b. to entertain you with a very imaginative science-fiction story
   - ☐ c. to describe the procedure for mining the raw materials of asteroids
   - ☐ d. to inform you about the potential benefits of mining raw materials from asteroids in outer space

2. Which of the following would be the best choice for another title of this selection?
   - ☐ a. "Raw Resources from Asteroids"
   - ☐ b. "Asteroids: A Threat to Earth?"
   - ☐ c. "Mining Meteors"
   - ☐ d. "A New Challenge for Astronauts"

3. Successfully mining an asteroid would be
   - ☐ a. very dangerous.
   - ☐ b. good training for astronauts.
   - ☐ c. too costly.
   - ☐ d. economically beneficial.

4. Which of the following best descibes the chances for mining asteroids in space to become a reality?
   - ☐ a. impossible
   - ☐ b. possible in time
   - ☐ c. a certainty
   - ☐ d. possible but highly unlikely

5. Which of the following is *not* one of the beneficial effects of mining asteriods in outer space?
   - ☐ a. Earth would aquire a new source of raw materials.
   - ☐ b. The pollution from industrial processing would be reduced.
   - ☐ c. Many new astronauts and space vehicles would be required.
   - ☐ d. The ravaging of Earth to obtain materials would be reduced.

6. Which of the following is a statment of opinion rather than fact?
   - ☐ a. Sometime in the next few decades, astronomers will discover a small asteroid approaching the Earth.
   - ☐ b. A half-kilometer asteroid would hit with the explosive force of thousands of megatons.
   - ☐ c. In the asteroid belt, just beyond Mars, there are thousands of still larger asteroids.
   - ☐ d. Asteroids this large hit Earth only about once every 100,000 years.

7. Mining an asteroid where it is in space would be preferable to diverting it to Earth because it would
   - ☐ a. require fewer workers.
   - ☐ b. be much safer.
   - ☐ c. be much easier.
   - ☐ d. be less costly.

8. Because of the asteroid's weak gravity, the astronauts' ship would
   - ☐ a. not be able to land on the asteroid.
   - ☐ b. descend rapidly to the asteroid.
   - ☐ c. descend slowly to the asteroid.
   - ☐ d. need extra rocket power to overcome the asteroid's gravity force.

9. Compared to an asteroid, a meteorite is
   - ☐ a. larger in area.
   - ☐ b. smaller in area.
   - ☐ c. made of different materials.
   - ☐ d. a planet.

10. Which of the following does *not* fit with the other three?
    - ☐ a. meteorite
    - ☐ b. comet
    - ☐ c. astronaut
    - ☐ d. asteroid

✎ _____ Number of correct answers
Enter this number on the Critical Thinking graph on page 166.

Vocabulary

Each numbered sentence contains an underlined word from the selection. Following are four definitions. Put an ✗ in the box next to the best meaning of the word as it is used in the sentence.

1. Planetary astronomers have been using spectroscopy to determine the composition of thousands of already <u>cataloged</u> asteroids.
   - ☐ a. explored
   - ☐ b. collided
   - ☐ c. mined
   - ☐ d. listed

2. An interplanetary <u>reconnaissance</u> ship departs from a space station in Earth's orbit.
   - ☐ a. military
   - ☐ b. rocket
   - ☐ c. scientific
   - ☐ d. exploration

3. While the ship is <u>maneuvering</u> to land, the astronauts descend to the asteroid's surface.
   - ☐ a. slowly drifting
   - ☐ b. changing direction and speed
   - ☐ c. speeding rapidly
   - ☐ d. waiting without moving

4. The total change in <u>velocity</u> that the ship's engines must produce could be less than the change in velocity required in the Apollo program to send astronauts from Earth's surface to the moon's surface and back.
   ☐ a. speed
   ☐ b. energy
   ☐ c. direction
   ☐ d. power

5. The asteroid is covered with a thin layer of powdery dry soil, created as micrometeorites <u>pulverized</u> its surface rocks and metals.
   ☐ a. crushed
   ☐ b. removed
   ☐ c. compared
   ☐ d. loosened

6. The mass driver is a magnetic device something like a giant <u>conveyer</u> belt.
   ☐ a. asteroid
   ☐ b. rocket
   ☐ c. carrier
   ☐ d. fan

7. Instead of <u>expelling</u> flaming fuel, it expels native asteroid dirt.
   ☐ a. ejecting forcefully
   ☐ b. releasing
   ☐ c. creating power
   ☐ d. pushing

8. The population of Earth will have acquired a new source of raw materials to replace the supplies that have dwindled during our <u>rapacious</u> mining of Earth's crust.
   ☐ a. fierce
   ☐ b. fragile
   ☐ c. greedy
   ☐ d. delicate

9. We will be on our way from being a global society with <u>finite</u> limits to being an interplanetary society with vastly wider horizons.
   ☐ a. enormous
   ☐ b. shrinking
   ☐ c. expanding
   ☐ d. measurable

10. Even a <u>modest</u> asteroid would supply 36 times as much material as our example.
   ☐ a. gigantic
   ☐ b. extremely tiny
   ☐ c. limited in size
   ☐ d. expansive

✎ _____ Number of correct answers
Enter this number on the Vocabulary graph on page 167.

Personal Response

Do you think the mining of asteroids in outer space will become a reality in your lifetime? Why or why not?

_____

_____

_____

Can you think of any reasons why such an idea should not be pursued? Explain.

_____

_____

_____

4 | Letter to Susan

by Margaret Culkin Banning

Margaret Culkin Banning wrote this letter to her daughter in college over 60 years ago. As you'll see, parents and children haven't changed much in all that time.

November 15, 1934

Dear Susan,

No, you can't drive to Detroit for Thanksgiving with the two boys and Ann. I thought I'd better put that simple, declarative sentence at the beginning of this letter so that you wouldn't be kept in suspense even if you are put in a bad temper. I'm sorry to have to be so definite and final. I would like to leave the decision to your own judgment, but this is one of the few times when I can't do that. For the judgment of so many people, young and old, is a little askew about just such propositions as four young people motoring together for most of two days and a night without any stops except for breath and coffee.

I do agree with much of what you wrote me. It would be delightful to be there for that Thanksgiving dance and it wouldn't be expensive to carry out your plan. I quite understand that you can manage the complicated schedules all around by leaving Wednesday afternoon, driving all that night and most of Thursday, and I don't doubt that you would have a grand time until Saturday noon and all be back in college by Sunday night. Also I know that Mark is probably the best driver of all your friends and that he behaves well. His father was like that too. He was also—though this bit of history may not interest you—rather dashing in his ways, like Mark. I don't know the other boy, David, or is it Daniel? (your handwriting certainly doesn't get any better) but I'll take your word for all the sterling qualities you say he has. Nobody need argue with me about Ann, after the way she measured up to family troubles and kept gay all last summer. Even you are all that I sometimes say that you are, but it doesn't affect the situation.

In fact, I think it aggravates it. Such young people as you four have no right to do things that confuse you with people who are quite different in habits and ideas of control. You write, quote, please don't say I can't go because of the looks of the thing because that's such rubbish and not like you, unquote. You're wrong on both counts. It is not rubbish and it is like me. I get a little angry about this highhanded scrapping of the looks of things. What else have we to go by? How else can the average person form an opinion of a girl's sense of values or even of her chastity except by the looks of her conduct? If looks are so unimportant, why do you yourself spend so much time on your physical looks before you go out with strangers? In your own crowd you will go around all day wearing shorts and a sweatshirt and that eternal and dreadful red-checked scarf that should be burned. But if you are going to be with people you don't know or who don't know who you are, it is different. Then you are careful to make yourself look as if you were decently bred, as if you could read and write, and as if you had good taste in clothes and cosmetics. You wouldn't be caught wearing cheap perfume, would you? Then why do you want to wear cheap perfume on your conduct?

Looks do matter and I do not mean just hair and skin and teeth and clothes. Looks are also your social contact with the world. Suppose you take this drive. How would it look to strangers? Two young men (of marriageable age) take two young women (also of marriageable age) on a 40-hour drive. Everyone knows that many girls go on 40-hour drives with men with extremely bad results, such as overexcited emotions, reckless conduct, and road accidents. How is anyone to make a special case of you? Why should anyone?

It looks as if you deliberately assumed the pathetic privileges of girls who want to be with men at any cost to their reputations.

You wrote also that you think that it is nobody's business except your own what you do, but you are wrong. This is the kind of world—and there doesn't seem to be any other—in which conduct is social as well as individual. The main point of your education, from kindergarten up, has been to make you understand that, and I don't want you to break down at this small test. Your conduct is not entirely your own business, though it begins there. Afterwards it affects other people's conduct. Other girls, seeing you go off on an unchaperoned motor jaunt, think it's all right to do the same thing. Parents doubt and wonder. Men, and even boys, grow skeptical and more careless. You confuse things by such conduct.

You wrote me that it would be such fun that you hope I'll see it your way. That's always a very disarming argument, but I think it's on my side this time. You see, if there were any necessity for this trip I would feel differently about it. If you were compelled for some real reason to travel that way, if there were a war or a siege to make it necessary, or if it were the only way you could see Mark for years, I would say that you could do it. But fun—that so-transient fun—of just missing being hit by a bus or finding the best hamburgers in the world at a roadside inn, or being cut in on 20 times at that Thanksgiving dance—isn't a good enough reason.

It is no fun for me either, to disappoint you like this. It isn't easy to be the person who sometimes has to try to preserve your happiness at the expense of your fun. After Thanksgiving—I know you probably can't do it until then—will you please believe that's true?

With love to you, Ann, Mark, and David-Daniel.

Mother ■

✔ **Enter your reading time below. Then look up your reading speed on the Words-per-Minute table on page 162.**

Reading Time   _____

Reading Speed   _____

Enter your reading speed on the Reading Speed graph on page 164.

Comprehension

Put an **X** in the box next to the correct answer for each question or statement. Do not look back at the selection.

1. Susan has asked her mother for permission to
   - ☐ a. go to a dance.
   - ☐ b. go to a party.
   - ☐ c. marry Mark.
   - ☐ d. take a vacation with her friends.

2. Susan has some time off from college because of the
   - ☐ a. Thanksgiving break.
   - ☐ b. Christmas break.
   - ☐ c. mid-year break.
   - ☐ d. spring vacation.

3. Susan wants to go because
   - ☐ a. her mother wants her to go.
   - ☐ b. all her friends are going.
   - ☐ c. it would be fun.
   - ☐ d. her mother doesn't want her to go.

4. Where does Susan want to go?
   - ☐ a. Dallas
   - ☐ b. Detroit
   - ☐ c. Chicago
   - ☐ d. Cleveland

5. How many people would make the trip together?
   - ☐ a. two
   - ☐ b. three
   - ☐ c. four
   - ☐ d. five

6. Susan and Mark are
   - ☐ a. daughter and father.
   - ☐ b. sister and brother.
   - ☐ c. cousins.
   - ☐ d. girlfriend and boyfriend.

7. Who is probably the best driver among those going?
   - ☐ a. Susan's father
   - ☐ b. Mark
   - ☐ c. Susan
   - ☐ d. David

8. How long would it take Susan and her friends to reach their destination?
   - ☐ a. all night
   - ☐ b. several days
   - ☐ c. 24 hours
   - ☐ d. 40 hours

9. What article of Susan's clothing did her mother think should be burned?
   - ☐ a. a red-checkered scarf
   - ☐ b. a gray sweatshirt
   - ☐ c. a pair of blue jeans
   - ☐ d. a pair of shorts

10. Susan wrote to her mother that she thought the issue of "the looks of things" was
    - ☐ a. important.
    - ☐ b. unimportant.
    - ☐ c. rubbish.
    - ☐ d. irrelevant.

✎ _____ **Number of correct answers**
Enter this number on the Comprehension graph on page 165.

Critical Thinking

Put an ✗ in the box next to the best answer for each question or statement. You may look back at the selection if you'd like.

1. The author's main purpose in this letter was to
   - ☐ a. change Susan's mind.
   - ☐ b. prove a point.
   - ☐ c. cheer Susan up.
   - ☐ d. enforce her will.

2. Which word best describes the tone of the letter?
   - ☐ a. humorous
   - ☐ b. happy
   - ☐ c. serious
   - ☐ d. sad

3. Why does the author think appearances are important?
   - ☐ a. They hide what you are thinking.
   - ☐ b. That's how people form opinions of you.
   - ☐ c. You could get in trouble if you don't dress right.
   - ☐ d. You are what you wear.

4. When she reads this letter, Susan will probably
   - ☐ a. cancel her trip plans.
   - ☐ b. drive to Detroit.
   - ☐ c. throw a tantrum.
   - ☐ d. fly to Detroit.

5. The main reason the author didn't want Susan to go on the trip was that
   - ☐ a. Susan would miss too much school time.
   - ☐ b. it would not look right.
   - ☐ c. her friends might act recklessly.
   - ☐ d. it would be too expensive.

Detroit for

I can't go

6. Which of the following is a statement of opinion rather than fact?
- ☐ a. No, you can't drive to Detroit for Thanksgiving with two boys and Ann.
- ☐ b. I don't know the other boy, David, or is it Daniel?
- ☐ c. Such young people as you four have no right to do things that confuse you with people who are quite different.
- ☐ d. I get a little angry about the highhanded scrapping of the look of things.

7. The word that best describes the author's emotional state is
- ☐ a. anger.
- ☐ b. love.
- ☐ c. fear.
- ☐ d. unconcern.

8. Which of the following does *not* fit with the other three?
- ☐ a. Mark
- ☐ b. David (or Daniel)
- ☐ c. Ann
- ☐ d. Margaret

9. In some ways, the author compares Susan's friend, Mark, to
- ☐ a. David.
- ☐ b. Daniel.
- ☐ c. his father.
- ☐ d. herself.

10. What does the author mean when she says "conduct is social as well as individual"?
- ☐ a. Only do things in groups.
- ☐ b. Live and let live.
- ☐ c. It's important how others perceive you.
- ☐ d. You can't live alone.

✎ _____ Number of correct answers
Enter this number on the Critical Thinking graph on page 166.

Vocabulary

Each numbered sentence contains an underlined word from the selection. Following are four definitions. Put an ✗ in the box next to the best meaning of the word as it is used in the sentence.

1. I thought I'd better put that simple, <u>declarative</u> sentence at the beginning of this letter
- ☐ a. giving a command
- ☐ b. showing excitement
- ☐ c. asking a question
- ☐ d. making a statement

2. The judgment of so many people, young and old, is a little <u>askew</u> about just such propositions.
- ☐ a. out of date
- ☐ b. slanted
- ☐ c. perfect
- ☐ d. unbelievable

3. He was also rather <u>dashing</u> in his ways, like Mark.
- ☐ a. punctual
- ☐ b. crazy
- ☐ c. exciting
- ☐ d. boring

4. You would have a <u>grand</u> time until Saturday noon.
- ☐ a. splendid
- ☐ b. sad
- ☐ c. one thousand
- ☐ d. one in a million

5. Please don't say that I can't go because of the looks of the thing because that's such <u>rubbish</u> and not like you.
- ☐ a. garbage
- ☐ b. vegetables
- ☐ c. nonsense
- ☐ d. snobbish behavior

6. In fact, I think it <u>aggravates</u> it.
- ☐ a. pleases
- ☐ b. slows down
- ☐ c. lessens
- ☐ d. makes worse

7. Then why do you want to wear cheap perfume on your <u>conduct</u>?
   - ☐ a. behavior
   - ☐ b. clothes
   - ☐ c. personality
   - ☐ d. leadership

8. Other girls, seeing you go off on an <u>unchaperoned</u> motor jaunt, think it's all right to do the same thing.
   - ☐ a. illegal
   - ☐ b. without supervision
   - ☐ c. uninsured
   - ☐ d. underage

9. If you were <u>compelled</u> for some real reason to travel that way, I would say that you could do it.
   - ☐ a. forced
   - ☐ b. inclined
   - ☐ c. thrilled
   - ☐ d. requested

10. But fun—that so-<u>transient</u> fun—of just missing being hit by a bus or finding the best hamburgers in the world isn't a good reason.
    - ☐ a. hobo
    - ☐ b. old-fashioned
    - ☐ c. silly
    - ☐ d. temporary

✎ _____ **Number of correct answers**
Enter this number on the Vocabulary graph on page 167.

Personal Response

From the point of view of Susan's mother, write two or three additional reasons why you would not permit Susan to make the trip.

_____

_____

_____

From Susan's point of view, write two or three additional reasons why you think Susan should be allowed to go on the trip.

_____

_____

_____

5 | All Creatures Great and Small

by James Herriot

James Herriot is well known for his many books about his experiences as a veterinarian in England. This passage shows that a little learning can be a dangerous thing.

I was back in Scotland. I was 17, and I was walking under the arch of the Veterinary College into Montrose Street. I had been a student for three days but not until this afternoon had I felt the thrill of fulfillment. Messing about with botany and zoology was all right but this afternoon had been the real thing; I had had my first lecture in animal husbandry.

The subject had been the points of the horse. Professor Grant had hung up a life-size picture of a horse and gone over it from nose to tail, indicating the withers, the stifle, the hock, the poll, and all the other rich, equine terms. And the professor had been wise; to make his lecture more interesting he kept throwing in little practical points like "This is where we find the curb," or "Here is the site for windgalls." He talked of thoroughpins and sidebones, splints and quittor; things the students wouldn't learn about for another four years, but it brought it all to life.

The words were still spinning in my head as I walked slowly down the sloping street. This was what I had come for. I felt as though I had undergone an initiation and become a member of an exclusive club. I really knew about horses. And I was wearing a brand-new riding mac with all sorts of extra straps and buckles which slapped against my legs as I turned the corner of the hill into busy Newton Road.

I could hardly believe my luck when I saw the horse. It was standing outside the library below Queen's Cross like something left over from another age. It drooped dispiritedly between the shafts of a coal cart which stood like an island in an eddying stream of cars and buses. Pedestrians hurried by, uncaring, but I had the feeling that fortune was smiling on me.

A horse. Not just a picture but a real, genuine horse. Stray words from the lecture floated up into my mind; the pastern, cannon bone, coronet, and all those markings—snip, blaze, white sock near hind. I stood on the pavement and examined the animal critically.

I thought it must be obvious to every passer-by that here was a true expert. Not just an inquisitive onlooker but a man who knew and understood all. I felt clothed in a visible aura of horsiness.

I took a few steps up and down, hands deep in the pockets of the new riding mac, eyes probing for possible shoeing faults or cubs or bog spavins. So thorough was my inspection that I worked round to the off side of the horse and stood perilously among the racing traffic.

I glanced around at the people hurrying past. Nobody seemed to care, not even the horse. He was a large one, at least 17 hands, and he gazed apathetically down the street, easing his hind legs alternately in a bored manner. I hated to leave him but I had completed my examination and it was time I was on my way. But I felt that I ought to make a gesture before I left; something to communicate to the horse that I understood his problems and that we belong to the same brotherhood. I stepped briskly forward and patted him on the neck.

Quick as a striking snake, the horse whipped downwards and seized my shoulder in his great strong teeth. He laid back his ears, rolled his eyes wickedly, and hoisted me up, almost off my feet. I hung there helplessly, suspended like a lopsided puppet. I wriggled and kicked but the teeth were clamped immovably in the material of my coat.

There was no doubt about the interest of the passers-by now. The grotesque sight of a man hanging from a horse's mouth brought them to a sudden halt and a crowd formed with people looking over each other's shoulders and others fighting at the back to see what was going on.

A horrified old lady was crying: "Oh, poor boy! Help him, somebody!" Some of the braver characters tried pulling at me but the horse whickered ominously and hung on tighter. Conflicting advice was shouted from all sides. With deep shame I saw two attractive girls in the front row giggling helplessly.

Appalled at the absurdity of my position, I began to thrash about wildly; my shirt collar tightened round my throat; a stream of the horse's saliva trickled down the front of my mac. I could feel myself choking and was giving up hope when a man pushed his way through the crowd.

He was very small. Angry eyes glared from a face blackened by coal dust. Two empty sacks were draped over his arm.

"Whit the devil's this?" he shouted. A dozen replies babbled in the air.

"Can ye no leave the bloody hoarse alone?" he yelled into my face. I made no reply, being pop-eyed, half throttled, and in no mood for conversation.

The coalman turned his fury on the horse. "Drop him, ya big bully! Go on, let go, drop him!"

Getting no response he dug the animal viciously in the belly with his thumb. The horse took the point at once and released me like an obedient dog dropping a bone. I fell on my knees and ruminated in the gutter for a while till I could breathe more easily. As from a great distance I could still hear the little man shouting at me.

After some time I stood up. The coalman was still shouting and the crowd was listening appreciatively. "Whit d'ye think you're playing at—keep yer hands off ma bloody hoarse—get the poliss tae ye."

I looked down at my new mac. The shoulder was chewed to a sodden mass. I felt I must escape and began to edge my way through the crowd. Some of the faces were concerned but most were grinning. Once clear I started to walk away rapidly and as I turned the corner the last faint cry from the coalman reached me.

"Dinna meddle wi' things ye ken nuthin' aboot!" ■

✔ Enter your reading time below. Then look up your reading speed on the Words-per-Minute table on page 162.

Reading Time _____

Reading Speed _____

Enter your reading speed on the Reading Speed graph on page 164.

Comprehension

Put an ✗ in the box next to the correct answer for each question or statement. Do not look back at the selection.

1. The story takes place in
   □ a. England.
   □ b. Ireland.
   □ c. Wales.
   □ d. Scotland.

2. James Herriot felt his first thrill of fulfillment after he had his first lecture in
   □ a. zoology.
   □ b. animal husbandry.
   □ c. botany.
   □ d. veterinary management.

3. When Herriot first saw the horse, it was
   □ a. running wild through the streets.
   □ b. plodding down the road.
   □ c. waiting patiently for its owner.
   □ d. attacking several passers-by.

4. Where was the horse when Herriot first spotted it?
   □ a. in front of the Veterinary College
   □ b. in the coal yard
   □ c. outside the library
   □ d. in the college's stables

5. How large was the horse?
   - [ ] a. at least 17 hands
   - [ ] b. at least a dozen hands.
   - [ ] c. larger than a moose
   - [ ] d. just under 10 hands

6. When Herriot patted the horse's neck, it
   - [ ] a. followed him home.
   - [ ] b. began to kick his legs.
   - [ ] c. bit the shoulder of his coat.
   - [ ] d. nuzzled him affectionately.

7. The horse was owned by
   - [ ] a. Professor Grant.
   - [ ] b. a coalman.
   - [ ] c. James Herriot.
   - [ ] d. the Veterinary College.

8. Herriot felt deep shame when
   - [ ] a. the coalman yelled at him.
   - [ ] b. an old lady cried, "Oh, poor boy! Help him, somebody!"
   - [ ] c. two attractive girls giggled helplessly.
   - [ ] d. some brave people tried to pull him away from the horse.

9. After the horse released him, Herriot wanted to
   - [ ] a. escape from the scene.
   - [ ] b. apologize to the coalman.
   - [ ] c. thank the crowd.
   - [ ] d. get his coat repaired.

10. As Herriot edged his way through the crowd, most of the people
    - [ ] a. were still concerned.
    - [ ] b. wished him well.
    - [ ] c. were grinning.
    - [ ] d. felt sorry for him.

✎ _____ Number of correct answers
Enter this number on the Comprehension graph on page 165.

Critical Thinking

Put an **X** in the box next to the best answer for each question or statement. You may look back at the selection if you'd like.

1. Which of the following best describes this selection?
   - [ ] a. a story of a real person's life written by someone else
   - [ ] b. a story of a real person's life written by that person
   - [ ] c. an imaginary story based in part on historical facts
   - [ ] d. a fanciful story about characters, places, and events that seem believable but don't really exist

2. The author tells his story mainly by
   - [ ] a. comparing different topics.
   - [ ] b. retelling personal experiences.
   - [ ] c. telling different stories about the same topic.
   - [ ] d. using his imagination and creativity.

3. Which word best describes the author's tone?
   - [ ] a. mysterious
   - [ ] b. gloomy
   - [ ] c. humorous
   - [ ] d. persuasive

4. After attending the lecture by Professor Grant, Herriot was
   - [ ] a. no longer interested in becoming a veterinarian.
   - [ ] b. tired and homesick.
   - [ ] c. excited about the subject matter.
   - [ ] d. ready to operate on the horse.

5. What caused the horse to release his hold on Herriot's shoulder?
   - [ ] a. He was frightened by the traffic.
   - [ ] b. Herriot patted him on his neck.
   - [ ] c. The coalman dug his thumb into the horse's belly.
   - [ ] d. Holding Herriot up almost off his feet made him tired.

6. Which of the following is a statement of opinion rather than fact?
   - ☐ a. I was back in Scotland, I was 17, and I was walking under the arch of the Veterinary College into Montrose Street.
   - ☐ b. I stood on the pavement and examined the animal critically.
   - ☐ c. He was a large one, at least 17 hands, and he gazed apathetically down the street.
   - ☐ d. It must be obvious to every passer-by that here was a true expert.

7. The reason Herriot examined the horse was
   - ☐ a. the horse looked sick.
   - ☐ b. he thought he was an expert on horses.
   - ☐ c. he wanted to buy it.
   - ☐ d. the coalman asked him to inspect it.

8. Which word best describes the coalman's mood?
   - ☐ a. concerned
   - ☐ b. amused
   - ☐ c. embarrassed
   - ☐ d. angry

9. Who or what did the author compare himself to?
   - ☐ a. a lopsided puppet
   - ☐ b. an obedient dog dropping a bone
   - ☐ c. a striking snake
   - ☐ d. a horrified old lady

10. After Herriot was bitten by the horse, the passers-by
    - ☐ a. were very interested in him.
    - ☐ b. never noticed him.
    - ☐ c. called an ambulance.
    - ☐ d. quietly waited for the coalman.

✎ _____ **Number of correct answers**
Enter this number on the Critical Thinking graph on page 166.

Vocabulary

Each numbered sentence contains an underlined word from the selection. Following are four definitions. Put an ✗ in the box next to the best meaning of the word as it is used in the sentence.

1. I had been a student for three days but not until this afternoon had I felt the thrill of <u>fulfillment</u>.
   - ☐ a. confusion
   - ☐ b. disappointment
   - ☐ c. frustration
   - ☐ d. satisfaction

2. To make his lecture more interesting he kept throwing in little <u>practical</u> points.
   - ☐ a. useful
   - ☐ b. funny
   - ☐ c. dull
   - ☐ d. unnecessary

3. It drooped <u>dispiritedly</u> between the shafts of a coal cart which stood like an island in an eddying stream of cars and buses.
   - ☐ a. briskly
   - ☐ b. intelligently
   - ☐ c. gloomily
   - ☐ d. affectionately

4. Not just an <u>inquisitive</u> onlooker but a man who knew and understood all.
   - ☐ a. noisy
   - ☐ b. shocked
   - ☐ c. curious
   - ☐ d. certified

5. So thorough was my inspection that I worked round to the off side of the horse and stood <u>perilously</u> among the racing traffic.
   - ☐ a. easily
   - ☐ b. dangerously
   - ☐ c. comfortably
   - ☐ d. silently

6. He gazed <u>apathetically</u> down the street, easing his hind legs alternately in a bored manner.
   - ☐ a. excitedly
   - ☐ b. hopefully
   - ☐ c. hungrily
   - ☐ d. indifferently

7. The <u>grotesque</u> sight of a man hanging from a horse's mouth brought them to a sudden halt.
   - ☐ a. cheerful
   - ☐ b. ordinary
   - ☐ c. ridiculous
   - ☐ d. festive

8. <u>Appalled</u> at the absurdity of my position, I began to thrash about wildly.
   - ☐ a. horrified
   - ☐ b. entertained
   - ☐ c. unsure
   - ☐ d. relaxed

9. I made no reply, being pop-eyed, half <u>throttled</u>, and in no mood for conversation.
   - ☐ a. drowned
   - ☐ b. talkative
   - ☐ c. curious
   - ☐ d. choked

10. I looked at my new mac. The shoulder was chewed to a <u>sodden</u> mass.
   - ☐ a. warm
   - ☐ b. soggy
   - ☐ c. blackened
   - ☐ d. starched

✎ _____ **Number of correct answers**
Enter this number on the Vocabulary graph on page 167.

Personal Response

In your own words, write what you think the coalman meant when he said, "Dinna meddle wi' things ye ken nuthin' aboot!"

_____

_____

_____

Describe a time when you probably should have followed the advice the coalman gave to the author.

_____

_____

_____

_____

6 Battle Tactics

by Farley Mowat

The Dog Who Wouldn't Be is one of a number of books written by Canadian author Farley Mowat about his experiences with animals. In this passage from the book, he recalls a time when his often-peculiar dog, Mutt, proved there was a method to his foolishness.

The canine population of River Road was enormous. Mutt had to come to terms with these dogs, and he found the going hard. His long, silken hair and his fine "feathers" tended to give him a soft and sentimental look that was misleading and that seemed to goad the roughneck local dogs into active hostility. They usually went about in packs, and the largest pack was led by a well-built bull terrier who lived next door to us. Mutt, who was never a joiner, preferred to go his way alone, and this made him particularly suspect by the other dogs.

He was not by nature the fighting kind. In all his life I never knew him to engage in battle unless there was no alternative. His pacific attitude used to embarrass my mother when the two of them happened to encounter a belligerent strange dog while they were out walking. At first glimpse of the stranger he would insinuate himself under Mother's skirt and no amount of physical force, nor scathing comment, could budge him from this sanctuary. Often the strange dog would not realize that it was a sanctuary and this was sometimes rather hard on Mother.

The local packs, and particularly the one led by the bull terrier next door, spared no pains to bring him to battle, and for some time he was forced to stay very close to home unless he was accompanied by Mother or by myself. It was nearly a month before he found a solution to this problem.

Almost all the back yards in Saskatoon were fenced with vertical planking nailed to horizontal two-by-fours. The upper two-by-four in each case was usually five or six feet above the ground, and about five inches below the projecting tops of the upright planks. For generations these elevated

gangways had provided a safe thoroughfare for cats. One fine day Mutt decided that they could serve him too.

I was brushing my teeth after breakfast when I heard Mutt give a yelp of pain and I went at once to the window and looked out. I was in time to see him laboriously clamber up on our back fence from a garbage pail that stood by the yard gate. As I watched he wobbled a few steps along the upper two-by-four, lost his balance, and fell off. Undaunted he returned at once to the garbage pail and tried again.

I went outside and tried to reason with him, but he ignored me. When I left he was still at it, climbing up, staggering along for a few feet, then falling off again.

I mentioned this new interest of his during dinner that night, but none of us gave it much thought. We were used to Mutt's peculiarities, and we had no suspicion that there was method behind this apparent foolishness. Yet method there was, as I discovered a few evenings later.

A squad of Bengal lancers, consisting of two of my friends and myself armed with spears made from bamboo fishing rods, had spent the afternoon riding up and down the back alleys on our bicycles hunting tigers (alley cats). As suppertime approached, we were slowly pedaling our way homeward along the alley behind River Road when one of my chums, who was a little in the lead, gave a startled yelp and swerved his bike so that I crashed into him, and we fell together on the sun-baked dirt. I picked myself up and saw my friend pointing at the fence ahead of us. His eyes were big with disbelief.

The cause of the accident, and of my chum's incredulity, was nonchalantly picking his way along the top of the fence not fifty yards away. Behind that fence lay the home of the Huskies, and although we could not see them, we—and most of Saskatoon—could hear them. Their frenzied howls were punctuated by dull thudding sounds as they leaped at their tormentor and fell back helplessly to earth again.

Mutt never hesitated. He ambled along his aerial route with the leisurely insouciance of an old gentleman out for an evening stroll.

We three boys had not recovered from our initial surprise when a new canine contingent arrived upon the scene. It included six or seven of the local dogs (headed by the bull terrier) attracted to the scene by the yammering of the Huskies. They spotted Mutt, and the terrier immediately led a mass assault. He launched himself against the fence with such foolhardy violence that only a bull terrier could have survived the impact.

Mutt remained unperturbed, although this may have been only an illusion, resulting from the fact that he was concentrating so hard on his balancing act that he could spare no attention for his assailants. He moved along at a slow but steady pace, and having safely navigated the Huskies' fence, he jumped up to the slightly higher fence next door and stepped along it until he came to a garage. With a graceful leap he gained the garage roof, where he lay down for a few moments, ostensibly to rest, but actually—I am certain—to enjoy his triumph.

Below him there was pandemonium. I have never seen a dog so angry as that bull terrier was. Although the garage wall facing on the alley was a good eight feet high, the terrier kept hurling himself impotently against it until he must have been one large quivering bruise.

Mutt watched the performance for two or three minutes; then he stood up and with one insolent backward glance jumped down to the dividing fence between two houses, and ambled along it to the street front beyond.

The tumult in the alley subsided and the pack began to disperse. Dispiritedly they began to drift off, until finally only the bull terrier remained.

He was still hurling himself at the garage wall in a paroxysm of fury when I took myself home to tell of the wonders I had seen. ■

✔ Enter your reading time below. Then look up your reading speed on the Words-per-Minute table on page 162.

Reading Time _____

Reading Speed _____

Enter your reading speed on the Reading Speed graph on page 164.

Comprehension

Put an **X** in the box next to the correct answer for each question or statement. Do not look back at the selection.

1. What seemed to goad the local dogs into being hostile to Mutt?
   - ☐ a. He wouldn't join their pack.
   - ☐ b. He would snarl at them.
   - ☐ c. He wouldn't share his food with them.
   - ☐ d. He had a soft and sentimental look.

2. The leader of the largest pack of dogs was a
   - ☐ a. Husky.
   - ☐ b. pit bull.
   - ☐ c. bull terrier.
   - ☐ d. bulldog.

3. Mutt would "insinuate himself under Mother's skirt" to
   - ☐ a. hide from other dogs.
   - ☐ b. make her mad.
   - ☐ c. not allow her to walk.
   - ☐ d. visit with neighboring dogs.

4. For generations the backyard fences in Saskatoon served as a safe thoroughfare for
   - ☐ a. cats.
   - ☐ b. dogs.
   - ☐ c. squirrels.
   - ☐ d. children.

5. How did Mutt learn to walk on the fence tops?
   - ☐ a. The author taught him.
   - ☐ b. He kept trying until he succeeded.
   - ☐ c. He went to obedience school.
   - ☐ d. none of the above

6. Why did the author's friend fall off his bicycle?
   - ☐ a. He was clumsy.
   - ☐ b. He hit a pothole in the road.
   - ☐ c. Mutt startled him.
   - ☐ d. The author pushed him.

7. Who lived behind the fence Mutt was on?
   - ☐ a. the author
   - ☐ b. the bull terrier
   - ☐ c. one of the author's friends
   - ☐ d. the Huskies

8. What attracted the dogs to the fence Mutt was on?
   - ☐ a. the yammering of the Huskies
   - ☐ b. Mutt's barking
   - ☐ c. the bull terrier's growling
   - ☐ d. the yelling of the author's friends

9. After climbing up on the fence, Mutt went on to the
   - ☐ a. next block.
   - ☐ b. garage roof.
   - ☐ c. alley.
   - ☐ d. park.

10. When the other dogs saw Mutt on the fence, they
   - ☐ a. ignored him.
   - ☐ b. jumped up with him.
   - ☐ c. barked at him.
   - ☐ d. bit him.

✎ _____ Number of correct answers
Enter this number on the Comprehension graph on page 165.

Critical Thinking

Put an **✗** in the box next to the best answer for each question or statement. You may look back at the selection if you'd like.

1. What mood does the author create in this story?
   - ☐ a. sinister
   - ☐ b. humorous
   - ☐ c. apprehensive
   - ☐ d. cheerful

2. Which of these titles comes closest to expressing the main idea of the selection?
   - ☐ a. "Brains Win Over Brawn"
   - ☐ b. "Mutt Meets New Friends"
   - ☐ c. "Mutt Learns a New Trick"
   - ☐ d. "Mutt Walks the Fence"

3. Mutt's plan for walking on fences probably came from
   - ☐ a. watching other dogs.
   - ☐ b. instinctive behavior.
   - ☐ c. seeing the author do it.
   - ☐ d. seeing cats do it.

4. The word that best describes Mutt's actions is
   - ☐ a. dangerous.
   - ☐ b. stupid.
   - ☐ c. witty.
   - ☐ d. clever.

5. What caused the bull terrier to get so angry?
   - ☐ a. Mutt had bit him.
   - ☐ b. The other dogs deserted him.
   - ☐ c. He couldn't get at Mutt.
   - ☐ d. The other dogs attacked him.

6. Which of the following is a statement of opinion rather than fact?
   - ☐ a. He launched himself against the fence with such foolhardy violence that only a bull terrier could survive.
   - ☐ b. For generations, these elevated gangways had provided a safe thoroughfare for cats.
   - ☐ c. Almost all the backyards in Saskatoon were fenced with vertical planking nailed to horizontal two-by-fours.
   - ☐ d. I have never seen a dog so angry as that bull terrier was.

7. Mutt wanted to walk on the fence top to
   - ☐ a. get into the neighbor's yard.
   - ☐ b. keep his feet from getting muddy.
   - ☐ c. escape the neighborhood dogs.
   - ☐ d. use a shortcut to the alley.

8. Which event happened first?
   - ☐ a. The Huskies howled in a frenzy.
   - ☐ b. Mutt kept falling off the fence.
   - ☐ c. The bull terrier kept hurling himself against the fence.
   - ☐ d. The author and his friends played Bengal lancers in the back alleys.

9. Which of the following does *not* fit with the other three?
   - ☐ a. Huskies
   - ☐ b. bull terrier
   - ☐ c. Mutt
   - ☐ d. Bengal lancers

10. Compared to the bull terrier, Mutt was
   - ☐ a. smarter.
   - ☐ b. braver.
   - ☐ c. stronger.
   - ☐ d. wilder.

✎ _____ Number of correct answers
Enter this number on the Critical Thinking graph on page 166.

Vocabulary

Each numbered sentence contains an underlined word from the selection. Following are four definitions. Put an ✗ in the box next to the best meaning of the word as it is used in the sentence.

1. The two of them happened to encounter a belligerent strange dog while they were out walking.
   - ☐ a. warlike
   - ☐ b. speckled
   - ☐ c. wounded
   - ☐ d. familiar

2. No amount of physical force, nor scathing comment, could budge him from this sanctuary.
   - ☐ a. verbal
   - ☐ b. unstated
   - ☐ c. stupid
   - ☐ d. bitter

3. I was in time to see him laboriously clamber up on our back fence from a garbage pail that stood by the yard gate.
   - ☐ a. with ease
   - ☐ b. with difficulty
   - ☐ c. with great speed
   - ☐ d. without looking

4. Undaunted he returned at once to the garbage pail and tried again.
   - ☐ a. defeated
   - ☐ b. slowly
   - ☐ c. not discouraged
   - ☐ d. not happy

5. Mutt was nonchalantly picking his way along the top of the fence not fifty yards away.
   - ☐ a. carefully
   - ☐ b. uneasily
   - ☐ c. swiftly
   - ☐ d. casually

6. He ambled along his aerial route with the leisurely <u>insouciance</u> of an old gentleman out for an evening stroll.
   - ☐ a. unconcern
   - ☐ b. gait
   - ☐ c. appearance
   - ☐ d. thrill

7. Mutt remained <u>unperturbed</u>, although this may have been only an illusion.
   - ☐ a. alone
   - ☐ b. calm
   - ☐ c. above
   - ☐ d. still

8. He lay down for a few moments, <u>ostensibly</u> to rest, but actually—I am certain—to enjoy his triumph.
   - ☐ a. merely
   - ☐ b. supposedly
   - ☐ c. mainly
   - ☐ d. curiously

9. Below him there was <u>pandemonium</u>.
   - ☐ a. nothing
   - ☐ b. organization
   - ☐ c. chaos
   - ☐ d. loudness

10. He was still hurling himself at the garage wall in a <u>paroxysm</u> of fury.
    - ☐ a. moment
    - ☐ b. outburst
    - ☐ c. feeling
    - ☐ d. threat

✎ _____ Number of correct answers
Enter this number on the Vocabulary graph on page 167.

Personal Response

Describe how a pet animal you have known found a solution to a problem it had.

_____

_____

_____

_____

What do you think was going through Mutt's mind as he watched the bull terrier continuously hurl himself against the garage wall?

_____

_____

_____

_____

7 | Watership Down

by Richard Adams

Watership Down, a popular novel by Richard Adams, chronicles the changes that occur when human beings disturb the peace of a rabbit warren. In this passage, some inhabitants of the warren discover the first hint of trouble.

The May sunset was red in clouds, and there was still half an hour to twilight. The dry slope was dotted with rabbits—some nibbling at the thin grass near their holes, others pushing further down to look for dandelions or perhaps a cowslip that the rest had missed. The warren was at peace.

At the top of the bank, close to the wild cherry where the blackbird sang, was a little group of holes almost hidden by brambles. In the green half-light, at the mouth of one of these holes, two rabbits were sitting together side by side. At length, the larger of the two came out, slipped along the bank under cover of the brambles and so down into the ditch and up into the field. A few moments later the other followed.

The first rabbit stopped in a sunny patch and scratched his ear with rapid movements of his hind leg. Although he was a yearling and still below full weight, he had not the harassed look of most "outskirters"—that is, the rank and file of ordinary rabbits in their first year who, lacking either aristocratic parentage or unusual size and strength, get sat on by their elders and live as best they can—often in the open—on the edge of their warren. He looked as though he knew how to take care of himself. His companion seemed less at ease. He was small, with wide, staring eyes and a way of raising and turning his head which suggested not so much caution as a kind of ceaseless, nervous tension. His nose moved continually, and when a bumblebee flew humming to a thistle bloom behind him, he jumped and spun round with a start that sent two nearby rabbits scurrying for holes before the nearest, a buck with black-tipped ears, recognized him and returned to feeding.

"Oh, it's only Fiver," said the black-tipped rabbit, "jumping at bluebottles again. Come on, Buckthorn, what were you telling me?"

"Fiver?" said the other rabbit. "Why's he called that?"

"Five in the litter, you know: he was the last—and the smallest. You'd wonder nothing had got him by now. I always say a man couldn't see him and a fox wouldn't want him. Still, I admit he seems to be able to keep out of harm's way."

The small rabbit came closer to his companion, lolloping on long hind legs.

"Let's go a bit further, Hazel," he said. "You know, there's something queer about the warren this evening, although I can't tell exactly what it is. Shall we go down to the brook?"

"All right," answered Hazel, "and you can find me a cowslip. If you can't find one, no one can."

He led the way down the slope, his shadow stretching behind him on the grass. They reached the brook and began nibbling and searching close beside the wheel ruts of the track. It was not long before Fiver found what they were looking for. Cowslips are a delicacy among rabbits, and as a rule there are very few left by late May in the neighborhood of even a small warren. This one had not bloomed and its flat spread of leaves was almost hidden under the long grass. They were just starting on it when two larger rabbits came running across from the other side of the nearby cattle wade.

"Cowslip?" said one. "All right—just leave it to us. Come on, hurry up," he added, as Fiver hesitated. "You heard me, didn't you?"

"Fiver found it, Toadflax," said Hazel.

"And we'll eat it," replied Toadflax. "Cowslips are for the Elders—don't you know that? If you don't we can easily teach you."

Fiver had already turned away. Hazel caught him up by the culvert.

"I'm sick and tired of it," he said. "It's the same all the time. 'These are my claws, so this is my cowslip.' 'These are my teeth, so this is my burrow.' I'll tell you if I ever get into the Elders, I'll treat outskirters with a bit of decency. I tell you what—shall we go across the brook? There'll be fewer rabbits and we can have a bit of peace. Unless you feel it isn't safe?" he added.

The way in which he asked suggested that he did in fact think that Fiver was likely to know better than himself, and it was clear from Fiver's reply that this was accepted between them.

"No, it's safe enough," he answered. "If I start feeling there's anything dangerous I'll tell you. But it's not exactly danger that I seem to feel about the place. It's—oh, I don't know— something oppressive, like thunder. I can't tell what; but it worries me. All the same, I'll come across with you."

They ran over the culvert. The grass was wet and thick near the stream and they made their way up the opposite slope, looking for drier ground. Part of the slope was in shadow, for the sun was sinking ahead of them, and Hazel, who wanted a warm, sunny spot, went on until they were quite near the lane. As they approached the gate he stopped, staring.

"Fiver, what's that? Look!"

A little way in front of them, the ground had been freshly disturbed. Two piles of earth lay on the grass. Heavy posts, reeking of creosote and paint, towered up as high as the holly trees in the hedge, and the board they carried threw a long shadow across the top of the field. Near one of the posts, a hammer and a few nails had been left behind. The two rabbits went up to the board at a hopping run and crouched in a patch of nettles on the far side, wrinkling their noses at the smell of a dead cigarette end somewhere in the grass. Suddenly Fiver shivered and cowered down.

"Oh, Hazel! This is where it comes from! I know now—something very bad! Some terrible thing—coming closer and closer."

He began to whimper with fear. ■

✔ Enter your reading time below. Then look up your reading speed on the Words-per-Minute table on page 162.

Reading Time _____

Reading Speed _____

Enter your reading speed on the Reading Speed graph on page 164.

Comprehension

Put an **X** in the box next to the correct answer for each question or statement. Do not look back at the selection.

1. The story takes place during
   - ☐ a. May.
   - ☐ b. July.
   - ☐ c. September.
   - ☐ d. November.

2. Who were the "outskirters"?
   - ☐ a. rabbits from a different warren
   - ☐ b. older and larger rabbits who ruled the warren
   - ☐ c. ordinary rabbits that lacked proper parentage or unusual size or strength
   - ☐ d. human beings who were beginning to invade the rabbits' habitat

3. Fiver was startled by
   - ☐ a. a clap of thunder.
   - ☐ b. Hazel.
   - ☐ c. Toadflax.
   - ☐ d. a bumblebee.

4. The young rabbit is called "Fiver" because he
   - ☐ a. was born in the fifth month of the year.
   - ☐ b. was the last in a litter of five.
   - ☐ c. is five months old.
   - ☐ d. is five years old.

5. The older rabbit says that Fiver is able to stay out of harm's way because
   - ☐ a. he has aristocratic parentage.
   - ☐ b. he is never worried about danger.
   - ☐ c. he is an Elder.
   - ☐ d. no man could see him and no fox would want him.

6. According to the selection, what is a delicacy among rabbits?
   - ☐ a. carrots
   - ☐ b. cowslips
   - ☐ c. dandelions
   - ☐ d. brambles

7. Why does Toadflax think he has a right to eat the cowslip?
   - ☐ a. He is the youngest.
   - ☐ b. He is the hungriest.
   - ☐ c. He is a teacher.
   - ☐ d. He is an Elder.

8. If Hazel became an Elder, he would
   - ☐ a. treat other rabbits decently.
   - ☐ b. get more cowslips to eat.
   - ☐ c. leave the warren for good.
   - ☐ d. get revenge on Toadflax.

9. Who first discovered that the ground had been freshly disturbed and two piles of earth lay on the grass?
   - ☐ a. Hazel
   - ☐ b. Buckthorn
   - ☐ c. Fiver
   - ☐ d. Toadflax

10. After seeing the heavy posts and the cigarette on the ground, Fiver was
    - ☐ a. angry.
    - ☐ b. relieved.
    - ☐ c. fearful.
    - ☐ d. excited.

✎ _____ Number of correct answers
Enter this number on the Comprehension graph on page 165.

Critical Thinking

Put an ✘ in the box next to the best answer for each question or statement. You may look back at the selection if you'd like.

1. The main purpose of this passage from *Watership Down* is
   - ☐ a. to emphasize the differences between the Elder rabbits and the "outskirters."
   - ☐ b. to express an opinion about humans invading the habitat of animals.
   - ☐ c. to inform you about the diet of rabbits.
   - ☐ d. to describe life in a rabbit warren.

2. Who is the narrator of this story?
   - ☐ a. Hazel
   - ☐ b. Fiver
   - ☐ c. an Elder
   - ☐ d. an outside observer

3. The author tells this story mainly by
   - ☐ a. retelling personal experiences.
   - ☐ b. telling different stories about the same incident.
   - ☐ c. using his imagination and creativity.
   - ☐ d. comparing two different kinds of rabbits.

4. Being an Elder allows one to
   - ☐ a. keep out of harm's way.
   - ☐ b. have the largest rabbit hole.
   - ☐ c. show decency to other rabbits.
   - ☐ d. have special privileges.

5. Why did Fiver suddenly shiver and cower down?
   - ☐ a. He felt very apprehensive after seeing signs of the presence of humans.
   - ☐ b. He was cold and wet from crossing the culvert.
   - ☐ c. He was frightened by the sound of thunder.
   - ☐ d. He was worried about what the Elders would say to him.

6. Which of the following is a statement of opinion rather than fact?
   - ☐ a. He looked as though he knew how to take care of himself.
   - ☐ b. The grass was wet and thick near the stream.
   - ☐ c. Heavy posts, reeking of creosote and paint, towered up as high as the holly trees in the hedge.
   - ☐ d. Near one of the posts, a hammer and a few nails had been left behind.

7. Just before Fiver and Hazel were scolded by the Elders,
   - ☐ a. Fiver was startled by a bumblebee.
   - ☐ b. Fiver found some cowslips.
   - ☐ c. Hazel and Fiver crossed over the culvert.
   - ☐ d. Hazel saw two piles of earth on the grass.

8. Which word best describes Fiver?
   - ☐ a. cautious
   - ☐ b. aggressive
   - ☐ c. nervous
   - ☐ d. bold

9. Which of the following does *not* fit with the other three?
   - ☐ a. Buckthorn
   - ☐ b. Elder
   - ☐ c. cowslip
   - ☐ d. outskirter

10. Compared to the Elders, the "outskirters"
   - ☐ a. are lower in class.
   - ☐ b. have aristocratic parents.
   - ☐ c. generally are much larger.
   - ☐ d. are older.

✎ _____ Number of correct answers
Enter this number on the Critical Thinking graph on page 166.

Vocabulary

Each numbered sentence contains an underlined word from the selection. Following are four definitions. Put an ✗ in the box next to the best meaning of the word as it is used in the sentence.

1. There was still half an hour to twilight.
   - ☐ a. dawn
   - ☐ b. faint light after sunset
   - ☐ c. faint light after sunrise
   - ☐ d. noon of the day

2. At the top of the bank was a little group of holes almost hidden by brambles.
   - ☐ a. animals difficult to see
   - ☐ b. tall oak-like trees
   - ☐ c. rough, prickly shrubs
   - ☐ d. small shacks

3. Although he was a yearling and still below full weight, he had not the harassed look of most "outskirters."
   - ☐ a. thin
   - ☐ b. worried
   - ☐ c. shaggy
   - ☐ d. lost

4. Lacking either aristocratic parentage or unusual size and strength, most "outskirters" get sat on by their elders.
   - ☐ a. expensive
   - ☐ b. strong
   - ☐ c. ordinary
   - ☐ d. upper-class

5. He had a way of raising and turning his head which suggested not so much caution as a kind of ceaseless, nervous tension.
   - ☐ a. without creases
   - ☐ b. continuous
   - ☐ c. anxious
   - ☐ d. serious

6. He jumped and spun round with a start that sent two nearby rabbits scurrying for holes.
   - ☐ a. running quickly
   - ☐ b. digging deeply
   - ☐ c. searching carefully
   - ☐ d. jumping playfully

7. "You know, there's something <u>queer</u> about the warren this evening, although I can't tell exactly what it is."
   - ☐ a. calm
   - ☐ b. odd
   - ☐ c. dignified
   - ☐ d. peaceful

8. Cowslips are a <u>delicacy</u> among rabbits.
   - ☐ a. poison
   - ☐ b. official status
   - ☐ c. a choice kind of food
   - ☐ d. antidote

9. "I'll treat outskirters with a bit of <u>decency</u>."
   - ☐ a. proper regard
   - ☐ b. disrespect
   - ☐ c. defiance
   - ☐ d. interest

10. "It's—oh, I don't know—something <u>oppressive</u>, like thunder."
   - ☐ a. friendly and welcoming
   - ☐ b. curious and shy
   - ☐ c. overwhelming and depressing
   - ☐ d. busy and unconcerned

✎ _____ Number of correct answers
Enter this number on the Vocabulary graph on page 167.

Personal Response

How do you feel about real estate developers being allowed to build on large areas of land that support many kinds of wildlife? Explain.

_____

_____

_____

_____

_____

Briefly describe how you would like this story to end.

_____

_____

_____

_____

_____

8 | How the Weather Works

by Ronald Kotulak

Love it or hate it (and we've all done both) it never goes away. It is the weather—a constant presence in all of our lives.

Throughout an average person's life span, nothing will have a more constant influence on his or her behavior than weather.

From the moment a person gets up in the morning, weather will determine mode of dress, plans for the day, and often changes in moods. For a farmer or outdoor worker, the weather could spell financial success or ruin.

Calm, violent, beautiful, or ugly, the weather is continuously changing. Its eternal motion is caused by the complex interplay of four main factors: air, land, sea, and sun.

The vast ocean of air that envelops our globe makes weather possible. Although it appears invisible to us, air has weight and other physical properties that can be twisted and turned, heated or cooled, and swollen or dried to create our weather.

The uneven heating of the earth by the sun sets huge masses of air in motion. Over the equator, which gets the most direct—and therefore the hottest—rays, the heated air rises, sucking up thousands of tons of water vapor from the oceans.

Water vapor is the critical final factor in producing weather. Without it there would be no clouds, storms, or life-giving rain. The rain that falls over land eventually makes its way back to the oceans. Thus it can be used repeatedly to replenish the land.

As the heated air rises over the equator, it travels north and south toward the poles, carrying its priceless treasure of moisture with it. At the same time cold temperatures at the poles cause the moisture to condense and the air to become heavier. As the air sinks, it pushes back toward the equator. Such massive air movements between the poles and the equator generate our prevailing winds.

Nowhere is the clash between the warm and cold fronts more dramatic and terrifying than on the Great Plains. The world's greatest extremes in weather occur in the area from the Rocky Mountains to the Mississippi River. The battle line shifts back and forth as the polar air from the Arctic and the moist, warm air from the Gulf of Mexico show their muscle. Bitter cold, blazing heat, floods, fearsome thunderstorms, and killing blizzards are the awesome aftermath.

On the West Coast, prevailing winds from the Pacific Ocean keep the climate relatively uniform year-round. The ocean is a giant air conditioner keeping the coast cool in the summer and warm in the winter. The Rocky Mountains bar the frigid cold from the Great Plains from reaching the coast in the winter and bottle up Plains heat in the summer.

The East Coast does not benefit as much from the Atlantic Ocean because prevailing westerly winds blow off the continent, making winters cold and summers hot.

The continents heat up quickly when the sun is up and cool off rapidly at night. The oceans, on the other hand, absorb much more of the sun's heat, so they remain basically at the same temperature day or night and often throughout the year.

Ocean currents that move warm water north have a big impact on climate. England should have the same climate as Labrador or Newfoundland because of its northern location. But the kindly Gulf Stream protects England with warm water, making it much warmer in winter than New York City.

The weather machine is made up of many different parts. Here are some important ones:

The sun, that enormous nuclear furnace 93 million miles away, constantly bathes the earth with energy equivalent to 126 trillion horsepower a second. The energy, however, is not distributed evenly. The equator gets the most direct rays, and consequently it is warmer. Away from the equator, the curvature of the earth causes the rays to slant, forcing them to cover a larger area, thereby scattering the heat energy.

The atmosphere is thickest close to the surface. This is the troposphere, and it is where the weather occurs. Air is made up of gases. The most prevalent are nitrogen (which accounts for 78 percent of our air) and oxygen (21 percent). Other gases occur in small amounts, but they are vital. Ozone, for instance, prevents ultraviolet rays from zapping us with potentially harmful radiation, and water vapor produces clouds and rain. Heat from the sun moves the air around, stirring it like soup.

Jet streams are rivers of rapidly moving air, 30,000 to 40,000 feet high, that blow around the globe from west to east. There are two main streams, one in each hemisphere. Over the United States the main stream path usually wanders between the Canadian border and the southern part of the country. The stream travels at 100 to 300 miles per hour. Although scientists do not know what causes the jet stream, it occurs where cold Arctic air butts up against warm, tropical air.

Clouds are created when warm, moist air rises. It cools, and the invisible water vapor in it condenses into tiny visible droplets or ice crystals. Fog is a cloud in air near the ground. Dew is confined to the surfaces of objects, occurring when the ground cools rapidly at night, causing moisture in the air to condense on the surfaces. Clouds often form when a cold front clashes with a warm front, pushing the warm, moist air up high enough to condense the water vapor.

Precipitation occurs in several forms. A typical raindrop contains a million times more water than a cloud droplet. For cloud droplets to form a raindrop, they must bump and attach to a nucleus like a dust particle or ice crystal. When they get heavy enough, they fall. Snow is not frozen rain. Snow forms when the air is supersaturated with water vapor and it is below freezing. Snowflakes crystallize on tiny nuclei such as dust or pollutants. Hail occurs when strong updrafts in supercooled clouds keep raindrops aloft, allowing them to freeze and build up successive layers of ice until they are heavy enough to fall.

There are two basic types of winds, local and prevailing. Local winds are caused by storms or the mixture of cold and warm air. Prevailing winds, such as the trade winds in the tropics and the westerlies over this country, are much more complex, and meteorologists do not completely understand how they work. If the earth did not spin, warmer and lighter air at the equator would rise into the upper atmosphere and flow to either pole. There the air would be cooled. It would then sink and make its way back along the surface to the equator. ■

✔ Enter your reading time below. Then look up your reading speed on the Words-per-Minute table on page 162.

Reading Time _____

Reading Speed _____

Enter your reading speed on the Reading Speed graph on page 164.

Comprehension

Put an ✗ in the box next to the correct answer for each question or statement. Do not look back at the selection.

1. What part of the earth gets the sun's most direct and hottest rays?
   - ☐ a. the equator
   - ☐ b. the South Pole
   - ☐ c. Europe
   - ☐ d. the Gulf of Mexico

2. According to the selection, the final critical factor in producing weather is
   ☐ a. sunshine.
   ☐ b. prevailing winds.
   ☐ c. water vapor.
   ☐ d. the oceans.

3. Cold temperatures at the North and South poles cause the air to
   ☐ a. expand and rise.
   ☐ b. become foggy.
   ☐ c. become heavier.
   ☐ d. turn into water vapor.

4. Prevailing winds from the Pacific Ocean keep the year-round climate on the West Coast
   ☐ a. relatively uniform.
   ☐ b. very unstable.
   ☐ c. cooler than the East Coast.
   ☐ d. drier than the East Coast.

5. Compared to New York City, England's winters
   ☐ a. have more snow.
   ☐ b. are warmer.
   ☐ c. are drier.
   ☐ d. are longer.

6. The earth's weather occurs in the
   ☐ a. hemisphere.
   ☐ b. troposphere.
   ☐ c. stratosphere.
   ☐ d. ionosphere.

7. What is the most prevalent gas found in air?
   ☐ a. ozone
   ☐ b. oxygen
   ☐ c. hydrogen
   ☐ d. nitrogen

8. Jet streams are rivers of rapidly moving air that travel around the globe at speeds of
   ☐ a. 20 to 50 miles per hour.
   ☐ b. 50 to 100 miles per hour.
   ☐ c. 100 to 300 miles per hour.
   ☐ d. more than 300 miles per hour.

9. Clouds often occur when
   ☐ a. a cold front clashes with a warm front.
   ☐ b. prevailing winds blow from the west.
   ☐ c. ocean currents move warm waters north.
   ☐ d. heat from the sun moves the air around.

10. When the ground cools at night and moisture in the air condenses on the surfaces of objects, that moisture is called
   ☐ a. fog.
   ☐ b. raindrops.
   ☐ c. crystallized water.
   ☐ d. dew.

✎ _____ Number of correct answers
Enter this number on the Comprehension graph on page 165.

Critical Thinking

Put an **X** in the box next to the best answer for each question or statement. You may look back at the selection if you'd like.

1. The author's main purpose in writing this selection was to
   ☐ a. emphasize how much the weather can affect the financial success or ruin of farmers and outdoor workers.
   ☐ b. entertain you with interesting facts about weather and its behavior.
   ☐ c. explain what causes the weather.
   ☐ d. inform you that the weather influences the lives of everyone in one way or another.

2. Which of the following statements best expresses the main idea of the selection?
   ☐ a. Weather is caused by a complex interplay of four main factors.
   ☐ b. Weather is continuously changing.
   ☐ c. Weather influences the lives of people more than any other single factor.
   ☐ d. Water vapor is the most critical factor in producing weather.

3. If you were traveling away from the equator, you should normally expect the air temperature to
   - ☐ a. gradually get warmer.
   - ☐ b. remain nearly the same.
   - ☐ c. gradually get cooler.
   - ☐ d. sometimes get warmer and sometimes get cooler.

4. Which of the following best describes weather?
   - ☐ a. predictable
   - ☐ b. often violent
   - ☐ c. consistent
   - ☐ d. continuously changing

5. When polar air meets moist, warm air, the result can be
   - ☐ a. blazing heat.
   - ☐ b. bitter cold.
   - ☐ c. floods.
   - ☐ d. all of the above

6. Which of the following is a statement of opinion rather than fact?
   - ☐ a. Throughout an average person's life span, nothing will have more constant influence on his or her behavior than weather.
   - ☐ b. The continents heat up quickly when the sun is up and cool off rapidly at night.
   - ☐ c. Snow forms when the air is super-saturated with water vapor and it is below freezing.
   - ☐ d. On the West Coast, prevailing winds from the Pacific Ocean keep the climate relatively uniform year-round.

7. If you wanted to avoid the worst weather in the United States, you would not move to the area
   - ☐ a. from the Rocky Mountains to the Mississippi River.
   - ☐ b. from the Pacific Ocean to the Rocky Mountains.
   - ☐ c. along the entire East Coast.
   - ☐ d. along the Gulf of Mexico.

8. England lies just about as far north as Newfoundland. Why, then, does it have a warmer climate than Newfoundland?
   - ☐ a. It gets more direct rays from the sun.
   - ☐ b. It lies closer to the equator.
   - ☐ c. The warm water of the Gulf Stream protects it.
   - ☐ d. It has more fog, which helps warm it.

9. Which of the following does *not* fit with the other three?
   - ☐ a. fog
   - ☐ b. cloud
   - ☐ c. dew
   - ☐ d. wind

10. One way prevailing winds differ from local winds is that prevailing winds are
   - ☐ a. caused by a mixture of cold and warm air.
   - ☐ b. simple and easy to understand.
   - ☐ c. complex and not completely understood.
   - ☐ d. caused by storms.

_____ Number of correct answers
Enter this number on the Critical Thinking graph on page 166.

Vocabulary

Each numbered sentence contains an underlined word or phrase from the selection. Following are four definitions. Put an ✘ in the box next to the best meaning of the word or phrase as it is used in the sentence.

1. Throughout an average person's life span, nothing will have a more <u>constant</u> influence on his or her behavior than weather.
   - ☐ a. continuous
   - ☐ b. important
   - ☐ c. necessary
   - ☐ d. occasional

2. Its <u>eternal</u> motion is caused by the complex interplay of four main factors: air, land, sea, and sun.
   - ☐ a. rapid
   - ☐ b. forward
   - ☐ c. circular
   - ☐ d. endless

3. The vast ocean of air that <u>envelops</u> our globe makes weather possible.
   - ☐ a. spins around
   - ☐ b. warms
   - ☐ c. encloses
   - ☐ d. inhabits

4. At the same time, cold temperatures at the poles cause the moisture to <u>condense</u>.
   - ☐ a. change to a liquid
   - ☐ b. change to a solid
   - ☐ c. change to a gas
   - ☐ d. become thinner

5. Bitter cold, blazing heat, floods, fearsome thunderstorms, and killing blizzards are the awesome <u>aftermath</u>.
   - ☐ a. display
   - ☐ b. result
   - ☐ c. forecast
   - ☐ d. disaster

6. The oceans, on the other hand, <u>absorb</u> much more of the sun's heat, so they remain basically at the same temperature.
   - ☐ a. block
   - ☐ b. take in
   - ☐ c. reflect
   - ☐ d. cool off

7. The most <u>prevalent</u> are nitrogen (which accounts for 78 percent of our air) and oxygen (21 percent).
   - ☐ a. unusual
   - ☐ b. common
   - ☐ c. serious
   - ☐ d. scarce

8. Other gases occur in small amounts, but they are <u>vital</u>.
   - ☐ a. not necessary
   - ☐ b. full of life
   - ☐ c. included
   - ☐ d. very important

9. Ozone, for instance, prevents ultraviolet rays from zapping us with <u>potentially</u> harmful radiation.
   - ☐ a. needlessly
   - ☐ b. dangerously
   - ☐ c. possibly
   - ☐ d. unfortunately

10. Clouds often form when a cold front <u>clashes with</u> a warm front.
    - ☐ a. comes in contact with
    - ☐ b. fights with
    - ☐ c. rises over
    - ☐ d. circles around

✎ _____ **Number of correct answers**
Enter this number on the Vocabulary graph on page 167.

Personal Response

One question I would like to ask the author about the weather is

_____

_____

Tell briefly about an experience in which the weather affected your life.

_____

_____

9 | The Martínez Family

by Oscar Lewis

Oscar Lewis, a well-known social scientist, spent many months observing and recording the lives of the members of five poor Mexican families. The results of his study are presented in his book *Five Families*. This passage from the book focuses on one of those families.

The ancient highland village of Azteca lay quiet and serene on the mountain slope in the early morning darkness. The air was cool and fresh after the long night rain. Spreading from the top of the slope to the broad valley below, eight barrios, each with its own chapel and patron saint, formed little communities within the larger village. Extending up and down the slope, the old terraced streets, laboriously constructed of blue-gray volcanic rock, were lined by small, one-story adobe houses with their patios of semi-tropical plants and trees set behind low stone walls.

In the barrio of San José, halfway between the highest and lowest point in the village, stood the house of Pedro Martínez, almost hidden by the overhanging branches of the native plum trees in his orchard. The tile-roofed house was typical of those in San José, the poorest of the eight barrios, and consisted of one windowless room and an attached kitchen flimsily built of cane stalks. The house site was called by its pre-Hispanic Nahuatl name, *Tlatlapancan*, or "the place where much was broken," referring to a local legend which told how the village god Azteco, said to be the son of the Virgin Mary, had broken one of his clay toys on this site. Forty-three years before, Pedro had thought the house site would be a propitious one and had bought it for 50 pesos.

Over the years Pedro had carefully worked on the little house and its neglected plot of ground, planting guave, coffee, avocado, hog plums, and other plants, all of which contributed to the family diet. Five years ago he and his sons had built the kitchen and had moved the simple hearth of three large stones from the smoky adobe room to the more airy kitchen where the smoke could filter through the spaces between the cane stalks of the walls. For all of its simplicity, it was the best house Pedro and his wife Esperanza had ever lived in.

It was still dark on this July morning when Esperanza opened her eyes. The house was quiet and no sounds came from the street. Esperanza got out of the hard bed in which she and Pedro slept, smoothed her dress, and wrapped a thin, dark-blue cotton shawl about her head and shoulders to ward off the morning chill. She walked barefoot across the dirt floor, found the big clay water jug, and dashed some cold water on her face; then she dried herself with the edge of her shawl.

Kneeling at the hearth, Esperanza uncovered the ashes of last night's fire and fanned some glowing chunks of charcoal into flames. She didn't want to use a match to light the fire for a box of matches cost five centavos and was still a luxury. Now the big clock in the plaza struck four. It was a half-hour earlier than she had thought. Well, her daughter Machrina could sleep a little longer. It was the time of year when the men planted and cultivated the corn, and the women had to rise early to prepare food for them. In the winter months, during the harvest, when the men sometimes worked all night and the women had to give them food at any hour, Esperanza and her daughter had to snatch sleep sitting on the low stools. It was only in September and October when the men were harvesting plums that the women could stay in bed as late as six o'clock.

Esperanza filled the clay pot and set the cinnamon tea to boil. More than 100 tortillas had to be made—25 each for Pedro and for Felipe, Martin, and Ricardo, the three oldest sons who worked in the fields, and 10 more for Pedro's dog. Esperanza lifted down one of the tin cans hanging from the rafters where she kept her supplies of food. It contained corn which had been ground at the mill the previous night. Before the coming of the mill, a few years back, Esperanza had got up at two in the morning during the farming season to grind soaked corn into a fine dough. Now the mill did most of that work for her; she had only to regrind the dough a bit to make it smoother and to give it the taste of the grinding stone. The men of the village had opposed the corn mill because, they said, hand-ground corn tasted better. But the women had won out; the mill was a success. Yes, it was good to have the mill. But all the same it was expensive. The 34 centavos paid to the miller would have bought half enough corn to feed the whole family for a meal. Machrina should do more grinding at home, Esperanza thought as she knelt before the grinding stone.

The first slapping of the tortillas into shape caused Pedro to stir, but the reassuring sound lulled him back to sleep. Their bed stood in the far corner of the kitchen behind an improvised wall of empty plum crates. The wall did not protect him from the noises of the kitchen but it did provide some privacy from the grown children, except during the plum season when the crates were used to haul plums. Until a year ago the whole Martínez family had slept in the other room, but Pedro had recently moved the metal, springless bed into the kitchen. It was embarrassing, he had come to realize, to lie down with one's wife in the presence of one's grown children.

Pedro's wish for privacy, however, had been partially thwarted when Machrina announced that she too wanted to sleep in the kitchen "since it was not nice for a girl to sleep all alone with her grown brothers." Machrina and little Herman, who had shared her bed since infancy, now slept in a cold and drafty corner of the kitchen. The four sons slept undisturbed in the adobe room. ∎

✔ Enter your reading time below. Then look up your reading speed on the Words-per-Minute table on page 162.

Reading Time   _____

Reading Speed   _____

Enter your reading speed on the Reading Speed graph on page 164.

Comprehension

Put an **X** in the box next to the correct answer for each question or statement. Do not look back at the selection.

1. The Martínez family lives in
   - ☐ a. Machrina, Mexico.
   - ☐ b. Tijuana, Mexico.
   - ☐ c. Azteca, Mexico.
   - ☐ d. Esperanza, Mexico.

2. How many barrios were contained in the larger village?
   - ☐ a. ten
   - ☐ b. eight
   - ☐ c. six
   - ☐ d. four

3. *Tlatlapancan,* the name of Pedro's house site, means the place where
   - ☐ a. nothing was found.
   - ☐ b. treasure was found.
   - ☐ c. none return from.
   - ☐ d. much was broken.

4. What had Pedro paid for his home site?
   - ☐ a. 100 pesos
   - ☐ b. 80 pesos
   - ☐ c. 50 pesos
   - ☐ d. 30 pesos

5. This selection describes a day in
   - ☐ a. July.
   - ☐ b. September.
   - ☐ c. October.
   - ☐ d. January.

6. Why doesn't Esperanza use matches to start the fire every morning?
   - [ ] a. Her husband won't let her.
   - [ ] b. They're too expensive.
   - [ ] c. She's afraid to use them.
   - [ ] d. She doesn't have any.

7. During the time of the year this story takes place, the men
   - [ ] a. harvest plums.
   - [ ] b. plant and cultivate corn.
   - [ ] c. harvest corn.
   - [ ] d. take time off from their work.

8. Esperanza gets up early to
   - [ ] a. tend the fire.
   - [ ] b. get ready to go to work.
   - [ ] c. care for the baby.
   - [ ] d. prepare food for her family.

9. How many tortillas does Esperanza make every morning?
   - [ ] a. just a few
   - [ ] b. 10 or 15
   - [ ] c. more than 100
   - [ ] d. several dozen

10. Why had the men of the village opposed the corn mill?
   - [ ] a. They thought hand-ground corn tasted better.
   - [ ] b. It was too expensive.
   - [ ] c. They didn't want their wives to have time for themselves.
   - [ ] d. People from other barrios would want to use it.

✎ _____ Number of correct answers
Enter this number on the Comprehension graph on page 165.

Critical Thinking

Put an **X** in the box next to the best answer for each question or statement. You may look back at the selection if you'd like.

1. The main purpose of the first paragraph of this selection is to
   - [ ] a. explain what a barrio is.
   - [ ] b. describe the setting of the story.
   - [ ] c. inform you where the village of Azteca is located.
   - [ ] d. express an opinion about the homes in the barrios.

2. Which of the following is the most important idea in the selection?
   - [ ] a. The Martínez family are close-knit, hard-working, and survive despite poor circumstances.
   - [ ] b. The Martínez family live in extreme poverty.
   - [ ] c. Though simple, Pedro Martínez's house is the best one his family has ever lived in.
   - [ ] d. In the Martínez family, the women are required to work harder than the men.

3. The Martínez family works hardest
   - [ ] a. in July and August.
   - [ ] b. in September and October.
   - [ ] c. during the winter harvest.
   - [ ] d. when they plant and cultivate the corn.

4. Which word best describes the author's feelings toward the Martínez family?
   - [ ] a. indifferent
   - [ ] b. compassionate
   - [ ] c. envious
   - [ ] d. happy

5. What effect did the coming of the mill have on Esperanza's life?
   - [ ] a. She could work at the mill.
   - [ ] b. She had to work harder.
   - [ ] c. She could gossip there with other women.
   - [ ] d. She did not have to work as hard.

6. Why does Esperanza store the food in tin cans hung from the rafters?
   ☐ a. The food needs to be dry.
   ☐ b. The food is safe there.
   ☐ c. The refrigerator is broken.
   ☐ d. It is hidden from the children.

7. Which of the following best describes how Pedro and Esperanza probably feel about their house?
   ☐ a. only a temporary home
   ☐ b. less than they deserve
   ☐ c. simple, but adequate
   ☐ d. too run-down to repair

8. Why did Pedro move the bed into the kitchen?
   ☐ a. It was warmer in the kitchen.
   ☐ b. He was embarrassed to lie down with his wife in the presence of his grown children.
   ☐ c. Esperanza would not disturb the children's sleep when she got up so early.
   ☐ d. There was no longer enough space in the other room.

9. Which of the following does *not* fit with the other three?
   ☐ a. Machrina
   ☐ b. Esperanza
   ☐ c. Azteco
   ☐ d. Pedro

10. Compared to the other barrios, San José was the
   ☐ a. poorest.
   ☐ b. largest.
   ☐ c. smallest.
   ☐ d. least poor.

✎ _____ Number of correct answers
Enter this number on the Critical Thinking graph on page 166.

Vocabulary

Each numbered sentence contains an underlined word from the selection. Following are four definitions. Put an ✗ in the box next to the best meaning of the word as it is used in the sentence.

1. The ancient highland village of Azteca lay quiet and <u>serene</u> on the mountain slope in the early morning darkness.
   ☐ a. calm
   ☐ b. disturbed
   ☐ c. dark
   ☐ d. dirty

2. Eight <u>barrios</u>, each with its own chapel and patron saint, formed little communities within the larger village.
   ☐ a. nightclubs
   ☐ b. stores
   ☐ c. neighborhoods
   ☐ d. slums

3. The old terraced streets, laboriously <u>constructed</u> of blue-gray volcanic rock, were lined by small, one-story adobe houses.
   ☐ a. destroyed
   ☐ b. built
   ☐ c. neglected
   ☐ d. bought

4. The tile-roofed house consisted of one windowless room and an attached kitchen <u>flimsily</u> built of cane stalks.
   ☐ a. shakily
   ☐ b. cleverly
   ☐ c. hazardously
   ☐ d. sturdily

5. Pedro had thought the house site would be a <u>propitious</u> one.
   ☐ a. cheap
   ☐ b. fertile
   ☐ c. handy
   ☐ d. favorable

6. A box of matches cost five centavos and was still a <u>luxury</u>.
   - ☐ a. very important thing
   - ☐ b. nonessential item
   - ☐ c. hot skillet
   - ☐ d. cheap item

7. It was the time of year when the men planted and <u>cultivated</u> the corn.
   - ☐ a. uprooted
   - ☐ b. ate
   - ☐ c. found
   - ☐ d. tended

8. The men of the village had <u>opposed</u> the corn mill.
   - ☐ a. welcomed
   - ☐ b. frequented
   - ☐ c. resisted
   - ☐ d. abandoned

9. The reassuring sound <u>lulled</u> him back to sleep.
   - ☐ a. bored
   - ☐ b. tricked
   - ☐ c. soothed
   - ☐ d. forced

10. Their bed stood in the far corner of the kitchen behind an <u>improvised</u> wall of plum crates.
    - ☐ a. made from material at hand
    - ☐ b. made from imported material
    - ☐ c. made from wooden material
    - ☐ d. made without nails

✎ _____ Number of correct answers
Enter this number on the Vocabulary graph on page 167.

Personal Response

One thing I admire about the Martínez family is

_____

_____

_____

Besides what the article tells you, what else would you like to know about the Martínezes' family life?

_____

_____

_____

_____

_____

10 | Challenger: The Final Countdown

by Henry and Melissa Billings

On a clear, cold January day in 1986, the National Aeronautics and Space Administration (NASA) prepared to launch another flight in its shuttle program. After 24 successful missions, these shuttle flights into space had become fairly routine. The 25th flight, however, would not be routine at all.

Christa McAuliffe. Francis Scobee. Ellison Onizuka. Judith Resnik. Michael Smith. Ronald McNair. Gregory Jarvis.

These were the crew members of the space shuttle *Challenger*. What happened to them on January 28, 1986, shocked millions of people and left a nation in mourning.

* * *

For Christa McAuliffe, the journey began in 1984. That was the year President Ronald Reagan announced that a teacher would be the next civilian to travel in space. McAuliffe, a social studies teacher from New Hampshire, eagerly applied for the job. She was among 11,000 teachers who sent applications to the National Aeronautics and Space Administration (NASA). Ever since childhood, McAuliffe had been fascinated with space. She told NASA how excited she was when she watched the first satellites being launched. And when Alan Shepard became the first American in space in 1961, McAuliffe was thrilled. She was always envious of astronauts and hoped that some day women would have careers in space too.

NASA chose McAuliffe for the teacher-in-space program in 1985. As part of her historic mission, she planned to teach two science classes in space. The lessons would be beamed live via satellite to classrooms across the country. McAuliffe, age 37, also planned to keep journals as a "pioneer space traveler."

Beginning in September of 1985, McAuliffe went through 114 hours of space flight training at the Johnson Space Center in Houston, Texas. There she trained with the other *Challenger* astronauts. All but Jarvis, a civilian engineer, had previously flown on shuttle missions. In 1984

Resnik became the second woman in space (Sally Ride was the first). That same year McNair became the second African American to travel in space. Onizuka flew on a secret Defense Department shuttle flight in 1985. Smith, the *Challenger*'s pilot, was one of NASA's most experienced pilots. And Scobee, who had piloted *Challenger* before, was the flight's mission commander.

Challenger's celebrated launch from Cape Canaveral, Florida, originally was scheduled for January 23, 1986. But bad weather postponed the flight several times. The astronauts remained in quarantine and in good spirits. They relaxed and studied flight plans while they waited in their quarters.

January 28 was a clear but unusually cold, windy day. In the VIP stands on the roof of Mission Control, the families of the *Challenger* crew shook with anticipation and huddled as the winds blew. The official countdown had begun. Across the nation, people were turning on their televisions. Students were gathered in auditoriums and classrooms to view the launch. At McAuliffe's school in Concord, New Hampshire, students and faculty were cheering loudly. Some wore party hats and waved noisemakers. In unison they chanted the countdown: "5! 4! 3! 2! 1!"

The 11:38 A.M. liftoff was spectacular. Christa McAuliffe's proud parents smiled and hugged each other as *Challenger* cleared the tower. McAuliffe's husband, Steve, and their children, Scott and Caroline, were jubilant. It was a great day. Then something went terribly wrong.

Seventy-five seconds into the flight, Mission Control told the shuttle crew: "*Challenger*, go at throttle up." *Challenger*'s pilot followed the order.

At that point, the shuttle's engines were thrust into full power. Suddenly the spacecraft erupted into a giant fireball. At first, spectators thought the brilliant burst of fire was the separation of the shuttle from its rocket boosters. But seconds later, trails of white and orange smoke streaked across the sky. There was silence for about 30 seconds. Then Mission Control announced that the shuttle had exploded.

The families of the crew members stood still in disbelief. McAuliffe's parents hugged but did not move. Jo Ann Jordan, McAuliffe's best friend, cried, "It didn't explode, it didn't explode." Everywhere people started to cry. At Concord High School, students stared blankly at the television screen. Many did not understand what had happened. Bonnie Wakeley, a sophomore, said later, "We were watching and then they [the crew] were gone. We couldn't believe it."

NASA immediately sent rescue crews to the crash site about 18 miles offshore. There was a slim chance that the astronauts might be found at sea. Ships and helicopters desperately searched the area. But later that afternoon, NASA gave the world the horrible news. Challenger's crew members died in the explosion. Rescuers had found only chunks of debris in the Atlantic Ocean. However, their search would continue and cover many miles. Later, in a huge warehouse, NASA investigators sifted through what was left of the 110-ton, $1.2 billion shuttle, looking for clues.

The Challenger disaster was a devastating setback for NASA and its shuttle program. Thirteen more flights had been scheduled for 1986, but those missions were canceled. McAuliffe's flight would have been the 25th for the shuttle program. In one of her last public statements, she said, "I realize there is a risk outside your everyday life, but it doesn't frighten me."

About a month after the tragic explosion, rescuers found Challenger's cabin and the crew's remains deep in the ocean. NASA was able to determine that the astronauts survived at least several seconds after the explosion. They may have even been alive but unconscious until they struck the ocean surface.

A presidential commission investigated the shuttle disaster for six months. It blamed NASA for allowing the spacecraft to take off in such cold weather. The 30-degree weather caused a rubber seal between segments of the right rocket booster to fail. Fiery gases then escaped through the defective seal. Like a blowtorch, the hot gases burned through the rocket and ignited the fuel in the shuttle's huge external tank. This created the catastrophic fireball that destroyed the shuttle. A film of the flight showed that Challenger was in trouble at least 14 seconds before the fatal blast. The crew may have sensed the impending danger. A split second before the spaceship blew apart, pilot Mike Smith said, "Uh-oh."

It would be 2 ½ years before the United States launched another shuttle. And there were no immediate plans for another civilian to travel in space.

The families of the Challenger crew still grieve for their loved ones. But in their grief, they carry on Challenger's mission—to educate. The families have praised various projects promoting space exploration and education. And together they founded the Challenger Center for Space Science Education in Virginia. They wanted to have something "dynamic" for children and teachers. "The eyes of those little children who were glued to television—you couldn't just let it end that way, with that terrible loss," said June Scobee, widow of Francis Scobee. "The Challenger center is a way to talk about how the mission continues. . . ." And not about how the mission ended. ∎

✔ Enter your reading time below. Then look up your reading speed on the Words-per-Minute table on page 162.

    Reading Time   _____

    Reading Speed   _____

Enter your reading speed on the Reading Speed graph on page 164.

Comprehension

Put an **X** in the box next to the correct answer for each question or statement. Do not look back at the selection.

1. The announcement that the first teacher was to ride the space shuttle was made by
   - ☐ a. NASA officials.
   - ☐ b. astronaut Sally Ride.
   - ☐ c. Senator John Glenn.
   - ☐ d. President Ronald Regan.

2. Who became the first American in space?
   - ☐ a. John Glenn
   - ☐ b. Neil Armstrong
   - ☐ c. Alan Shepard
   - ☐ d. Michael Smith

3. Christa McAuliffe went through her space flight training at the Johnson Space Center in
   - ☐ a. Cocoa Beach, Florida.
   - ☐ b. Houston, Texas.
   - ☐ c. San Diego, California.
   - ☐ d. Baltimore, Maryland.

4. The first woman astronaut to travel in space was
   - ☐ a. Christa McAuliffe.
   - ☐ b. Judith Resnik.
   - ☐ c. Sally Ride.
   - ☐ d. Jo Ann Jordan.

5. Christa McAuliffe taught school in
   - ☐ a. New Hampshire.
   - ☐ b. Florida.
   - ☐ c. Texas.
   - ☐ d. Washington, D.C.

6. What caused the *Challenger's* launch to be postponed?
   - ☐ a. Some astronauts were ill.
   - ☐ b. The rocket booster had to be refueled.
   - ☐ c. The space shuttle needed some repair.
   - ☐ d. The weather was bad.

7. The space shuttle exploded because
   - ☐ a. there was too much fuel in the tank.
   - ☐ b. a rubber seal was defective.
   - ☐ c. static electricity caused a spark that ignited the fuel.
   - ☐ d. the computer system on board failed.

8. From where was the *Challenger* launched?
   - ☐ a. Houston, Texas
   - ☐ b. Cape Canaveral, Florida
   - ☐ c. Tampa, Florida
   - ☐ d. Washington, D.C.

9. Christa McAuliffe's flight would have been the shuttle program's
   - ☐ a. 25th flight.
   - ☐ b. 20th flight.
   - ☐ c. 13th flight.
   - ☐ d. 10th flight.

10. During her flight aboard the *Challenger,* McAuliffe planned to
    - ☐ a. observe the other astronauts.
    - ☐ b. record the technical aspects of the flight.
    - ☐ c. keep a journal and teach two science classes.
    - ☐ d. take detailed notes for a book she was going to write.

✎ _____ **Number of correct answers**
Enter this number on the Comprehension graph on page 165.

Critical Thinking

Put an **X** in the box next to the best answer for each question or statement. You may look back at the selection if you'd like.

1. The main purpose of the first paragraph of the selection is to tell you the
   - ☐ a. names of the crew members of successful space shuttle flights.
   - ☐ b. name of the teacher who died on *Challenger*.
   - ☐ c. date of the tragic event to be reported in the selection.
   - ☐ d. names of the crew members who died on *Challenger*.

2. Which of the following statements best expresses the main idea of the selection?
   - ☐ a. The United States was stunned when the first shuttle launch to include a teacher, Christa McAuliffe, exploded.
   - ☐ b. The space program in the United States slowed down because of the *Challenger* explosion.
   - ☐ c. Investigators blamed NASA for allowing the *Challenger* to take off in such cold weather.
   - ☐ d. The launch date for the *Challenger* had been postponed several times because of bad weather.

3. Based on what you've read, you can conclude that
   - ☐ a. civilians shouldn't travel in space.
   - ☐ b. women will not be allowed to fly on future shuttle flights.
   - ☐ c. despite the disaster, the families of the *Challenger* crew will continue to believe in and support the space program.
   - ☐ d. it is too dangerous to continue space flights.

4. Based on the information in the selection, you can predict that *Challenger* might not have exploded if
   - ☐ a. there were fire extinguishers aboard.
   - ☐ b. there were fewer astronauts aboard.
   - ☐ c. the launch took place on a warm day.
   - ☐ d. Mike Smith had been a more experienced pilot.

5. What was the immediate effect of the *Challenger* disaster on NASA's shuttle program?
   - ☐ a. NASA continued to launch shuttle missions in 1986.
   - ☐ b. Thirteen flights scheduled for 1986 were canceled.
   - ☐ c. NASA founded the Challenger Center for Space Science Education.
   - ☐ d. NASA permanently canceled the shuttle program.

6. Which of the following is a statement of opinion rather than fact?
   - ☐ a. It would be 2 ½ years before the U. S. launched another shuttle.
   - ☐ b. NASA chose McAuliffe for the teacher-in-space program in 1985.
   - ☐ c. They may have been alive but unconscious until they struck the ocean surface.
   - ☐ d. Onizuka flew on a secret Defense Department shuttle flight in 1985.

7. Which of the following statements do you think the authors would agree with?
   - ☐ a. NASA officials acted irresponsibly when they insisted on launching *Challenger* on an unusually cold day.
   - ☐ b. NASA should not have canceled the other planned shuttle flights in 1986.
   - ☐ c. After the *Challenger* disaster, many people lost faith in NASA and its shuttle program.
   - ☐ d. Christa McAuliffe did not realize her mission on the *Challenger* space shuttle could be dangerous.

8. Which of the following does *not* fit with the other three?
   - ☐ a. Ellison Onizuka
   - ☐ b. Francis Scobee
   - ☐ c. Ronald McNair
   - ☐ d. Ronald Reagan

9. In what way was Gregory Jarvis different from Michael Smith?
   - ☐ a. He was an African American.
   - ☐ b. He was an experienced pilot.
   - ☐ c. He had flown a secret shuttle flight in 1985.
   - ☐ d. He had not previously flown a shuttle mission.

10. Choose the best one-sentence paraphrase for the following sentence from the selection: "In the VIP stands on the roof of Mission Control, the families of the *Challenger* crew shook with anticipation and huddled as the winds blew."
    - ☐ a. The families of the crew members shook with fear as they waited for the *Challenger* launch.
    - ☐ b. The families of the crew members trembled with excitement and pressed close together against the wind as they waited for the *Challenger* launch.
    - ☐ c. The families of the crew members clung to each other to keep from being blown off the roof of Mission Control.
    - ☐ d. The families of the crew members, in worried anticipation, huddled together in prayer.

✎ _____ Number of correct answers
Enter this number on the Critical Thinking graph on page 166.

Vocabulary

Each numbered sentence contains an underlined word from the selection. Following are four definitions. Put an ✖ in the box next to the best meaning of the word as it is used in the sentence.

1. She was always <u>envious</u> of astronauts and hoped that some day women would have careers in space too.
   - ☐ a. feeling dislike for
   - ☐ b. feeling proud
   - ☐ c. desiring what another has
   - ☐ d. resentful

2. *Challenger's* <u>celebrated</u> launch from Cape Canaveral, Florida, originally was scheduled for January 23, 1986.
   - ☐ a. famous
   - ☐ b. little known
   - ☐ c. forgettable
   - ☐ d. happy

3. The astronauts remained in <u>quarantine</u> and in good spirits.
   - ☐ a. a state of readiness
   - ☐ b. protective custody
   - ☐ c. isolation
   - ☐ d. the hospital

4. In the VIP stands, the families of the *Challenger* crew shook with <u>anticipation</u> and huddled as the wind blew.
   - ☐ a. cold
   - ☐ b. relief
   - ☐ c. boredom
   - ☐ d. expectation

5. McAuliffe's husband, Steve, and their children, Scott and Caroline, were <u>jubilant</u>.
   - ☐ a. restless and impatient
   - ☐ b. tired and happy
   - ☐ c. very joyous and excited
   - ☐ d. depressed and unhappy

6. The *Challenger* disaster was a <u>devastating</u> setback for NASA and its shuttle program.
   - ☐ a. temporary
   - ☐ b. unexpected
   - ☐ c. overwhelming
   - ☐ d. disappointing

7. Thirteen more flights had been scheduled for 1986, but those missions were <u>canceled</u>.
   - ☐ a. delayed
   - ☐ b. rescheduled
   - ☐ c. criticized
   - ☐ d. done away with

8. Fiery gases then escaped through the <u>defective</u> seal.
   - ☐ a. faulty
   - ☐ b. enlarged
   - ☐ c. repaired
   - ☐ d. frozen

9. Like a blowtorch, the hot gases burned through the rocket and ignited the fuel in the shuttle's huge <u>external</u> tank.
   - ☐ a. storage
   - ☐ b. outer
   - ☐ c. rustproof
   - ☐ d. inner

10. They [the families of the crew] wanted to have something "<u>dynamic</u>" for children and teachers.
    - ☐ a. relaxing
    - ☐ b. interesting
    - ☐ c. full of energy
    - ☐ d. new

✎ _____ Number of correct answers
Enter this number on the Vocabulary graph on page 167.

Personal Response

Should NASA continue its shuttle program? Why or why not?

_____

_____

_____

I think Christa McAuliffe is a genuine hero because

_____

_____

_____

✔ Check Your Progress
Study the graphs you completed for lessons 1–10 and answer the How Am I Doing? questions on page 168.

11 | The Yellow Emperor

by Tao Tao Liu Sanders

In this ancient myth from China, a powerful god's throne is threatened by a scheming lower god.

The Yellow Emperor was an important god in ancient times. He was a very powerful figure and had many children, some of whom were gods and some humans. He took a great interest in the human race and because he protected them and helped them to lead a peaceful, settled life, he was often considered to be an earthly emperor, the first to rule over China.

One of his greatest deeds was his defeat of a monster named Chiyou. Chiyou started life as quite a lowly god whose task was to be a runner for the Yellow Emperor, one who cleared the way for him when he went on a journey. Chiyou was, however, very ambitious and he planned to overthrow the Yellow Emperor and take his throne. Chiyou gathered as his followers some 80 minor gods who were discontented with the Yellow Emperor's reign. These gods were terrible to look at: they had iron heads and copper faces with four eyes, six hands, and cloven feet. Their food was stones and metal and their special skill was making iron weapons of every kind—sharp lances, spears, axes, and strong bows. When Chiyou had trained and organized these demon gods in Heaven, he went down to earth. There he visited the barbarian tribe of the Miao in the south of China, stirring up rebellion and discontent against the Yellow Emperor.

All this time the Yellow Emperor was living comfortably in his palace in Heaven, unaware of the scheming and plotting that was going on all around him. It was therefore a great surprise when Chiyou suddenly attacked with his fearsome army of copper-faced demons. At first the Yellow Emperor tried to reason with Chiyou, but Chiyou was too obsessed with ambition and refused to listen.

The battle began in earnest. Swords and armor clanged and clashed and the peaceful air was filled with battle cries. Chiyou was determined to win by any means and at the height of the battle he used his magic powers to surround the Yellow Emperor's army in a thick fog. The Yellow Emperor tried to muster his men and break out of the all-enveloping cloud, but it was no use. Try as they might, they simply found themselves marching in circles, while the sinister fog swirled around them.

Just when everything looked desperate, one of the Yellow Emperor's ministers, who was fighting with him in the royal chariot, had an idea. "If only we could see the stars through this cloud we could find our direction easily. Now, I wonder. What if we had something that would keep its direction like the North Star. Something that would guide us all out of the mist . . ."

The minister set to work at once with his magical powers and within minutes he had invented and made the first compass. With this marvelous new instrument the Emperor and his army easily found their way out of the fog and the battle began again as fiercely as ever.

Now the Yellow Emperor summoned another of his warriors, Yinglong (his name means Dragon Ying), a god who could make rain at will. "Bring me a storm that will flood this rebel out of Heaven," he commanded. But Chiyou was once again too clever for him. Before Yinglong had even started his magic, Chiyou brought a downpour of rain that stranded the Yellow Emperor's entire army. Still the Yellow Emperor was undismayed. He called one of his daughters, a goddess who was always burning hot, and as soon as she arrived the heat from her fiery body dried up the rain, leaving only small, steaming puddles which quickly evaporated. The army was saved, but the Yellow Emperor's daughter had quite exhausted her powers and could no longer remain in Heaven. No one on earth wanted her either, for wherever she went she dried up the rivers, wells, and fields and people drove her from village to village, a feared and hated outcast. Yinglong, the rainmaker, was also unable to remain in Heaven, for he had been beaten by a superior force and was therefore discredited. He, too, stayed on earth, where he became king in the south. To this day the south of China is frequently wet from his rain-making.

The Yellow Emperor now seemed to be winning the war, but his army was exhausted and their morale was very low. Chiyou was still a threat, and the Yellow Emperor knew that he must find some way to encourage his soldiers. After much thought he decided that what he needed was a war drum louder and more powerful than anyone had ever heard before, a drum that would really put heart into his army and fear into his enemies.

In the Eastern Sea lived a monster called Kui, a strange creature rather like an ox with one foot which lived floating in the sea, keeping company with the storms, opening its great mouth to spit out fangs of lightning and roaring like the thunder itself.

"From this Kui I will make my drum," said the Yellow Emperor and he sent his strongest warriors to capture and kill the monster. A great drum was made from its skin but though the men beat upon it with their hands, the sound was not loud enough to please the Yellow Emperor. Then he thought of the Thunder God. With hardly a moment's hesitation he commanded the Thunder God to be killed, removed his thigh bone, and gave it to the principal drummer. The great drum thundered at last: the Yellow Emperor's forces marched into battle, and the copper-faced demons were routed.

The war was over in Heaven but the Miao tribes on earth were still in revolt. It did not take the Yellow Emperor long to overpower them, however, and at the same time to capture Chiyou and bind him with manacles and chains. Still Chiyou refused to surrender. The Yellow Emperor had no alternative but to have him executed.

Chiyou struggled so fiercely that the manacles around his wrists were stained with his blood. After Chiyou had been killed, the Yellow Emperor threw the manacles into the wilderness. There they became maple trees, and when the leaves turned bright red each year, people said the color was the blood and anger of Chiyou. ■

✔ Enter your reading time below. Then look up your reading speed on the Words-per-Minute table on page 162.

Reading Time   _____

Reading Speed   _____

Enter your reading speed on the Reading Speed graph on page 164.

Comprehension

Put an **X** in the box next to the correct answer for each question or statement. Do not look back at the selection.

1. Who was Chiyou?
   - ☐ a. a lowly god who served as a runner for the Yellow Emperor
   - ☐ b. one of the Emperor's ministers
   - ☐ c. the Emperor's rainmaker
   - ☐ d. the Thunder God

2. What did Chiyou want?
   - ☐ a. to be a more important god
   - ☐ b. to lead the Emperor's army
   - ☐ c. to be the Emperor's chief assistant
   - ☐ d. to overthrow the Emperor and take his throne

3. Chiyou gathered together some 80 minor gods who
   - ☐ a. refused to join Chiyou.
   - ☐ b. wanted their own kingdoms.
   - ☐ c. were discontented with the Emperor's reign.
   - ☐ d. were content to be minor gods.

4. For food, the demon gods ate
   - ☐ a. stones and metal.
   - ☐ b. trees and rocks.
   - ☐ c. the meat of monsters.
   - ☐ d. glass and copper.

5. The Miao were
   - ☐ a. minor gods.
   - ☐ b. barbarians.
   - ☐ c. demon gods.
   - ☐ d. sea monsters.

6. The Emperor and his army were able to find their way out of the fog that surrounded them when
   - ☐ a. the Wind God blew the fog away.
   - ☐ b. a minister invented the first compass
   - ☐ c. the fog lifted by itself.
   - ☐ d. the sun burned through the fog.

7. Who was Yinglong?
   - ☐ a. the leader of the Miao tribes
   - ☐ b. Chiyou's rainmaker
   - ☐ c. the Emperor's rainmaker
   - ☐ d. the Emperor's minister who invented the compass

8. The Emperor's daughter was not allowed to remain in Heaven because
   - ☐ a. she had disobeyed the Emperor.
   - ☐ b. she had exhausted her powers.
   - ☐ c. heat from her body had dried up all the rivers.
   - ☐ d. she wanted her own kingdom on earth.

9. To encourage his soldiers, the Emperor had a great war drum made from the
   - ☐ a. thigh bone of the Thunder God.
   - ☐ b. skin of Kui.
   - ☐ c. body of Chiyou.
   - ☐ d. copper faces of the demon gods.

10. The Emperor threw Chiyou's manacles into the wilderness where they became
    - ☐ a. maple trees.
    - ☐ b. red rose bushes.
    - ☐ c. cedar trees.
    - ☐ d. olive trecs.

✎ _____ Number of correct answers
Enter this number on the Comprehension graph on page 165.

Critical Thinking

Put an **X** in the box next to the best answer for each question or statement. You may look back at the selection if you'd like.

1. The main purpose of the first paragraph is to
   - ☐ a. inform you who the first emperor of China was.
   - ☐ b. identify the setting of the story.
   - ☐ c. introduce the main character.
   - ☐ d. inform you that the first emperor of China was also a god.

2. Which is the best description of this story?
   - ☐ a. a story made up by the author using his imagination and creativity
   - ☐ b. a retelling of a very old story
   - ☐ c. a story of a real person's life written by that person
   - ☐ d. a story of a real person's life written by someone else

3. Since the Emperor cast out his own daughter from Heaven, you can conclude that he
   - ☐ a. would not allow any god or goddess who had lost his or her power to remain in Heaven.
   - ☐ b. preferred to have gods rather than goddesses in his service.
   - ☐ c. punished her for disobeying him.
   - ☐ d. wanted her to have her own kingdom on earth.

4. Which word best describes how the Yellow Emperor must have felt when Chiyou, a lower god in the Emperor's own service, suddenly attacked him?
   - [ ] a. foolish
   - [ ] b. sad
   - [ ] c. disappointed
   - [ ] d. betrayed

5. The Emperor's daughter became a feared and hated outcast on earth because
   - [ ] a. she flooded the land with her rainmaking.
   - [ ] b. the Emperor had cast her out of Heaven.
   - [ ] c. she was believed to be an evil goddess.
   - [ ] d. she dried up all the rivers, wells, and fields.

6. Which of the following events happened first?
   - [ ] a. The Emperor sent warriors to capture and kill Kui.
   - [ ] b. Chiyou brought a downpour of rain that stranded the Emperor's army.
   - [ ] c. The Emperor's minister invented and made the first compass.
   - [ ] d. The Emperor had the Thunder God killed.

7. What was the main reason the Yellow Emperor was able to defeat Chiyou's attempt to take his throne?
   - [ ] a. Chiyou decided to establish his own kingdom on earth instead.
   - [ ] b. Chiyou's allies, the Miao tribe, deserted him.
   - [ ] c. The Emperor could draw upon greater magical powers than Chiyou could.
   - [ ] d. The thundering of the Emperor's great drum frightened Chiyou's demon gods into surrendering.

8. The Emperor's minister invented and made the first compass because the
   - [ ] a. Emperor wanted to know where the North Star was.
   - [ ] b. minister wanted to impress the Emperor.
   - [ ] c. Emperor's army was surrounded by fog and couldn't find its way out.
   - [ ] d. Emperor wanted to know in which direction the south of China was.

9. Which of the following does *not* fit with the other three?
   - [ ] a. Chiyou
   - [ ] b. Kui
   - [ ] c. Yellow Emperor
   - [ ] d. Yinglong

10. In which one of the following ways were the Emperor's daughter and Yinglong alike?
   - [ ] a. Both were unable to remain in Heaven.
   - [ ] b. Both were rainmakers.
   - [ ] c. Both were goddesses.
   - [ ] d. Both were children of the Emperor.

_____ Number of correct answers
Enter this number on the Critical Thinking graph on page 166.

Vocabulary

Each numbered sentence contains an underlined word from the selection. Following are four definitions. Put an ✗ in the box next to the best meaning of the word as it is used in the sentence.

1. Chiyou was, however, very <u>ambitious</u> and he planned to overthrow the Yellow Emperor and take his throne.
   - [ ] a. full of jealousy
   - [ ] b. desirous of achieving power
   - [ ] c. patient
   - [ ] d. organized

2. At first the Yellow Emperor tried to <u>reason</u> with Chiyou, but Chiyou was too obsessed with ambition and refused to listen.
   - ☐ a. talk sensibly
   - ☐ b. argue
   - ☐ c. make an agreement
   - ☐ d. cooperate

3. The Yellow Emperor tried to <u>muster</u> his men and break out of the all-enveloping cloud, but it was no use.
   - ☐ a. control
   - ☐ b. criticize
   - ☐ c. assemble
   - ☐ d. console

4. They simply found themselves marching in circles, while the <u>sinister</u> fog swirled around them.
   - ☐ a. damp
   - ☐ b. thick
   - ☐ c. evil
   - ☐ d. gray

5. Still, the Yellow Emperor was <u>undismayed</u>.
   - ☐ a. uncertain
   - ☐ b. in charge
   - ☐ c. not surrendering
   - ☐ d. not discouraged

6. The army was saved but the Yellow Emperor's daughter had quite <u>exhausted</u> her powers.
   - ☐ a. grown tired of
   - ☐ b. displayed
   - ☐ c. used up
   - ☐ d. wrongly used

7. The Yellow Emperor now seemed to be winning the war but his army was exhausted and their <u>morale</u> was very low.
   - ☐ a. food supplies
   - ☐ b. chances of winning
   - ☐ c. physical condition
   - ☐ d. mental attitude

8. The great drum thundered at last; the Yellow Emperor's forces marched into battle and the copper-faced demons were <u>routed</u>.
   - ☐ a. caught off guard
   - ☐ b. met in battle
   - ☐ c. soundly defeated
   - ☐ d. forced to take a different route

9. The war was over in Heaven but the Miao tribes on earth were still in <u>revolt</u>.
   - ☐ a. a state of rebellion
   - ☐ b. a state of surrender
   - ☐ c. a state of confusion
   - ☐ d. a fighting mood

10. Still Chiyou refused to surrender and the Yellow Emperor had no <u>alternative</u> but to have him executed.
    - ☐ a. regrets
    - ☐ b. choice
    - ☐ c. desire
    - ☐ d. hesitation

✎ _____ Number of correct answers
Enter this number on the Vocabulary graph on page 167.

Personal Response

If I were the author, here's how I would end the story.

_____

_____

Would you recommend this selection to other students? Explain.

_____

_____

12 | Ishi, the Last Yahi

by Ernest R. May

During the early 1900s, a lone Indian wandered into a California town. Soon people began to realize that he was the only survivor of his tribe and that this was his first exposure to the modern world. He was the last relic of a way of life that was long gone.

On August 29, 1911, the story in the *Oroville* (California) *Register* began this way:

An Indian, clad in a rough canvas shirt which reached to his knees, beneath which was a frayed undershirt that had been picked up somewhere in his wanderings, was taken into custody last evening at the Ward slaughterhouse on the Quincy road. He had evidently been driven by hunger to the slaughterhouse, as he was almost in a starving condition. At the sheriff's office he ate ravenously of the food that was set before him. Not a single word of English did he know.

In addition to beans and bread, the Indian was provided with bananas, apples, oranges, and tomatoes. "He knows how to eat none of them," the story continued. "The banana he started to eat skin and all, with an evident lack of relish. When he was showed how to peel the fruit, he enjoyed it hugely." He started to peel the tomato too, "but there he bumped against some of the inconsistencies of civilization, and was shown that he must eat it without peeling it." However, in only a short time the stranger developed a taste for nearly every new food that he tried.

When found, he appeared to be about 45 years of age. No one ever learned his real Indian name. For that reason he was given the name *Ishi*, which in his own language meant "man." It was soon determined that Ishi was a member of the Yahi tribe. As it turned out, he was the last Yahi.

The Yahi were part of the Yana group who lived east of the Sacramento River. The beginning of the end for them came in 1848, when gold was discovered in California. Miners flocked to the area and, among other things, they brought new diseases such as chicken pox, smallpox, and measles. These illnesses killed Yahi by the hundreds. Other Yahi died as a result of quarrels with whites.

In 1872 hunters spotted five Yahi—two men, two women, and a child. The Indians disappeared into the brush. Thirty years later, a group of surveyors found four Yahi who had continued to live a traditional life in the wild. They, too, fled. Then, in 1911, Ishi appeared in Oroville. He may have been the child whom those hunters saw in 1872.

Alfred L. Kroeber and other anthropologists at the University of California took Ishi under their wing. *Anthropologists* study people and their cultures. For the first time, Ishi rode a train, a ferryboat, and a streetcar. He was also given a room in which to live at the university's Museum of Anthropology.

In addition, Ishi also received a job as a janitor at the museum. He soon learned to use money that he earned wisely; "How much?" and "Too much!" were among his first English expressions. Ishi was also given modern clothes to wear, including a shirt, a tie, trousers, and shoes. He never really got used to the shoes and usually managed to leave them behind.

The anthropologists communicated with Ishi through an Indian who knew the Yana language. Ishi himself eventually mastered between 500 and 600 English words, and Kroeber learned some Yana.

Ishi demonstrated the ancient crafts of bow and arrow making and of chipping flint into arrow points. He showed how his people made fire with a wooden drill. Out of wood and flint points he fashioned a harpoon that the Yahi had used to fish for salmon. He knew about plants that were good as medicines and collected them for the museum. Ishi had learned all these things from his father. He also knew how to weave baskets, but he refused to do so since, he said, that was "women's work."

Accepting the modern world with little trouble, Ishi found life pleasant. He was given a watch, which he wound but never set. He had his own way of telling time by the sun and the stars. Streetcars fascinated him, and he could watch them for hours. Automobiles, however, did not impress him very much. He enjoyed nearly every new food that he tasted.

At one time Ishi led a group from the museum to his homeland. He pointed out village sites where he had lived with his parents and grandparents, as well as a cave in which bones of the dead had been buried. With Ishi's aid, anthropologists were able to map the Yahi country and to learn much about the Yahi way of life. Ishi was very pleased to show his new friends how he and his family had lived for many years.

Disease from the modern world finally caught up with Ishi, just as it had with many of his ancestors. In December, 1914, he developed a cough, and his ailment was found to be tuberculosis. Ishi grew steadily worse, and he died on March 25, 1916. "Death came at noon," wrote a person who knew him, "in the time of year when new clover was painting green his native hills and when Deer Creek and Mill Creek were swollen with the rush of the spring salmon run." Saxton T. Pope, an anthropologist, said of Ishi:

And so, stoic and unafraid, departed the last wild Indian in America. He closes a chapter in history. He looked upon us as sophisticated children—smart, but not wise. We knew many things, and much that is false. He knew nature, which is always true. His were the qualities of character that last forever. He was kind; he had courage and self-restraint; though all had been taken from him, there was no bitterness in his heart. His soul was that of a child, his mind that of a philosopher.

Ishi had offered a glance far back through the mists of time to an ancient way of living and of looking at the world—a way of life he himself had known. During the final years of his life, the last Yahi had contributed much to scientists' knowledge about Indians. ■

✔ Enter your reading time below. Then look up your reading speed on the Words-per-Minute table on page 162.

Reading Time _____

Reading Speed _____

Enter your reading speed on the Reading Speed graph on page 164.

Comprehension

Put an **X** in the box next to the correct answer for each question or statement. Do not look back at the selection.

1. In what year was Ishi discovered?
   - ☐ a. 1872
   - ☐ b. 1911
   - ☐ c. 1914
   - ☐ d. 1916

2. When he was discovered, Ishi was
   - ☐ a. living in a cave.
   - ☐ b. ill with chicken pox.
   - ☐ c. wearing a canvas shirt.
   - ☐ d. fishing for salmon.

3. Ishi was a native of
   - ☐ a. New Mexico.
   - ☐ b. Arizona.
   - ☐ c. California.
   - ☐ d. Colorado.

4. Ishi's tribe was called the
   - ☐ a. Yana.
   - ☐ b. Oroville.
   - ☐ c. Sacramento.
   - ☐ d. Yahi.

5. When Ishi was discovered, he appeared to be about
   - ☐ a. 30 years old.
   - ☐ b. 35 years old.
   - ☐ c. 40 years old.
   - ☐ d. 45 years old.

6. What does the name *Ishi* mean in the Indian's own language.
   - ☐ a. "man"
   - ☐ b. "warrior"
   - ☐ c. "leader"
   - ☐ d. "wise one"

7. Ishi made a harpoon out of wood and flint points which he used for
   - ☐ a. weaving.
   - ☐ b. fishing.
   - ☐ c. hunting.
   - ☐ d. protection.

8. Why wouldn't Ishi weave baskets?
   - ☐ a. He considered it women's work.
   - ☐ b. He didn't know how.
   - ☐ c. He had arthritis.
   - ☐ d. He had no time because of his job as a janitor.

9. In a tribute to Ishi, Saxon T. Pope referred to him as
   - ☐ a. the last of the great Indian chiefs.
   - ☐ b. the last wild Indian in America.
   - ☐ c. the most famous Indian of his time.
   - ☐ d. an Indian who was more child than man.

10. Ishi died from
    - ☐ a. smallpox.
    - ☐ b. chicken pox.
    - ☐ c. tuberculosis.
    - ☐ d. old age.

✎ _____ **Number of correct answers**
Enter this number on the Comprehension graph on page 165.

Critical Thinking

Put an ✘ in the box next to the best answer for each question or statement. You may look back at the selection if you'd like.

1. The author's main purpose in writing "Ishi, The Last Yahi" was to
   - ☐ a. entertain you with an amusing story.
   - ☐ b. shock you with an amazing story.
   - ☐ c. inform you about an event of historical and cultural significance.
   - ☐ d. teach you a lesson in Indian history.

2. Another good title for this selection would be
   - ☐ a. "Ishi and the Indians."
   - ☐ b. "How the Gold Rush Affected the Indians."
   - ☐ c. "The Ways of the Modern World."
   - ☐ d. "Ishi: A Link to a Lost Culture."

3. Why was setting his watch not important to Ishi?
   - ☐ a. He had another way of telling time.
   - ☐ b. He never cared what time it was.
   - ☐ c. He didn't know how to set his watch.
   - ☐ d. He wore the watch just for show.

4. Based on this selection, the best word to describe Ishi is
   - ☐ a. adaptable.
   - ☐ b. greedy.
   - ☐ c. secretive.
   - ☐ d. mistrustful.

5. What effect did the California Gold Rush have on the Yahi people?
   - ☐ a. Most of them became rich.
   - ☐ b. They were driven out of California by the gold miners.
   - ☐ c. They were forced to work in the mines.
   - ☐ d. Hundreds died from diseases brought by miners.

6. Which of the following is a statement of opinion rather than fact?
   - ☐ a. Miners flocked to the area and brought new diseases.
   - ☐ b. The Yahi were part of the Yana group who lived east of the Sacramento River.
   - ☐ c. His soul was that of a child, his mind that of a philosopher.
   - ☐ d. He developed a cough, and his ailment was found to be tuberculosis.

7. It became apparent that Ishi grew up on a diet that did not include
   - ☐ a. bread.
   - ☐ b. fruit.
   - ☐ c. fish.
   - ☐ d. cornmeal.

8. Which event happened first?
   - ☐ a. A newspaper reported that a starving Indian had been found.
   - ☐ b. Hundreds of Yahi Indians died of illnesses.
   - ☐ c. Gold was discovered in California.
   - ☐ d. Hunters spotted five Yahi—two men, two women, and a child.

9. Which of the following does *not* fit with the other three?
   - ☐ a. Yahi
   - ☐ b. Ishi
   - ☐ c. Oroville
   - ☐ d. Yana

10. Compared to the Yahi way of life, life in the modern world is
   - ☐ a. more complex.
   - ☐ b. more satisfying.
   - ☐ c. simpler.
   - ☐ d. less advanced.

✎ _____ Number of correct answers
Enter this number on the Critical Thinking graph on page 166.

Vocabulary

Each numbered sentence contains an underlined word from the selection. Following are four definitions. Put an ✗ in the box next to the best meaning of the word as it is used in the sentence.

1. "At the sheriff's office he ate ravenously of the food that was set before him."
   - ☐ a. like a raven
   - ☐ b. predatorily
   - ☐ c. hungrily
   - ☐ d. cautiously

2. "The banana he started to eat skin and all, with an evident lack of relish."
   - ☐ a. seasoning
   - ☐ b. haste
   - ☐ c. enjoyment
   - ☐ d. hunger

3. Miners flocked to the area.
   - ☐ a. flew
   - ☐ b. joined
   - ☐ c. walked together
   - ☐ d. came in numbers

4. A group of surveyors found four Yahi who had continued to live a traditional life in the wild.
   - ☐ a. nearly normal
   - ☐ b. according to custom
   - ☐ c. hunting and fishing
   - ☐ d. rapidly changing

5. "How much?" and "Too much!" were among his first English expressions.
   - ☐ a. symbolic mathematical forms
   - ☐ b. facial aspects conveying feeling
   - ☐ c. words or phrases
   - ☐ d. parts of a vocabulary list

6. Ishi demonstrated the ancient crafts of bow and arrow making and of chipping flint into arrow points.
   - ☐ a. native
   - ☐ b. very old
   - ☐ c. hunting
   - ☐ d. clever

7. Out of wood and flint points he <u>fashioned</u> a harpoon that the Yahi had used to fish for salmon.
   - ☐ a. drew
   - ☐ b. constructed
   - ☐ c. illustrated
   - ☐ d. modeled

8. He developed a cough, and his <u>ailment</u> was found to be tuberculosis.
   - ☐ a. illness
   - ☐ b. pain
   - ☐ c. wound
   - ☐ d. awareness

9. "He looked upon us as <u>sophisticated</u> children—smart, but not wise."
   - ☐ a. well-dressed
   - ☐ b. foolish
   - ☐ c. complex
   - ☐ d. fancy

10. During the final years of his life, the last Yahi had <u>contributed</u> much to scientists' knowledge about Indians.
    - ☐ a. given
    - ☐ b. hidden
    - ☐ c. discovered
    - ☐ d. explained

✎ _____ **Number of correct answers**
Enter this number on the Vocabulary graph on page 167.

Personal Response

If you had been the last Yahi experiencing your first exposure to the modern world, what two or three things do you think would have amazed you the most?

_____

_____

_____

_____

If you could have asked Ishi one question, what would it be?

_____

_____

_____

_____

13 | Just Like Bernard Shaw

by James Herriot

In this passage from *The Lord God Made Them All*, James Herriot, the Yorkshire, England, veterinarian and writer, describes a day when he would have been wise to remain silent.

It was in 1950 that one of my heroes, George Bernard Shaw, broke his leg while pruning apple trees in his garden.

I was shocked when I read about the calamity, and there was no doubt the national press shared my feelings. For weeks bulletins were published for the benefit of an anxious public. It was right that this should be, and I agreed with all the phrases that rolled off the journalists' typewriters. "Literary genius . . ." "Inspired musical critic who sailed fearlessly against the tide of public opinion . . ." "Most revered playwright of our age . . ."

It was just about then that the Caslings' calf broke its leg, too, and I was called to set it. The Casling farm was one of a group of homesteads set high on the heathery Yorkshire moors. They were isolated places and often difficult to find.

The Caslings' place was perched on the moor top, with a fine disregard for the elements. The only concession was a clump of hardy trees that had been planted to the west of the farm to give shelter from the prevailing wind.

Mr. Casling and his two big sons slouched towards me as I got out of the car. The farmer was the sort of man you would expect to find in a place like this, his 60-year-old face purpled and roughened by the weather, wide, bony shoulders pushing against the ragged material of his jacket. His sons, Alan and Harold, were in their 30s and resembled their father in almost every detail, even to the way they walked, hands deep in pockets, heads thrust forward, heavy boots trailing over the cobbles. Also, they didn't smile. They were good chaps, all of them, in fact, a nice family, but they weren't smilers.

"Now, Mr. Herriot," Mr. Casling peered at me under the frayed peak of his cap and came to the point without preamble. "Calf's in t'field."

We set off through a gate with two stringy little sheep dogs slinking at our heels, and the wind met us with savage joy, swirling over the rolling bare miles of that high plateau.

About a score of calves were running with their mothers on a long rectangle of green cut from the surrounding heather. At a few barked commands from Mr. Casling the dogs darted among the cattle, snapping at heels, baring their teeth at defiant horns till they had singled out cow and calf. They stood guard then till the young men rushed in and bore the little animal to the ground.

My patient was expertly immobilized, held flat on the sparse turf by Harold at the head, Alan at the tail, and their father in the middle.

As I dipped my plaster bandages in water and began to apply them to the fracture, I noticed that our heads were very close together. It was a very small calf—about a month old—and at times the three human faces were almost in contact. And yet nobody spoke.

Veterinary work passes blithely by when there is good conversation, and it is a positive delight when you are lucky enough to have one of those dry Yorkshire raconteurs among your helpers. At times I have had to lay down my scalpel and laugh my fill before I was able to continue. But here all was silence.

I began to feel embarrassed. With all my heart I wished somebody would say something. Then, like a glorious flash of inspiration, I remembered the recent clamor in the newspapers.

"Just like Bernard Shaw, eh?" I said with a light laugh.

The silence remained impenetrable, and for about half a minute it seemed that I was going to receive no reply.

Then Mr. Casling cleared his throat. " 'oo?" he inquired.

"Bernard Shaw, George Bernard Shaw, you know. He's broken his leg, too." I was trying not to gabble.

The silence descended again, and I had a strong feeling that I had better leave it that way. I got on with my job, dousing the white cast with water and smoothing it over.

It was Harold who came in next. "Does 'e live about 'ere?"

"No . . . no . . . not really." I decided to put on one more layer of bandage, wishing fervently that I had never started this topic.

I was tipping the bandage from the tin when Alan chipped in.

"Darrowby feller, is 'e?"

Things were becoming more difficult. "No," I replied airily. "I believe he spends most of his time in London."

"London!" The conversation, such as it was, had been carried on without any movement of the heads, but now the three faces jerked up towards me with undisguised astonishment and the three voices spoke as one.

After the initial shock had worn off the men looked down at the calf again, and I was hoping that the subject was dead when Mr. Casling muttered form the corner of his mouth. "He won't be in t' farmin' line, then?"

"Well, no . . . he writes plays." I could see by the flitting side glances that I was in deep enough, already.

"We'll just give the plaster time to dry," I said. I sat back on the springy turf as the silence descended again.

After a few minutes I tapped a finger along the length of the white cast. It was as hard as stone. "Right, you can let him go now."

"I'll take it off in a month," I said, but there was no further talk as we made our way over the field towards the gate.

Still, I knew very well what the remarks would be over the farmhouse dinner table. "Queer lad, that vitnery. Kept on about some friend of his in London broke his leg."

"Aye. Kept on just like the man knows us."

"Aye. Queer lad."

And my last feeling as I drove away was not just that all fame is relative but that I would take care in the future not to start talking about somebody who doesn't live about 'ere. ∎

✔ Enter your reading time below. Then look up your reading speed on the Words-per-Minute table on page 162.

Reading Time _____

Reading Speed _____

Enter your reading speed on the Reading Speed graph on page 164.

Comprehension

Put an **X** in the box next to the correct answer for each question or statement. Do not look back at the selection.

1. This story takes place in the
   - ☐ a. 1930s.
   - ☐ b. 1940s.
   - ☐ c. 1950s.
   - ☐ d. 1960s.

2. George Bernard Shaw was a famous
   - ☐ a. veterinarian.
   - ☐ b. soldier.
   - ☐ c. playwright.
   - ☐ d. farmer.

3. Why was Shaw's name in the newspaper?
   - ☐ a. He recently died.
   - ☐ b. He won an award.
   - ☐ c. He broke his leg.
   - ☐ d. He won an election.

4. The author went to the Caslings' farm to
   - ☐ a. help a cow giving birth.
   - ☐ b. buy some cattle.
   - ☐ c. walk on the moor.
   - ☐ d. set a broken leg.

5. Where is the story's setting?
   - [ ] a. on a farm in Yorkshire
   - [ ] b. on a farm in Montana
   - [ ] c. in a theater in London
   - [ ] d. on a dairy farm in Wisconsin

6. James Herriot earns his living as a
   - [ ] a. journalist.
   - [ ] b. playwright.
   - [ ] c. veterinarian.
   - [ ] d. farmer.

7. How many sons does Mr. Casling have?
   - [ ] a. one
   - [ ] b. two
   - [ ] c. three
   - [ ] d. four

8. What bothered Herriot the most while he was tending the calf?
   - [ ] a. Mr. Casling's criticism
   - [ ] b. the constant talking
   - [ ] c. the mother cow's interference
   - [ ] d. the silence

9. What emotion was Herriot beginning to feel that prompted him to mention George Bernard Shaw?
   - [ ] a. anger
   - [ ] b. embarassment
   - [ ] c. joy
   - [ ] d. fear

10. Herriot told the Caslings that George Bernard Shaw spent most of his life in
    - [ ] a. Darrowby.
    - [ ] b. London.
    - [ ] c. Yorkshire.
    - [ ] d. Wales.

_____

✎ _____ **Number of correct answers**
Enter this number on the Comprehension graph on page 165.

Critical Thinking

Put an ✗ in the box next to the best answer for each question or statement. You may look back at the selection if you'd like.

1. What was the author's main purpose in writing the selection?
   - [ ] a. to entertain you with a good story
   - [ ] b. to describe life on the isolated Yorkshire moors
   - [ ] c. to express an opinion about the intelligence of Yorkshire farmers
   - [ ] d. to inform you about the important role veterinarians play in isolated farm communities

2. The author tells this story mainly by
   - [ ] a. telling it from the point of view of the Yorkshire farmer.
   - [ ] b. using his imagination and creativity.
   - [ ] c. retelling a personal experience.
   - [ ] d. comparing two similar stories.

3. In this story, the author's tone is
   - [ ] a. critical.
   - [ ] b. humorous.
   - [ ] c. serious.
   - [ ] d. apprehensive.

4. Why did the author tell the Caslings about George Bernard Shaw's broken leg?
   - [ ] a. to be polite
   - [ ] b. to make them laugh
   - [ ] c. to warn them to be careful
   - [ ] d. to break the silence

5. What effect did Herriot's story about George Bernard Shaw have on the Caslings?
   - [ ] a. They laughed uproariously.
   - [ ] b. They expressed sympathy for Shaw.
   - [ ] c. They wondered who Shaw was.
   - [ ] d. They wanted to discuss the situation with Herriot.

6. Which of the following is a statement of opinion rather than fact?
   - [ ] a. They were good chaps, all of them, in fact, a nice family.
   - [ ] b. His sons were in their thirties.
   - [ ] c. The Casling farm was set high on the heathery Yorkshire moors.
   - [ ] d. It was in 1950 that one of my heroes, George Bernard Shaw, broke his leg.

7. Why didn't Herriot want to explain to the Caslings who Shaw was?
   - [ ] a. It was time to leave.
   - [ ] b. He didn't care what they thought.
   - [ ] c. He didn't want to reveal the secret.
   - [ ] d. He thought it would only confuse them.

8. Which word best describes Mr. Casling?
   - [ ] a. unfriendly
   - [ ] b. carefree
   - [ ] c. simple
   - [ ] d. stubborn

9. Why does Herriot say he'll be careful in the future not to talk to anyone from the Yorkshire moors about someone who doesn't live there?
   - [ ] a. One shouldn't talk about strangers.
   - [ ] b. They wouldn't know who he was talking about.
   - [ ] c. They might ask him too many questions.
   - [ ] d. He wouldn't want to bore them.

10. If James Herriot is asked to visit the Caslings again, you can predict that he will
    - [ ] a. not go to the farm.
    - [ ] b. talk very little.
    - [ ] c. tell them some stories.
    - [ ] d. bring them a newspaper.

✎ _____ Number of correct answers
Enter this number on the Critical Thinking graph on page 166.

Vocabulary

Each numbered sentence contains an underlined word from the selection. Following are four definitions. Put an **X** in the box next to the best meaning of the word as it is used in the sentence.

1. I was shocked when I read about the calamity.
   - [ ] a. disaster
   - [ ] b. injury
   - [ ] c. fall
   - [ ] d. illness

2. "Most revered playwright of our age . . ."
   - [ ] a. respected
   - [ ] b. forgotten
   - [ ] c. holy
   - [ ] d. despised

3. The Caslings' house was perched on the moor top, with fine disregard for the elements.
   - [ ] a. built
   - [ ] b. set in a valley
   - [ ] c. set up high
   - [ ] d. clustered

4. We set off through a gate with two stringy little sheep dogs slinking at our heels.
   - [ ] a. creeping
   - [ ] b. nipping
   - [ ] c. barking
   - [ ] d. sniffing

5. They stood guard then till the young men rushed in and bore the little animal to the ground.
   - [ ] a. tied
   - [ ] b. forced
   - [ ] c. tripped
   - [ ] d. threw

6. My patient was expertly immobilized, held flat on the sparse turf.
   - [ ] a. branded
   - [ ] b. avoided
   - [ ] c. held still
   - [ ] d. put to sleep

74

7. It is a positive delight when you are lucky enough to have one of those dry Yorkshire <u>raconteurs</u> among your helpers.
   - ☐ a. storytellers
   - ☐ b. veterinarians
   - ☐ c. shepherds
   - ☐ d. politicians

8. Then, like a glorious flash of inspiration, I remembered the recent <u>clamor</u> in the newspaper.
   - ☐ a. article
   - ☐ b. uproar
   - ☐ c. outcry
   - ☐ d. picture

9. I decided to put on one more layer of bandage, wishing <u>fervently</u> that I had never started this topic.
   - ☐ a. happily
   - ☐ b. sadly
   - ☐ c. slowly
   - ☐ d. intensely

10. I sat back on the springy <u>turf</u> as the silence descended again.
    - ☐ a. bushes
    - ☐ b. sod
    - ☐ c. couch
    - ☐ d. rocks

✎ _____ Number of correct answers
Enter this number on the Vocabulary graph on page 167.

Personal Response

A time when I would have been wiser if I had remained silent was

_____

_____

_____

_____

If it had been you setting the calf's broken leg, what would you have said to the Caslings to break the silence?

_____

_____

_____

14 | Engineers of the Woods

Some of the best structural engineers are found working in the streams and rivers in the woods of North America. They are beavers, and the dams and lodges they construct are engineering marvels.

In the forests of North America, where the winters are often long and cold, small ponds can be found along the streams. Sometimes these ponds are natural; sometimes they are man-made; and sometimes they are the constructions of beavers. You can tell a beaver by its dam. To make the dams, the beavers lay sticks and branches on top of each other to form an effective barrier against the water of the stream. Near the dam the beavers build a mud-covered, rounded pile of other sticks and branches. Usually this mound resembles a small island surrounded by the water of the pond. This is the house where a beaver family spends the winter, protected from its enemies and from the cold. The beavers are able to keep dry in the center of the house, which is above water level.

The beavers work hard to make their house. They cut down trees, gather branches and twigs, and put them together with mud. Most of the summer is spent in this kind of work, but in the winter the beavers' work proves worthwhile. Their house protects them even from bears.

During the American Revolution, when the armies made roads through the woods, they often tore down the beaver dams to drain swamps and make dry roads. However, the beavers returned again and again to their former dam sites and rebuilt their dams.

The beaver is related to other rodents, or gnawing animals, such as rats, mice, and squirrels. The beaver, however, is much bigger than its rodent cousins. An adult beaver may weigh more than 50 pounds, and its body may be about three feet long. Its tail will add 10 or 12 more inches to its length. Its hind feet are webbed, which helps it swim rapidly. Its front paws are similar to a pair of strong hands. With them it can carry logs and stones. Its eyes, nose, and ears are small, but it has two huge front teeth. These teeth are always growing, and it must keep them sharpened by constant use. The teeth of an adult beaver are yellow from the bark of trees that it gnaws.

The beaver's tail is particularly useful. It is broad and oval, in the shape of a paddle blade. The beaver uses it as an oar or rudder when in the water, and for balance when sitting on the ground. The beaver often uses its tail to strike the ground or water as a warning to other beavers that danger is near. It can remain under water for 10 minutes, using its tail as a sort of propeller.

People attach great value to the beaver because of its fur. The beaver has practically disappeared from Europe because fur hunters and trappers killed so many beavers for their pelts. The beaver might easily have become extinct in America, too, but laws were passed to protect the beavers before they were all killed.

The beaver likes family life, and lives with the same mate all of its life. Several young—usually two to five—are born every year. The little beavers stay with their parents two years before mating and setting out on their own. The whole family lives in the same mound, or lodge. Generally there are several lodges in the same area, and the beaver families help each other in their community life. They share the work of building dams, constructing mounds, and raising the young (who require more space to live each year).

When there are too many beavers in one place, some of them will start a new colony in another place. They usually choose a spot near some fairly deep lake or river, where there are birch, poplar, or willow trees. The bark of the birch, poplar, or willow is eaten as food. Then the wood is used in building.

Sometimes the lodges are built on the bank of the pond or river, but usually they are built on an island in the water. Beavers feel most secure when surrounded by water. If there is no island already there, the beavers make one by piling sticks and mud on the bed of the river until the top is a few inches above the level of the water. This top is carpeted with small pieces of wood, leaves, or moss. A dome-shaped roof of sticks and lots of mud is then built over this "floor." Food for the winter is taken to the lodge before the weather gets too cold. Some of it—the larger pieces—is stored on the bottom of the lake or river, near the entrance to a tunnel leading up to the lodge. There are sometimes several such entrances, under the surface of the water. Wood that is kept under water may be stuck in the mud, or weighted down with stones.

Beavers prefer to work at night. One beaver, in a single night, can fell a tree that is eight inches in diameter. After felling the tree, the beaver gnaws the trunk into pieces that can be carried. It uses these as the base for the dam. The dam is built in a straight line, or in a curve, depending on the location. A small dam may be augmented after several years, in order to flood a larger surface and provide living space for more beavers. Under favorable conditions, a dam may last for 100 years or more. Naturally, other animals use these dams as bridges, forcing the beavers to keep the dams in good repair. The dams must be strong enough to resist the pressure of ice in the spring; and sometimes holes are made by the beavers, after heavy rains, to allow excess water to run off.

Another type of work beavers do is canal digging. When they have used the good trees near their homes, they must bring more wood from farther away. To accomplish this, they may dig a canal to float the trees to the place where they are needed.

Beaver dams help people because they prevent floods and make irrigation easier. It is fortunate that these animals have not been allowed to disappear completely. ■

✔ Enter your reading time below. Then look up your reading speed on the Words-per-Minute table on page 162.

Reading Time _____

Reading Speed _____

Enter your reading speed on the Reading Speed graph on page 164.

Comprehension

Put an **X** in the box next to the correct answer for each question or statement. Do not look back at the selection.

1. Where are beaver dams mostly found?
   - ☐ a. South America
   - ☐ b. North America
   - ☐ c. Europe
   - ☐ d. arctic regions

2. Most of the beavers' work in building their houses is done in the
   - ☐ a. summer.
   - ☐ b. fall.
   - ☐ c. winter.
   - ☐ d. spring.

3. Beavers are related to
   - ☐ a. cats.
   - ☐ b. dogs.
   - ☐ c. skunks.
   - ☐ d. rats.

4. Beavers use their tails to help them
   - ☐ a. climb.
   - ☐ b. swim.
   - ☐ c. cut trees.
   - ☐ d. carry wood.

5. The beaver has practically disappeared from Europe because
   - ☐ a. they migrated into Asia.
   - ☐ b. the winters were too severe there.
   - ☐ c. a disease wiped most of them out.
   - ☐ d. hunters and trappers killed so many for their pelts.

6. How many beavers are born to a beaver family each year?
   - ☐ a. one or two
   - ☐ b. two or three
   - ☐ c. two to five
   - ☐ d. three to six

7. The entrances to beaver houses are
   - ☐ a. level with the water surface.
   - ☐ b. at the ends of the dam.
   - ☐ c. under the water.
   - ☐ d. under trees.

8. Beavers feel most secure when they
   - ☐ a. are surrounded by water.
   - ☐ b. are surrounded by other beavers.
   - ☐ c. have finished building their dams.
   - ☐ d. have stored away their food for the winter.

9. The most important reason for the beavers' popularity is their
   - ☐ a. prevention of floods.
   - ☐ b. fur.
   - ☐ c. ability to cut down trees.
   - ☐ d. being a source of food.

10. Under favorable conditions, a beaver dam may last for
   - ☐ a. 10 to 20 years.
   - ☐ b. 20 to 50 years.
   - ☐ c. 50 to 100 years.
   - ☐ d. 100 years or more.

✎ _____ **Number of correct answers**
Enter this number on the Comprehension graph on page 165.

Critical Thinking

Put an ✘ in the box next to the best answer for each question or statement. You may look back at the selection if you'd like.

1. The main purpose of this selection is to
   - ☐ a. persuade you of the need to keep beavers protected.
   - ☐ b. entertain you with a story about the beaver's family life.
   - ☐ c. give you detailed information about beavers—their work, their homes, and their family and community life.
   - ☐ d. inform you how beavers build dams.

2. Which of the following best expresses the main idea of the selection?
   - ☐ a. Beavers build their homes on islands for protection against enemies.
   - ☐ b. Beavers must be protected because people greatly value their fur.
   - ☐ c. Beaver dams help people because they prevent floods and make irrigation easier.
   - ☐ d. Beavers are hard-working, resourceful animals with strong family and community values.

3. Based on the selection, you can conclude that people are gradually learning that animals
   - ☐ a. should be limited in number.
   - ☐ b. should never be protected by laws.
   - ☐ c. are often necessary in ways they did not realize.
   - ☐ d. often need to be killed in certain numbers.

4. A general characteristic of beavers is their
   - ☐ a. sense of community.
   - ☐ b. lonely existence.
   - ☐ c. friendliness to humans.
   - ☐ d. fighting spirit.

5. Beavers have not become extinct in America because
   - [ ] a. their population is so huge.
   - [ ] b. they build their homes on small islands for protection from enemies.
   - [ ] c. laws were passed to protect them.
   - [ ] d. beavers are not good game for hunters.

6. Which of the following is a statement of opinion rather than fact?
   - [ ] a. It is fortunate that these animals have not been allowed to disappear completely.
   - [ ] b. The beaver is related to other rodents, or gnawing animals, such as rats, mice, and squirrels.
   - [ ] c. The beaver has practically disappeared from Europe because fur hunters and trappers killed so many beavers for their pelts.
   - [ ] d. One beaver, in a single night, can fell a tree that is eight inches in diameter.

7. Which of the following does *not* fit with the other three?
   - [ ] a. beaver
   - [ ] b. raccoon
   - [ ] c. mouse
   - [ ] d. squirrel

8. Compared to the other rodents, beavers
   - [ ] a. are much larger.
   - [ ] b. are not as smart.
   - [ ] c. like to live alone.
   - [ ] d. are lazier.

9. During the American Revolution, beavers often had to rebuild their dams because
   - [ ] a. they were blown up during the fighting.
   - [ ] b. soldiers damaged them while crossing rivers.
   - [ ] c. supply boats traveling down the rivers destroyed them.
   - [ ] d. armies tore down the dams to drain swamps and make roads.

10. The last paragraph of the selection is intended to show that the author believes
    - [ ] a. only a limited number of beavers should be protected.
    - [ ] b. beaver dams often cause floods.
    - [ ] c. beavers can be used to help irrigate farmland.
    - [ ] d. beavers are helpful to humans and should be protected.

✎ _____ Number of correct answers
Enter this number on the Critical Thinking graph on page 166.

Vocabulary

Each numbered sentence contains an underlined word from the selection. Following are four definitions. Put an X in the box next to the best meaning of the word as it is used in the sentence.

1. To make the dams, the beavers lay sticks to form an <u>effective</u> barrier against the water of the stream.
   - [ ] a. really outrageous
   - [ ] b. very useful
   - [ ] c. almost unnoticeable
   - [ ] d. too elaborate

2. To make the dams, the beavers lay sticks to form an effective <u>barrier</u> against the water of the stream.
   - [ ] a. a hideout
   - [ ] b. a lookout tower
   - [ ] c. a wall
   - [ ] d. a weak bridge

3. Usually this mound <u>resembles</u> a small island surrounded by the water of the pond.
   - [ ] a. looks like
   - [ ] b. is located near
   - [ ] c. is built on
   - [ ] d. floods

4. However, the beavers returned again and again to their former dam <u>sites</u> and rebuilt their dams.
   - ☐ a. places or locations
   - ☐ b. unsightly views
   - ☐ c. feeding grounds
   - ☐ d. destroyed structures

5. The beaver is related to other rodents, or <u>gnawing</u> animals, such as rats, mice, and squirrels.
   - ☐ a. chewing
   - ☐ b. swift-moving
   - ☐ c. small
   - ☐ d. meat-eating

6. The beaver might easily have become <u>extinct</u> in America, too, but laws were passed.
   - ☐ a. very rare
   - ☐ b. almost suppressed
   - ☐ c. seriously hunted
   - ☐ d. no longer living

7. <u>Generally</u> there are several lodges in the same area.
   - ☐ a. usually
   - ☐ b. once in a while
   - ☐ c. at some time
   - ☐ d. consistently

8. After <u>felling</u> the tree, the beaver gnaws the trunk into pieces that can be carried.
   - ☐ a. finishing off
   - ☐ b. cutting down
   - ☐ c. climbing up
   - ☐ d. losing balance

9. A small dam may be <u>augmented</u> after several years, in order to flood a larger surface.
   - ☐ a. rotted
   - ☐ b. removed
   - ☐ c. enlarged
   - ☐ d. destroyed

10. To <u>accomplish</u> this, they may dig a canal to float the trees to the place where they are needed.
   - ☐ a. make an agreement
   - ☐ b. aid someone
   - ☐ c. increase by growth
   - ☐ d. succeed in doing

✎ _____ **Number of correct answers**
Enter this number on the Vocabulary graph on page 167.

Personal Response

What do you think of the practice of using fur from animal skins to make fur coats and jackets?

_____

_____

_____

I find it hard to believe that

_____

_____

_____

15 | The Medieval Castle

by Fiona MacDonald

In western Europe during the Middle Ages (A.D. 500 to about 1450), life centered on the castle—a large fortified building or set of buildings. While most of these ancient relics have been destroyed or now lie in ruins, many of the huge stone castles built centuries ago are still standing.

The earliest castles were built of earth and wood. Local timber was used, if possible, for economy and convenience. A vast amount of wood was needed to build a big castle: over 8,000 oaks (about 950,000 square yards of forest) were felled to construct the huge fortress of Trelleborg in Sweden.

By the 12th century, most new castles were being built of stone, which made them better able to withstand attack. Unlike wood, stone could not be set on fire; and, unlike the earlier wooden fences and towers, stone walls could be built several yards thick. It was almost impossible for enemy forces to batter holes in them, until gunpowder was brought to Europe from China in the 14th century. These new castles were designed with more space for the lord and his family, and with better quarters for the servants and soldiers.

A castle under siege had to be able to provide for all its inhabitants for many months. Capacious storerooms for food, fuel, and weapons were therefore essential. They occupied the ground floor of the castle keep. The upper floors, where people lived and worked, could not usually be reached from the courtyard. Instead, a ladder gave access to the upper rooms, but could be hauled inside if an enemy approached. In some castles the staircase was in a separate building, linked to the main rooms by a drawbridge.

The men who built the medieval castles worked extremely hard. They had some machinery to help them—pulleys, winches, and other lifting gear—but the difficult work of construction was done by hand. Stone was cut to size and lifted into position using hand tools. The huge timbers used for scaffolding and to construct the castles' floors and rafters were sawed and shaped by hand. Some castle inhabitants lived in the middle of a building site for years; it might easily take a lifetime to rebuild a great castle in the latest style.

In emergencies, however, castles could be erected with amazing speed. King Edward I's eight new castles, built under wartime conditions as English strongholds against the Welsh, were ready to occupy in less than 10 years. By 1296, the king was employing over 2,630 workmen in a hurried attempt to finish Conwy castle, at a cost roughly equivalent to $124,000 a week in today's money.

Skilled workmen were organized into teams led by a master mason (or master carpenter, or master plumber, if they worked in wood or lead). They were helped by gangs of unskilled laborers and by local workers and apprentices. Often, the laborers were unwilling "volunteers": soldiers drafted in to help, out-of-work farmhands, and prisoners released on parole.

A castle was usually the largest building for miles around. Often it stood in wild and lonely countryside, but even when it was built on the edge of a town its walls towered over everything else, except, perhaps, the spires of a newly finished cathedral. Its looming presence meant safety and security for everyone who lived nearby.

For this reason, many villages and towns grew up under the protection of great castles. Such new settlements were usually encouraged by the lord. The villagers, men and women, provided a labor force to work in his fields, while their sons and daughters were useful as servants in the castle.

In return for permission to settle on the lord's land, the villagers had to work part of the time for him, and also give him a share of their crops, or else a yearly money rent. He insisted that they use his mill to grind all their corn into flour (and he charged them for doing it), and he collected tolls on all goods sold in the village marketplace. Sometimes, villagers even contributed to the cost of keeping the castle walls in good repair.

In spite of these charges, which poor villagers could ill afford, castle settlements grew and prospered. If a marauding army was on the rampage, the presence of a strong castle nearby was one of the best guarantees of a village's safety. In this way, castles helped to prevent war too.

What was it like to live in a medieval castle? Today we see them as grim ruins, open to the sky, with bitter winds whistling around their crumbling walls. But for people in the Middle Ages, a castle was the most luxurious building they were ever likely to see. As well as greater comfort and luxury, by the 14th century there was also much more privacy. The castle's inhabitants no longer ate and slept in the great hall; different members of the household had separate apartments. There were nurseries and schoolrooms for the lord's children, an elegant sitting room for the lady, a chapel, a library, and several bedrooms.

Upstairs rooms had wooden floors, plastered walls, and painted ceilings—a favorite pattern was the signs of the zodiac. There might be glass in the windows to replace the old wooden shutters. The narrow slit-windows still did not let in much light, but great lords and ladies could afford to burn tallow lamps and candles. Many rooms had fireplaces. It was cozy to sit around the glowing embers, although the most usual seats were still just hard wooden benches. Only the greatest lords and ladies had chairs. When it was time for bed, instead of a straw mattress thrown down on the cold stone floor, you would now find huge four-posters, with soft pillows filled with feathers or wool and heavy curtains to keep out the drafts. ■

✔ Enter your reading time below. Then look up your reading speed on the Words-per-Minute table on page 162.

Reading Time _____

Reading Speed _____

Enter your reading speed on the Reading Speed graph on page 164.

Comprehension

Put an **X** in the box next to the correct answer for each question or statement. Do not look back at the selection.

1. What were the earliest castles made of?
   - a. stone
   - b. cement
   - c. earth and wood
   - d. brick

2. One important reason stone was preferred over wood in building castles was
   - a. it was less expensive.
   - b. it could not be set on fire.
   - c. there were not enough trees to provide the needed wood.
   - d. it was much easier to build with.

3. Gunpowder was brought to Europe from China in the
   - a. 11th century.
   - b. 12th century.
   - c. 13th century.
   - d. 14th century.

4. Why were ladders used to reach the upper floors of a castle rather than stairs?
   - a. It was too expensive to build stairways that high.
   - b. Ladders could be hauled inside if an enemy approached.
   - c. Wooden ladders were much easier to build than stone stairways.
   - d. The upper floors were seldom used.

5. The most difficult work in constructing a castle was done by
   - ☐ a. hand.
   - ☐ b. pulleys.
   - ☐ c. winches.
   - ☐ d. scaffolding.

6. How long did it take to build King Edward I's eight new castles?
   - ☐ a. a lifetime
   - ☐ b. under five years
   - ☐ c. under 10 years
   - ☐ d. over 10 years

7. The workers brought in to help build a castle were
   - ☐ a. out-of-work farmhands.
   - ☐ b. soldiers.
   - ☐ c. prisoners released on parole.
   - ☐ d. all of the above

8. For permission to settle on the land of a castle lord, villagers had to
   - ☐ a. pay rent or share their crops with him.
   - ☐ b. fight against any enemy that attacked the lord's castle.
   - ☐ c. sell their goods only to him.
   - ☐ d. allow the lord to use their mill, for free, to grind his corn.

9. For people in the Middle Ages, a castle was
   - ☐ a. a damp and dreary place to live.
   - ☐ b. a place that required too much money to keep in good repair.
   - ☐ c. a place that offered opportunities for work.
   - ☐ d. the most luxurious place they were ever likely to see.

10. While there were some luxuries in later castles, only the greatest lords and ladies had
    - ☐ a. fireplaces.
    - ☐ b. chairs.
    - ☐ c. painted ceilings.
    - ☐ d. glass in the windows.

✎ _____ Number of correct answers
Enter this number on the Comprehension graph on page 165.

Critical Thinking

Put an **X** in the box next to the best answer for each question or statement. You may look back at the selection if you'd like.

1. The main purpose of the first two paragraphs of the selection is to
   - ☐ a. inform you what medieval castles were built of.
   - ☐ b. describe how castles were built.
   - ☐ c. convince you of the superiority of stone over wood for building castles.
   - ☐ d. inform you that gunpowder was brought to Europe from China in the 14th century.

2. Which of the following statements best expresses the main idea of the selection?
   - ☐ a. Most new castles were built of stone because it made them better able to withstand attack.
   - ☐ b. Older castles were quite uncomfortable, but those built in the 14th century provided greater comfort and luxury.
   - ☐ c. Medieval castles served several purposes: as a residence for a lord and his family; as a refuge from attack; and as a focal point for the castle community.
   - ☐ d. The presence of a strong castle nearby was one of the best guarantees of a village's safety.

3. By the year 1500, the era of the castle had come nearly to an end. Based on the selection, you can conclude that a major reason for this was
   - ☐ a. castles became too expensive to build.
   - ☐ b. castles were still too uncomfortable to live in.
   - ☐ c. any castle could easily be destroyed with gunpowder weapons.
   - ☐ d. the villagers would no longer work for the castle lords.

4. Which of the following events happened last?
   - ☐ a. The huge fortress of Trelleborg in Sweden was built.
   - ☐ b. Gunpowder was brought to Europe from China.
   - ☐ c. The first stone castles were built.
   - ☐ d. King Edward I built eight new castles.

5. The lord of a castle encouraged people to settle in a village around his castle because he
   - ☐ a. needed them to work in his fields and in his castle.
   - ☐ b. could enlist villagers into his army if an enemy attacked.
   - ☐ c. thought it would make it more difficult for an enemy to attack it.
   - ☐ d. wanted to provide protection for the villagers from any enemy.

6. Which of the following is a statement of opinion rather than fact?
   - ☐ a. Today we see them as grim ruins, open to the sky, with bitter winds whistling around their crumbling walls.
   - ☐ b. A castle was usually the largest building for miles around.
   - ☐ c. By the 12th century, most new castles were being built in stone.
   - ☐ d. In some castles the staircase was in a separate building, linked to the main rooms by a drawbridge.

7. Which word best describes the way the lord of a castle treated the villagers of his castle community?
   - ☐ a. fairly
   - ☐ b. harshly
   - ☐ c. kindly
   - ☐ d. unjustly

8. Based on the selection, which of these building materials does not fit with the other three?
   - ☐ a. earth
   - ☐ b. stone
   - ☐ c. steel
   - ☐ d. wood

9. One advantage a castle built with earth and wood had over one built with stone was
   - ☐ a. it could not be set on fire.
   - ☐ b. its walls could be built several yards thick.
   - ☐ c. it was impossible for any forces to batter holes in its walls.
   - ☐ d. none of the above

10. Based on the selection, you can conclude that the primary purpose of a castle was to
   - ☐ a. provide an impressive residence for the lord and his family.
   - ☐ b. provide work for carpenters and stonecutters.
   - ☐ c. provide a self-contained community that did not rely on outsiders.
   - ☐ d. provide protection from attack.

✎ _____ **Number of correct answers**
Enter this number on the Critical Thinking graph on page 166.

Vocabulary

Each numbered sentence contains an underlined word from the selection. Following are four definitions. Put an **X** in the box next to the best meaning of the word as it is used in the sentence.

1. Most new castles were built in stone, which made them better able to <u>withstand</u> attack.
   - ☐ a. prevent
   - ☐ b. launch
   - ☐ c. resist successfully
   - ☐ d. prepare for

2. <u>Capacious</u> storerooms for food, fuel, and weapons were therefore essential.
   - ☐ a. hidden
   - ☐ b. protected
   - ☐ c. very large
   - ☐ d. limited

3. A ladder gave <u>access</u> to the upper rooms.
   - ☐ a. a way of approach
   - ☐ b. an alternative means
   - ☐ c. a secret entrance
   - ☐ d. the location of

4. King Edward I's eight new castles were ready to <u>occupy</u> in less than 10 years.
   - ☐ a. defend
   - ☐ b. abandon
   - ☐ c. live in
   - ☐ d. take possession of

5. Its <u>looming</u> presence meant safety and security for everybody who lived nearby.
   - ☐ a. comforting
   - ☐ b. lonely
   - ☐ c. familiar
   - ☐ d. appearing of great size

6. Sometimes, villagers even <u>contributed</u> to the cost of keeping the castle walls in good repair.
   - ☐ a. objected
   - ☐ b. agreed
   - ☐ c. added
   - ☐ d. donated

7. In spite of these charges, castle settlements grew and <u>prospered</u>.
   - ☐ a. became poorer
   - ☐ b. remained loyal
   - ☐ c. failed
   - ☐ d. thrived

8. If a marauding army was <u>on the rampage</u>, the presence of a strong castle nearby was one of the best guarantees of a villager's safety.
   - ☐ a. on the horizon
   - ☐ b. acting violently
   - ☐ c. in the region
   - ☐ d. approaching quickly

9. Today we see them as grim ruins with bitter winds whistling around their <u>crumbling</u> walls.
   - ☐ a. timeworn
   - ☐ b. sturdy
   - ☐ c. falling to pieces
   - ☐ d. interesting

10. A castle was the most <u>luxurious</u> building they were ever likely to see.
    - ☐ a. above ordinary
    - ☐ b. important
    - ☐ c. mysterious
    - ☐ d. fanciful

✎ _____ **Number of correct answers**
Enter this number on the Vocabulary graph on page 167.

Personal Response

One thing not mentioned in the selection that I would like to know about castles (or castle life) is

_____

_____

16 | Turquoise: The Sky Stone

While it may not be rare as gold or diamonds, turquoise has a long and fascinating history. And its popularity has been growing.

Turquoise is an opaque mineral that has been widely used as a gemstone. The name of the gem comes from the French word *turquoyse,* meaning "Turkish," indicating the Middle Eastern origin of the stones. Turquoise has always been a popular gemstone. Many years ago it was mined by the ancient Egyptians in the Sinai peninsula. It is recorded that Queen Zer of the first Egyptian dynasty owned turquoise jewelry. Turquoise is said to bring success in love and money. It is also the birthstone for December.

Technically, turquoise is a mineral belonging to the copper group. It is found in arid regions of the southwestern United States and parts of Asia. It is formed when surface rocks that are rich in aluminum undergo a chemical change. In most cases turquoise results from the weathering of lava. Water deposits the mineral in veins within existing rock. This surrounding rock creates the characteristic turquoise markings, or matrix, which appear in the gem as thin, colored lines, spots and blotches of various colors, shiny flakes of quartz, and even glittering, gold-colored iron pyrite. This matrix gives each stone its own unique natural beauty.

Turquoise is found in many locations all over the world. Major, high-grade deposits are found in Iran and Tibet; the mines around Nishapur, in Iran, yield the high-quality stones known as Persian turquoise. Low- to medium-grade turquoise is also found in Africa, Australia, and China. Copious quantities of turquoise, ranging all the way from low-quality to high-quality gems, are found in the southwestern United States, especially in Arizona, Nevada, New Mexico, and Colorado.

The "sky stone," as it is called, has been part of southwestern American Indian cultures for centuries. Native people were mining turquoise centuries before the arrival of the Europeans on the North American continent. Turquoise deposits found in the West have shown evidence of prehistoric mining. The oldest well-documented record of the use of turquoise was the discovery of two turquoise ornaments at southeastern Arizona's Snaketown ruin, estimated to have been made before A.D. 300. To the Indians, turquoise has the life-giving power of sky and water, and the stones are held in high esteem. The beautiful blue gem found in the earth is a sign of wealth, as well as a symbol of protection from the forces of evil.

Turquoise is prized for its color, which ranges from bright blue to blue-green. It is relatively soft and is easy to shape and polish. Unlike crystals, which are cut in angular shapes, turquoise gemstones are usually cut in a smooth, rounded dome shape. The stones are cut so that the finished gem includes some of the matrix in which the turquoise is found. The matrix can be brown, black, yellow, red, or even white. Although turquoise is considered most valuable when it is "pure," or completely blue and free of matrix, many people judge a stone by how much matrix it contains. Some people find the matrix an extremely attractive feature. One form of matrix that is very popular today is known as "spiderweb." In this type of turquoise, the matrix is formed in very fine lines that show patterns similar to lifelike spiderwebs.

In the same way that the color of turquoise varies from light blue to deep blue and green, the gem itself comes in various grades. Only a small percentage of the stones found in any turquoise mine are of the high-grade quality. High-grade stones are those with the greatest density, hardest consistency, and deepest color, as well as those with the finest matrix pattern. Turquoise is sold by carat weight, with high-grade stones costing considerably more per carat because of their quality and scarcity.

As turquoise grades go downward, the hardness decreases accordingly and the color gets noticeably lighter. These medium to lower grades of turquoise are more abundant than the high-grade stones. Most often they are stabilized, or chemically hardened, to increase durability and deepen the color of the stones. Naturally, stabilized turquoise is less expensive than the higher grades, but it commands a greater price than unstabilized stones of the same grade. Much confusion exists as to the merits of stabilized turquoise. Many people are under the impression that stabilization alters the true stone, covers faults, and makes it less valuable. On the contrary, proper stabilization of turquoise enhances the color and durability of the stone so that it will resist cracking and retain its sky-blue color through the years.

In the past few years turquoise has become very popular. Turquoise jewelry is worn by people from all walks of life. The jewelry comes in many forms—earrings, rings, bracelets, necklaces, and pins. Turquoise is also used to decorate such things as silver spoons, vases, dishes, and many other household items. Turquoise is quite popular with men and is used in making belt buckles, tie tacs, rings, watchbands, money clips, and western neckties.

One unfortunate problem has arisen regarding the selling of turquoise jewelry. Many people who are not Native Americans are making and selling turquoise jewelry while advertising it as American Indian–made. If you desire true American Indian–made items, make sure that the person you are dealing with can guarantee that what you have purchased is authentic. Many turquoise items, however, are quite lovely even though they are not authentically Indian-made.

When seeking to purchase turquoise, beware of plastic sold as turquoise, or inferior turquoise mixed with plastic, or dyed turquoise sold as genuine turquoise. Iodine and shoe polish can be used to produce a phony matrix. The authentic turquoise gemstone is indeed a beautiful and valuable item that will surely give its owner great pleasure. ■

✔ Enter your reading time below. Then look up your reading speed on the Words-per-Minute table on page 163.

Reading Time _____

Reading Speed _____

Enter your reading speed on the Reading Speed graph on page 164.

Comprehension

Put an **X** in the box next to the correct answer for each question or statement. Do not look back at the selection.

1. From which language does the word *tourquoyse* originally come?
   - ☐ a. Turkish
   - ☐ b. Spanish
   - ☐ c. French
   - ☐ d. English

2. Turquoise belongs to which mineral group?
   - ☐ a. lead
   - ☐ b. silver
   - ☐ c. gold
   - ☐ d. copper

3. Generally, turquoise results
   - ☐ a. from the stabilization of gemstones.
   - ☐ b. from the weathering of lava.
   - ☐ c. when lava is mixed with plastic.
   - ☐ d. when a matrix appears in crystals.

4. Persian turquoise comes from
   - ☐ a. Turkey.
   - ☐ b. France.
   - ☐ c. America.
   - ☐ d. Iran.

5. American Indians have been using turquoise
   - [ ] a. since Columbus came to America.
   - [ ] b. for many centuries.
   - [ ] c. for 300 years.
   - [ ] d. since 1990.

6. Turquoise is prized for its
   - [ ] a. shape.
   - [ ] b. smoothness.
   - [ ] c. matrix patterns.
   - [ ] d. color.

7. Turquoise is sold by
   - [ ] a. the ounce.
   - [ ] b. the pound.
   - [ ] c. carat weight.
   - [ ] d. the dozen.

8. The matrix of a turquoise stone is the
   - [ ] a. color of the stone.
   - [ ] b. fine lines in the stone.
   - [ ] c. weight of the stone.
   - [ ] d. hardness of the stone.

9. As turquoise grades go downward,
   - [ ] a. hardness decreases.
   - [ ] b. hardness increases.
   - [ ] c. the matrix turns blue.
   - [ ] d. colors become darker.

10. The proper stabilization of a turquoise stone will
   - [ ] a. make it less valuable.
   - [ ] b. enhance its color and durability.
   - [ ] c. alter its color.
   - [ ] d. cover its faults.

✎ _____ Number of correct answers
Enter this number on the Comprehension graph on page 165.

Critical Thinking

Put an **X** in the box next to the best answer for each question or statement. You may look back at the selection if you'd like.

1. The main purpose of the second paragraph of the selection is to
   - [ ] a. express an opinion about the beauty of turquoise.
   - [ ] b. explain what turquoise is and how it is formed.
   - [ ] c. emphasize that the matrix is what gives each stone its natural beauty.
   - [ ] d. inform you where turquoise is found.

2. Which of the following best expresses the main idea of the selection's first paragraph?
   - [ ] a. Turquoise is said to bring success in love and money.
   - [ ] b. Turquoise is the birthstone for December.
   - [ ] c. The name of the gem comes from the French word *turquoyse*.
   - [ ] d. Turquoise has always been a popular gemstone.

3. Why might a dealer pretend that a piece of jewelry is Indian-made?
   - [ ] a. Indian jewelry is tax exempt.
   - [ ] b. The jewelry can be sold more cheaply.
   - [ ] c. The jewelry can be sold for more money.
   - [ ] d. The dealer would show his or her respect for Indians.

4. Which phrase best describes turquoise?
   - [ ] a. extremely expensive
   - [ ] b. very popular
   - [ ] c. very scarce
   - [ ] d. dull in appearance

5. What causes turquoise to vary in color?
   - [ ] a. It has different amounts of various minerals in it.
   - [ ] b. It is treated differently by manufacturers.
   - [ ] c. It is treated differently by different cultures.
   - [ ] d. It has different amounts of gold in it.

6. Which event happened first?
   - ☐ a. The Europeans arrived in North America.
   - ☐ b. American Indians mined turquoise in Arizona.
   - ☐ c. The Egyptians mined turquoise in the Sinai peninsula.
   - ☐ d. Turquoise ornaments were found in Arizona's Snaketown.

7. What effect does stabilization have on turquoise?
   - ☐ a. It makes it harder and less valuable.
   - ☐ b. It makes it softer and less valuable.
   - ☐ c. It makes it softer and more valuable.
   - ☐ d. It makes it harder and more valuable.

8. Which of the following is a characteristic of crystals and not of turquoise gemstones?
   - ☐ a. They are cut in angular shapes.
   - ☐ b. They are cut in smooth, rounded shapes.
   - ☐ c. They are blue or blue-green in color.
   - ☐ d. They are a mineral belonging to the copper group.

9. Choose the best one-sentence paraphrase for the following sentence: "Many people who are not Native Americans are making and selling turquoise jewelry while advertising it as American Indian–made."
   - ☐ a. Many people make and sell turquoise jewelry in a deceitful way by falsely claiming it is American Indian–made.
   - ☐ b. Many people sell turquoise jewelry made by Native Americans.
   - ☐ c. Many people who are not Native Americans buy turquoise.
   - ☐ d. Many Native Americans make turquoise jewelry and sell it to people who are not Native American.

10. Why is plastic sometimes mixed with turquoise?
    - ☐ a. to make it harder
    - ☐ b. to make it darker
    - ☐ c. to fool people
    - ☐ d. to make it waterproof

✎ _____ Number of correct answers
Enter this number on the Critical Thinking graph on page 166.

Vocabulary

Each numbered sentence contains an underlined word from the selection. Following are four definitions. Put an ✗ in the box next to the best meaning of the word as it is used in the sentence.

1. Technically, turquoise is a mineral belonging to the copper group.
   - ☐ a. frankly speaking
   - ☐ b. strictly speaking
   - ☐ c. loosely speaking
   - ☐ d. happily speaking

2. Copious amounts of turquoise are found in the southwestern United States.
   - ☐ a. very large
   - ☐ b. very small
   - ☐ c. occasional
   - ☐ d. nearly used up

3. To the Indians, turquoise has the life-giving power of sky and water, and the stones are held in high esteem.
   - ☐ a. demand
   - ☐ b. fear
   - ☐ c. awareness
   - ☐ d. regard

4. The finished gem includes some of the matrix in which the turquoise is found.
   - ☐ a. surrounding dirt
   - ☐ b. surrounding rock
   - ☐ c. surrounding air
   - ☐ d. none of the above

5. Turquoise is sold by carat weight, with high-grade stones costing considerably more per <u>carat</u> because of their quality and scarcity.
 ☐ a. measure of weight
 ☐ b. measure of counting
 ☐ c. measure of volume
 ☐ d. measure of color intensity

6. These medium to lower grades of turquoise are more <u>abundant</u> than the high-grade stones.
 ☐ a. precious
 ☐ b. scarce
 ☐ c. plentiful
 ☐ d. hard

7. Naturally, stabilized turquoise is less expensive than the higher grades, but it <u>commands</u> a greater price than unstabilized stones of the same grade.
 ☐ a. desires
 ☐ b. requests
 ☐ c. forfeits
 ☐ d. demands

8. On the contrary, proper stabilization of turquoise <u>enhances</u> the color and durability of the stone.
 ☐ a. creates
 ☐ b. removes
 ☐ c. increases
 ☐ d. reflects

9. Turquoise jewelry is worn by people from all <u>walks of life</u>.
 ☐ a. countries
 ☐ b. classes
 ☐ c. ages
 ☐ d. civilizations

10. Many turquoise items, however, are quite lovely even though they are not <u>authentically</u> Indian-made.
 ☐ a. genuinely
 ☐ b. originally
 ☐ c. officially
 ☐ d. formerly

✏ _____ **Number of correct answers**
Enter this number on the Vocabulary graph on page 167.

Personal Response

What do you think of people who are not Native Americans making and selling turquoise while advertising it as American Indian–made?

_____

_____

_____

I wonder why

_____

_____

_____

17 | A Dying Art

by Dan Wulffson

Zach Wallace and his 12-year-old sister Dora live across the road from Derek Hyesmith III, a sculptor. Hyesmith lives alone except for his housekeeper, Ruth Quinlan, who moved into the mansion after the mysterious death of Hyesmith's wife nine years ago. One afternoon Zach, who does chores for Hyesmith, overhears him and Ms. Quinlan arguing loudly, with Ms. Quinlan finally yelling that she is quitting. Later that evening, Zach and Dora see Hyesmith carrying a suitcase to his car and driving off alone, returning later empty-handed. Their suspicions aroused, they decide to find out what is going on.

The next day, Zach was excited to go to work at the mansion. He looked around the grounds for anything unusual but found nothing. He did manage to gather some information and couldn't wait to get home to tell Dora about it.

"Mr. Hyesmith came downstairs when I was cleaning the fireplace," he told Dora a short time later. "He was even more nervous and weird than usual, and he told me he'd fired Ms. Quinlan."

Dora frowned. "I thought you said she quit."

"She did," Zach said. "I kept wondering why he was lying to me. Anyway, then he started telling me all this junk about Hippolyta."

"Hippo—who?" Dora asked.

"Hippolyta. She's an Amazon queen in Greek mytholology. Mr. Hyesmith knows all about her, since she's the subject of his next sculpture."

"So get to the interesting part," Dora said impatiently.

"Well, finally he went upstairs and left me alone, so I snuck into Ms. Quinlan's room." Zach paused. "And all her stuff was gone."

"But we never saw her leave!" exclaimed Dora.

"Right!" Zach nearly shouted. "And we kept watch on the house almost all night!"

"Do you think he killed her?" asked Dora in a whisper.

"Don't know," said Zach. "But I'm going to find out, and you can help. Mr. Hyesmith gave me the day off tomorrow. I'll go into town to the library to see what I can dig up on him. Meanwhile, you keep a careful watch on his house."

When Zach got back from the library that afternoon, he was full of news for Dora. "Guess what?" he said excitedly. "I found out that Hyesmith's wife was actually murdered nine years ago, supposedly by a prowler in the house. But the case was never solved. And get this," Zach added, his eyes widening. "His wife's maiden name was Crookston. So when I thought I heard Hyesmith yell, 'You're a crook's son,' what he was really saying was Crookston."

"Cool!" Dora yelped, and she jumped up from her chair and started pacing the room like a detective thinking about clues. "That means he was saying that Ms. Quinlan was related to his murdered wife!"

"Exactly!" Zach exclaimed. "Anyway, the article I read about the murder said the Crookston family believed Mr. Hyesmith had his wife killed by a hit man named Jenkins, a former boxer who disappeared right after the killing. But so far they haven't been able to prove it."

Dora stopped dead in her tracks. "That would explain why Mr. Hyesmith accused Ms. Quinlan of being a Crookston," she said. "In fact, maybe she did come to work for him just to nose around!"

"And she probably found something," Zach continued, "so he killed her."

"And listen to this," Dora said, about to burst. "I saw smoke coming out of one of the chimneys around noon. And it was hot today!"

Zach's eyes lit up. "Maybe he was burning evidence of some kind. I say it's about time we called the police."

Hyesmith was polite and no more nervous than usual when the police showed up with Zach and Dora the next day. "I fired Ms. Quinlan two days ago," he told the sheriff as deputies searched the mansion. "In fact, I drove her to the train station myself."

The sheriff sat on the sofa opposite Hyesmith. "The kids say they saw you drive off the other night with a suitcase, but they never saw Ms. Quinlan get into the car. And the boy here claims he heard the housekeeper say she quit—when you told him she was fired."

"The children are mistaken on both accounts," replied Hyesmith.

"All right," the sheriff said. "Assuming that you did take Ms. Quinlan to the train station, where was she going?"

"Some town in the Midwest. I even gave her money for train fare, then left. That's the last I saw of her."

"Did you know it hit 90 degrees at noon yesterday?" the sheriff asked, writing down some information in his notepad. "A little warm for a fire, wouldn't you say?"

"That was my kiln," Hyesmith answered simply. "I'm an artist, as you may know, and I was firing clay."

The sheriff looked at Zach and Dora. Frowning, he stood up. "Sorry to have troubled you, Mr. Hyesmith." Then, flipping his notepad closed, he headed for the door, his deputies trailing after him.

But Zach and Dora were still convinced that Hyesmith had killed Ms. Quinlan. They continued to keep watch on the mansion but saw nothing. Then one day they were surprised to see the sheriff's patrol car pull up in front of their house.

"I've got some interesting news," said the sheriff as the kids came out to greet him. "After looking into the stationmaster's records, we found that an unclaimed suitcase belonging to a Ruth Quinlan turned up in Florida."

"So Mr. Hyesmith put her stuff on the train to get rid of it," Zach guessed. "But how did he get rid of her?"

"My deputies have been over every square inch of his house," said the sheriff. "So far there's no trace of Ms. Quinlan . . . or her body."

"I don't know if it means anything," added Dora, "but according to Zach, Mr. Hyesmith said something about Ms. Quinlan 'snoopin around Pollux.' I looked up the word Pollux in the encyclopedia, and he's a mythological Greek hero famous for his skill in boxing."

"That's it!" cried Zach. "Let's go pay Mr. Hyesmith another visit!" Within minutes Hyesmith, polite as usual, was ushering in Zach, Dora, and the sheriff. They sat in his living room, surrounded by paintings and statues.

"I have just one question," Zach said, looking around the room. "Is Mr. Jenkins here?"

"Pardon me?" replied Hyesmith, blinking nervously.

"Jenkins," said Zach. "Don't you remember? He was the man you hired to kill your wife."

Hyesmith's eyes suddenly grew wide as Zach made his way to a statue of man in a boxing pose. "Pollux the boxer," said Zach. "A perfect statue of a boxer—because it is a boxer—inside of a statue!"

Hyesmith look almost amused, and the sheriff looked dumbfounded.

"Dora, would you like to show us where Ms. Quinlan ended up once she discovered Mr. Jenkins?" Zach asked.

"Certainly," said Dora, walking over to a fresh-looking statue of a huge woman—Hippolyta, the Amazon queen. "This is what you encased your housekeeper in," she said, touching the statue. "Am I right, Mr. Hyesmith?"

"You—you mean you actually live in a house with the bodies of two people you murdered?" the sheriff asked Hyesmith with disgust.

"No," said Hyesmith, looking around the statue-filled room. "Not just two," he said with a giggle. ■

✔ Enter your reading time below. Then look up your reading speed on the Words-per-Minute table on page 163.

Reading Time _____

Reading Speed _____

Enter your reading speed on the Reading Speed graph on page 164.

Comprehension

Put an **X** in the box next to the correct answer for each question or statement. Do not look back at the selection.

1. Mr. Hyesmith told Zach that
   - ☐ a. Ms. Quinlan quit her job.
   - ☐ b. he had fired Ms. Quinlan.
   - ☐ c. Ms. Quinlan was on vacation.
   - ☐ d. Ms. Quinlan was visiting her mother.

2. Who was Hippolyta?
   - ☐ a. an Amazon queen
   - ☐ b. a Greek hero
   - ☐ c. Mr. Hyesmith's wife
   - ☐ d. Mr. Hyesmith's housekeeper

3. What did Zach find out at the library?
   - ☐ a. Hyesmith's wife disappeared nine years ago and was never found.
   - ☐ b. Ms. Quinlan was the sister of Hyesmith's wife.
   - ☐ c. Hyesmith's wife was murdered nine years ago.
   - ☐ d. Ms. Quinlan disappeared right after the murder of Hyesmith's wife.

4. Mrs. Hyesmith's maiden name was
   - ☐ a. Quinlan.
   - ☐ b. Jenkins.
   - ☐ c. Pollux.
   - ☐ d. Crookston.

5. Mrs. Hyesmith's family believed that she was killed by a hit man who was a former
   - ☐ a. gardener.
   - ☐ b. butler.
   - ☐ c. boxer.
   - ☐ d. artist.

6. When the police showed up with Zach and Dora at Hyesmith's mansion, he seemed
   - ☐ a. happy to see them.
   - ☐ b. polite and not unusually nervous.
   - ☐ c. impolite and very nervous.
   - ☐ d. surprised and uneasy.

7. According to Hyesmith, he
   - ☐ a. put Ms. Quinlan on a bus.
   - ☐ b. called a taxi for her.
   - ☐ c. drove her to a town in the Midwest.
   - ☐ d. drove her to the train station.

8. The sheriff reported that an unclaimed suitcase showed up in Florida, and it belonged to
   - ☐ a. Mrs. Hyesmith.
   - ☐ b. Mr. Jenkins.
   - ☐ c. Ms. Quinlan.
   - ☐ d. Mr. Hyesmith.

9. Whose body was encased in the statue of Hippolyta?
   - ☐ a. Ms. Quinlan
   - ☐ b. Mr. Jenkins
   - ☐ c. Mrs. Hyesmith
   - ☐ d. There was no body in the statue.

10. How did Hyesmith react when the sheriff asked him if he actually lived in a house with the bodies of two people he murdered.
   - ☐ a. He denied it.
   - ☐ b. He admitted it.
   - ☐ c. He giggled.
   - ☐ d. He began to cry.

✎ _____ **Number of correct answers**
Enter this number on the Comprehension graph on page 165.

Critical Thinking

Put an **X** in the box next to the best answer for each question or statement. You may look back at the selection if you'd like.

1. The author tells this story mainly by
   - ☐ a. using his own imagination and creativity.
   - ☐ b. retelling a personal experience.
   - ☐ c. retelling an experience told to him by others.
   - ☐ d. telling two different versions of the same story.

2. Who is the narrator of this story?
   - ☐ a. Zach
   - ☐ b. Dora
   - ☐ c. Mr. Hyesmith
   - ☐ d. an outside observer

3. What mood does the author create in this story?
   - ☐ a. frightening
   - ☐ b. mysterious
   - ☐ c. lonely
   - ☐ d. amusing

4. Why did Hyesmith giggle at the end of the story?
   - ☐ a. He thought the accusations made against him were funny.
   - ☐ b. He is mentally unbalanced.
   - ☐ c. He thought it funny that the murders had been found out by two young people instead of the sheriff.
   - ☐ d. He thought that what he had done was funny.

5. Why did Hyesmith have a fire going on such a hot day?
   - ☐ a. He was chilly inside his mansion.
   - ☐ b. He was burning the evidence of his crime.
   - ☐ c. He was drying out his work area, which was damp.
   - ☐ d. He was firing clay in his kiln.

6. Which of the following is a statement of opinion rather than fact?
   - ☐ a. "I saw smoke coming out of one of the chimneys around noon."
   - ☐ b. "Hippolyta. She's an Amazon queen in Greek mythology."
   - ☐ c. "Maybe he was burning evidence of some kind."
   - ☐ d. "I found out that Hyesmith's wife was actually murdered nine years ago."

7. Based on what you've read, you can predict that probably
   - ☐ a. more bodies will be found.
   - ☐ b. no more bodies will be found.
   - ☐ c. the sheriff will be unable to prove Mr. Hyesmith committed the murders.
   - ☐ d. Mr. Hyesmith will escape.

8. Which word best describes Zach?
   - ☐ a. disloyal
   - ☐ b. reliable
   - ☐ c. suspicious
   - ☐ d. unconcerned

9. Which of the following does *not* fit with the other three?
   - ☐ a. Mr. Jenkins
   - ☐ b. Mr. Hyesmith
   - ☐ c. Mrs. Hyesmith
   - ☐ d. Ms. Quinlan

10. Which event happened shortly after Mrs. Hyesmith was killed?
    - ☐ a. Ms. Quinlan disappeared.
    - ☐ b. Zach and Dora called the police.
    - ☐ c. Mr. Hyesmith made a sculpture of the Amazon queen Hippolyta.
    - ☐ d. Mr. Jenkins disappeared.

_____ **Number of correct answers**
Enter this number on the Critical Thinking graph on page 166.

Vocabulary

Each numbered sentence contains an underlined word or phrase from the selection. Following are four definitions. Put an ✗ in the box next to the best meaning of the word or phrase as it is used in the sentence.

1. "His wife's <u>maiden</u> name was Crookston."
   - ☐ a. married
   - ☐ b. favorite
   - ☐ c. unmarried
   - ☐ d. legal

2. She jumped up from her chair and started <u>pacing</u> the room like a detective thinking about clues.
   - ☐ a. rushing around
   - ☐ b. walking with slow, regular steps
   - ☐ c. searching
   - ☐ d. studying

3. "That would explain why Mr. Hyesmith <u>accused</u> Ms. Quinlan of being a Crookston."
   - ☐ a. reminded
   - ☐ b. informed
   - ☐ c. charged
   - ☐ d. question

4. "In fact, maybe she did come to work for him just to <u>nose around</u>!"
   - ☐ a. look for something
   - ☐ b. hang around
   - ☐ c. walk around
   - ☐ d. hide something

5. "And the boy here <u>claims</u> he heard the housekeeper say she quit when you told him she was fired."
   - ☐ a. states positively
   - ☐ b. denies strongly
   - ☐ c. believes
   - ☐ d. recalls

6. "<u>Assuming</u> that you did take Ms. Quinlan to the train station, where was she going?"
   - ☐ a. forgetting
   - ☐ b. remembering
   - ☐ c. supposing
   - ☐ d. pretending

7. "I'm an artist, as you may know, and I was <u>firing</u> clay."
   - ☐ a. burning
   - ☐ b. shaping
   - ☐ c. making red hot
   - ☐ d. drying by heat

8. Hyesmith's eyes grew wide as Zach made his way to a statue of a man in a boxing <u>pose</u>.
   - ☐ a. picture
   - ☐ b. ring
   - ☐ c. trunks
   - ☐ d. position

9. Hyesmith look almost amused, and the sheriff looked <u>dumbfounded</u>.
   - ☐ a. disturbed
   - ☐ b. confused
   - ☐ c. surprised
   - ☐ d. determined

10. "You mean you actually live in a house with the bodies of two people you murdered?" the sheriff asked Hyesmith with <u>disgust</u>.
    - ☐ a. great interest
    - ☐ b. much doubt
    - ☐ c. strong dislike
    - ☐ d. great difficulty

✎ _____ **Number of correct answers**
Enter this number on the Vocabulary graph on page 167.

Personal Response

Would you recommend this story to other students? Explain why or why not.

_____

_____

18 | Shot Down Behind Enemy Lines

Among the many traditions of the United States military, there is one of which its members are particularly proud. Whenever one of their own is in grave danger, every possible means is used to rescue him or her from that danger. An example of this tradition in action is described in this selection.

In February 1991, Captain Scott O'Grady found himself alone, cold, and hungry in the mountains of Washington State. He had to eat black ants and grasshoppers in order to survive. He had to start fires using the rays of the sun and make tools out of tree branches. And to ward off boredom, he played "entire rounds of golf and chess" in his mind. Yes, it was a brutal and grueling test for O'Grady, but it was only a test. The jet pilot was taking the U.S. Air Force's three-week Survival, Evasion, Resistance, and Escape (SERE) course just in case he ever needed these skills.

He did. On June 2, 1995, Captain O'Grady took off in his F-16 jet fighter for a routine air patrol over Bosnia. On this mission, Captain Bob Wright flew alongside in a second F-16. Both pilots were part of a multinational military force trying to stop Serbian attacks in Bosnia.

As O'Grady and Wright flew their patrol, the Serbs launched two surface-to-air missiles at the two F-16s. O'Grady's instruments picked up the incoming missiles, but he could not see them because the sky was cloudy. One missile exploded in the air, doing no harm to either plane, but the second missile sheared O'Grady's jet in half. As the front section of the jet tumbled toward the ground, O'Grady pulled a special cord that blew away his canopy and ejected him from the cockpit. He then parachuted into the Serb-held hills of western Bosnia.

Right after landing, O'Grady got rid of his parachute and dashed into the woods, hoping to avoid capture. He fell face down on the ground and covered his head and ears with his camouflaged gloves to make himself harder to see. Civilians and soldiers were all around. Once

O'Grady saw armed soldiers walking nearby. He whispered a silent prayer thanking them for *not* having sniffing dogs.

Now O'Grady really needed the training he had received in the SERE course. He had the necessary equipment to evade the enemy and to survive for several days—a radio, a compass, flares, a first-aid kit, a knife, a pistol, and other such items. And the SERE course had taught him how to live off the land. He used a sponge to soak up rainwater, and he ate grass, bugs, and grasshoppers. He slept during the day, hidden under a camouflaged cover, and traveled only after midnight.

O'Grady didn't use his radio to call for help right away. His training had taught him that downed pilots are often captured because they radio too soon, giving away their position. So he watched and waited for the right time. After 5½ days, O'Grady finally took a chance and at 2:08 A.M. on June 8, broadcast his call sign: "Basher 52." His voice was picked up by a patrolling F-16 jet. This was the first time anyone actually knew that O'Grady had survived the missile attack and was still alive. Captain Wright had last seen him going down through the clouds and hadn't seen his parachute open.

A rescue operation had already been planned just in case O'Grady was still alive. It was a huge effort involving 40 aircraft, a half-dozen ships, and more than 100 soldiers. There was a primary team as well as backup teams—all willing to risk their lives to save the downed pilot. As it turned out, the backup teams were not needed because the primary team did its job so well.

At 5:50 A.M., less than three hours after O'Grady's message was received, the rescue got underway. Two Super Stallion helicopters, two Super Cobra helicopters, and four jet fighters took off from a ship in the Adriatic Sea. Each aircraft had a special job to do. The Super Stallions carried a total of 40 combat Marines. They would land and rescue O'Grady. The two Super Cobra gunships, armed with missiles and machine guns, would hover overhead and deal with any enemy who might show up. And the jets would provide additional air support.

As the choppers moved into position, the Marines aboard spotted a yellow smoke signal—O'Grady's sign. The Super Stallions landed within 50 yards of his hiding place. The 40 Marines piled out and formed a tight defensive circle. Moments later, O'Grady rushed out of the bushes. He appeared to be very cold, so one Marine gave him a blanket. Then he was helped into one of the choppers. From touchdown to takeoff, the rescue took less than two minutes. It was perfect—a "textbook" rescue.

Colonel Martin Berndt, the commander of the rescue team, later said, "To see him [Captain O'Grady] running through the brush covered with sweat, with his pistol in his hand making his way to the aircraft, [was] not a scene that I'll soon forget."

Still, the whole enterprise could have ended in disaster. After all, they were in Serb-held territory. Shortly after O'Grady was picked up, Serbs fired one or maybe two missiles at the choppers, but they both missed. The Serbs also fired on the choppers with automatic weapons. Luckily, they left nothing but a few holes; everyone escaped unharmed.

After O'Grady was safely back on American soil, President Bill Clinton called to congratulate him. The President also told the media that the pilot was "one amazing kid." But Captain Scott O'Grady saw things differently. To him, the real heroes were the men who came to rescue him. "They say they were just doing their job," he said. "But they risked their lives to get me out. If you want to find some heroes, that's where you should look." ∎

✔ Enter your reading time below. Then look up your reading speed on the Words-per-Minute table on page 163.

Reading Time   _____

Reading Speed   _____

Enter your reading speed on the Reading Speed graph on page 164.

Comprehension

Put an **X** in the box next to the correct answer for each question or statement. Do not look back at the selection.

1. SERE stands for
   - ☐ a. Survival, Evasion, Resistance, and Escape.
   - ☐ b. Staying Ever Ready to Escape.
   - ☐ c. Surviving Every Returning Enemy.
   - ☐ d. Surviving Enemy Retaliation with Energy.

2. Captain O'Grady was the pilot of a
   - ☐ a. jet fighter.
   - ☐ b. reconnaissance plane.
   - ☐ c. air transport plane.
   - ☐ d. helicopter.

3. Captain O'Grady was on a routine flying mission over
   - ☐ a. Serbia.
   - ☐ b. Somalia.
   - ☐ c. Washington State.
   - ☐ d. Bosnia.

4. Captain O'Grady's plane was shot down by
   - ☐ a. anti-aircraft guns.
   - ☐ b. an air-to-air missile from an enemy plane.
   - ☐ c. surface-to-air missiles.
   - ☐ d. automatic-weapons fire from soldiers on the ground.

5. O'Grady landed in an area that was held by the
   - ☐ a. United Nations forces.
   - ☐ b. Serbs.
   - ☐ c. United States.
   - ☐ d. NATO forces.

6. O'Grady was very fortunate that the soldiers did not have any
   - ☐ a. weapons.
   - ☐ b. observation towers.
   - ☐ c. interest in finding him.
   - ☐ d. sniffing dogs.

7. When did Captain O'Grady travel?
   - ☐ a. only after midnight
   - ☐ b. only after sunrise
   - ☐ c. just before sunset
   - ☐ d. only on foggy days

8. O'Grady did not use his radio
   - ☐ a. at all.
   - ☐ b. for at least two weeks.
   - ☐ c. for five hours.
   - ☐ d. for more than five days.

9. How far from O'Grady's hiding place did the rescue team land?
   - ☐ a. one-half mile
   - ☐ b. 100 yards
   - ☐ c. 50 yards
   - ☐ d. 25 yards

10. To help the rescue team find his exact location, O'Grady used a
   - ☐ a. flashing light.
   - ☐ b. signal flag.
   - ☐ c. flare gun.
   - ☐ d. yellow smoke signal.

✎ _____ Number of correct answers
Enter this number on the Comprehension graph on page 165.

Critical Thinking

Put an ✗ in the box next to the best answer for each question or statement. You may look back at the selection if you'd like.

1. What was the author's main purpose in writing "Shot Down Behind Enemy Lines"?
   - ☐ a. to express an opinion about war
   - ☐ b. to inform you about an exciting and heroic rescue
   - ☐ c. to provide instruction in survival techniques
   - ☐ d. to persuade you to take a course in survival techniques

2. The main purpose of the first paragraph of the selection is to
   - ☐ a. describe the wilderness of the state of Washington.
   - ☐ b. explain how Scott O'Grady prepared for the adventure to follow.
   - ☐ c. raise your curiosity about the SERE training course.
   - ☐ d. identify the setting of the rescue adventure.

3. Which of the following statements best expresses the main idea of the selection?
   - ☐ a. Scott O'Grady, a pilot trained in survival techniques, was rescued in Bosnia in a perfect "textbook" rescue.
   - ☐ b. U.S. Air Force pilot Scott O'Grady was shot down over Bosnia, but was later rescued.
   - ☐ c. One of the most frightening situations for any soldier is to be all alone behind enemy lines.
   - ☐ d. The exciting rescue of Scott O'Grady involved 40 aircraft, at least 6 ships, and more than 100 military personnel.

4. Why didn't the pilot of the other F-16 jet fighter try to rescue Captain O'Grady?
   - ☐ a. His plane was nearly out of fuel.
   - ☐ b. He didn't want to get shot down too.
   - ☐ c. He didn't know O'Grady had been shot down.
   - ☐ d. It would be impossible to land his plane in such a hilly, forest-covered land.

5. Why didn't Captain O'Grady use his radio for 5½ days?
   - ☐ a. He didn't want to run the radio batteries down.
   - ☐ b. It took time to assemble the radio.
   - ☐ c. He didn't want to give away his location to the Serb soldiers.
   - ☐ d. The radio was damaged in his parachute fall and had to be repaired.

6. What does the author imply by saying "the Super Stallions landed within 50 yards of his [O'Grady's] hiding place"?
   - ☐ a. The helicopter pilots were careless and landed too far from O'Grady's hiding place.
   - ☐ b. It was fortunate that the helicopters landed so unbelievably close to O'Grady's hiding place.
   - ☐ c. O'Grady was almost injured when the helicopters landed dangerously close to him.
   - ☐ d. The helicopters gave away O'Grady's position to the Serbs by landing so close to him.

7. If Captain O'Grady had not been rescued, what would have likely happened?
   - ☐ a. He would have surrendered.
   - ☐ b. He would have escaped on his own.
   - ☐ c. He would have been captured.
   - ☐ d. He would decide to stay and live in Bosnia.

8. Which word best describes Captain O'Grady during his ordeal?
   - ☐ a. disciplined
   - ☐ b. careless
   - ☐ c. confident
   - ☐ d. relaxed

9. Which of the following does *not* fit with the other three?
   - ☐ a. Bob Wright
   - ☐ b. Bill Clinton
   - ☐ c. Scott O'Grady
   - ☐ d. Martin Berndt

10. Choose the best one-sentence paraphrase for the following sentence: "Captain Wright had last seen him [O'Grady] going down through the clouds and hadn't seen his parachute open."
    - ☐ a. Captain Wright saw O'Grady last as he himself was parachuting down through the clouds.
    - ☐ b. Without opening his own parachute, Captain Wright saw O'Grady going down through the clouds.
    - ☐ c. Captain Wright saw O'Grady open his parachute before he went down through the clouds.
    - ☐ d. The last time Captain Wright had seen O'Grady, O'Grady had been falling through the clouds and his parachute was not open.

✎ _____ **Number of correct answers**
Enter this number on the Critical Thinking graph on page 166.

Vocabulary

Each numbered sentence contains an underlined word or phrase from the selection. Following are four definitions. Put an **X** in the box next to the best meaning of the word or phrase as it is used in the sentence.

1. And to <u>ward off</u> boredom, he played "entire rounds of golf and chess" in his mind.
   - ☐ a. welcome
   - ☐ b. extend
   - ☐ c. think about
   - ☐ d. prevent

2. On June 2, 1995, Captain O'Grady took off in his F-16 jet fighter for a <u>routine</u> air patrol.
   - ☐ a. dangerous
   - ☐ b. regular
   - ☐ c. unusual
   - ☐ d. important

3. O'Grady pulled a special cord that blew away his canopy and <u>ejected</u> him from the cockpit.
   - ☐ a. threw out
   - ☐ b. pulled in
   - ☐ c. photographed
   - ☐ d. restrained

4. Covering his head and ears with his <u>camouflaged</u> gloves made him harder to see.
   - ☐ a. patterned to be obvious
   - ☐ b. specially-heated
   - ☐ c. patterned so as to be unnoticed
   - ☐ d. brown-colored

5. He had the necessary equipment to <u>evade</u> the enemy and to survive for several days.
   - ☐ a. battle
   - ☐ b. confuse
   - ☐ c. join
   - ☐ d. avoid

6. There was a <u>primary</u> team as well as backup teams.
   - ☐ a. experienced
   - ☐ b. organized
   - ☐ c. main
   - ☐ d. trained

7. The Super Stallions carried a total of 40 <u>combat</u> marines.
   - ☐ a. trained to fight
   - ☐ b. trained to rescue
   - ☐ c. trained to fly
   - ☐ d. trained to patrol

8. The two Super Cobra gunships would <u>hover</u> overhead.
   - ☐ a. hang suspended in air
   - ☐ b. circle rapidly
   - ☐ c. observe quietly
   - ☐ d. attract attention

9. The Serbs fired on the choppers with <u>automatic</u> weapons.
   - ☐ a. hand-loading
   - ☐ b. self-loading
   - ☐ c. modern
   - ☐ d. outdated

10. The President also told the <u>media</u> that the pilot was "one amazing kid."
    - ☐ a. pilot's family
    - ☐ b. other pilots
    - ☐ c. news reporters
    - ☐ d. audience

✎ _____ Number of correct answers
Enter this number on the Vocabulary graph on page 167.

Personal Response

Do you think the lives of many people should be risked to save one life? Explain your answer.

_____

_____

19 | An Empire and Its Problems

Once just a small Italian trading post, Rome eventually grew into one of the world's most powerful empires. But like all advanced nations since then, the Roman Empire had its share of problems, inequality, and injustice. As it grew, it solved some problems and ignored others.

A thousand years before Christ, Rome was merely a small Italian trading post on the banks of the Tiber River. For a time it was ruled by Etruscan kings who came down from the north. Soon, however, the merchants of Rome, who traded with the Greek cities in southern Italy as well as the towns to the north, began to resent the domination of kings. The merchants preferred to set up a city-state, as the Greeks had done, governed by a senate of influential people. These people were generally aristocrats who owned lands, and they were appointed to the Senate by two consuls who were elected by the citizens.

For a long time the common people, or *plebeians*, had little money or power. At one point the plebeians showed their discontent by leaving Rome and settling down in another city. This incident frightened the upper classes, or *patricians*, because they could not get along without the plebeians. As a result the patricians gave the plebeians some privileges, and the latter returned to Rome. Little by little it became possible for plebeians to attain high positions, even positions as high as senator. Representatives of the plebeians, called tribunes, could veto the actions of the Senate, and even those of the consuls, if necessary.

Romans had great respect for the government and its officials. Some plebeian families rose to positions of importance because of the service their members had rendered to Rome. After a time, the Senate, composed of highly respected men, became even more powerful than the consuls, who could not make decisions without Senate approval.

There were, however, a large number of people who had no power and no rights. These were the slaves, who were brought from conquered territory, sometimes from very far away. They could be bought or sold, punished or liberated at the will of the masters. As Rome grew, the patricians became richer and often exploited the plebeians. Both groups exploited the slaves.

Rome began its expansion by taking possession of land around the city. Sometimes colonies of Roman citizens were settled in this land. Other times, the people living there were given the privileges of citizenship in return for their support. Thus, more and more people served in the Roman army, which became stronger and more powerful.

In the third and fourth centuries before Christ, the Roman army fought in a series of wars. At the conclusion of these wars, Rome had become the most important city in Italy. Its only important rival at that point was Carthage, across the Mediterranean in northern Africa.

The Carthaginians were descendants of the Phoenicians, who had established a very rich, successful city. They were seamen and traders. When the Greeks, who had established cities in southern Italy, tried to stop Rome from expanding, the Carthaginians helped the Romans because they did not want the Greeks to become more powerful. After the Greeks were driven out, the Romans took possession of southern Italy and the Carthaginians took possession of Sicily.

Rome and Carthage did not remain friendly for long. They were too close together; and both cities were too powerful for peaceful coexistence. Carthage had already gained control of the coast of North Africa from the Greek territory of Cyrene to the Straits of Gibraltar and southern

Spain. The Carthaginians did not permit ships from any other city to sail through the straits or into the ports that they controlled. Unlike the Roman army, the Carthaginian army was composed of paid soldiers from many places. Carthage was ruled by a group of rich merchants who made up the aristocracy. The Carthaginians also had large numbers of slaves.

In 264 B.C. the first of three long wars between Rome and Carthage began. These three wars were spread out over more than 100 years, with intervals of peace in between. They were called the Punic Wars, and they ended with the complete destruction of Carthage by the Romans. The best-known figure during these wars was the Carthaginian general Hannibal, who harassed Rome for 15 years during the second Punic War.

After the defeat of Carthage, Rome had no rival in the western Mediterranean world. Shortly afterward Rome established provinces in the eastern Mediterranean too. Gold and slaves poured into Rome from the conquered lands. The lives of the rich Romans became more and more luxurious. The Roman governors who went out to rule the new provinces were interested chiefly in getting as rich as they could. They accomplished this by imposing high taxes and taking advantage of all they could get.

In Rome the demand for clothes, spices, and luxuries from other parts of the Roman Empire grew tremendously. To satisfy this demand, Roman ships sailed regularly between Rome and the outposts. The ship owners became rich merchants, and banks had to be established to handle all the money that was being amassed. The banks at Rome filled a line of booths on both sides of the marketplace called the Forum. When a government official returned to Rome and built a beautiful new house, others wanted to do the same. Some made their old houses bigger by adding more rooms, a court with columns, and libraries. They installed expensive furniture, statues, mosaics, and paintings in their new or enlarged houses. The new houses sometimes had running water, baths, and sanitary conveniences. Sometimes there was central heating with a furnace that sent hot air through pipes into the rooms. Greek literature was translated, theaters were built, books were copied. Roman writers and artists not only copied Greek models, but created new works as well. Freed Greek slaves began to open schools for the education of Roman children, who, in former years, had seldom learned to read and write.

Some people felt that there was too much luxury. Laws were passed to restrain expensive habits, such as wearing showy jewelry and using carriages. However, these laws had little effect on the rich people who wished to display the luxuries that they could afford. ■

✔ **Enter your reading time below. Then look up your reading speed on the Words-per-Minute table on page 163.**

Reading Time   _____

Reading Speed   _____

Enter your reading speed on the Reading Speed graph on page 164.

Comprehension

Put an **X** in the box next to the correct answer for each question or statement. Do not look back at the selection.

1. When Rome was just a small trading post on the banks of the Tiber River, it was ruled by the
   - ☐ a. Etruscans.
   - ☐ b. Carthaginians.
   - ☐ c. Greeks.
   - ☐ d. Phoenicians.

2. The consuls in Rome were
   - ☐ a. appointed by the Senate.
   - ☐ b. elected by the citizens.
   - ☐ c. appointed by the king.
   - ☐ d. elected by the landowning aristocrats.

3. The plebeians, who had little power or money, showed their discontent by
   - ☐ a. refusing to work.
   - ☐ b. revolting against the patricians.
   - ☐ c. leaving Rome and settling down in another city.
   - ☐ d. begging the patricians for some privileges.

4. What group of people had no power or rights?
   - ☐ a. the slaves
   - ☐ b. the plebeians
   - ☐ c. the Etruscans
   - ☐ d. the Phoenicians

5. The Carthaginians helped the Romans at one time because they
   - ☐ a. needed many slaves.
   - ☐ b. wanted to trade with Rome.
   - ☐ c. wanted to conquer Rome.
   - ☐ d. wanted to stop Greek power.

6. Rome began its expansion by
   - ☐ a. taking possession of Sicily.
   - ☐ b. driving the Greeks out.
   - ☐ c. taking possession of land around the city of Rome.
   - ☐ d. conquering the Phoenicians.

7. The only serious rival of Rome in the third century B.C. was in
   - ☐ a. Africa.
   - ☐ b. Italy.
   - ☐ c. Greece.
   - ☐ d. Asia.

8. The Carthaginian army was composed of
   - ☐ a. slaves from conquered lands.
   - ☐ b. common people of Carthage.
   - ☐ c. paid soldiers from many places.
   - ☐ d. rich merchants who made up the aristocracy.

9. The Punic Wars were spread out over
   - ☐ a. 30 years.
   - ☐ b. 70 years.
   - ☐ c. more than 100 years.
   - ☐ d. more than 200 years.

10. What was the Forum?
    - ☐ a. a marketplace
    - ☐ b. a sports stadium
    - ☐ c. the emperor's palace
    - ☐ d. the Roman Senate's building

✎ _____ Number of correct answers
Enter this number on the Comprehension graph on page 165.

Critical Thinking

Put an **X** in the box next to the best answer for each question or statement. You may look back at the selection if you'd like.

1. The main purpose of the first paragraph of the selection is to
   - ☐ a. express an opinion about rule by kings versus rule by elected officials.
   - ☐ b. explain the form of government chosen for the city-state of Rome.
   - ☐ c. inform you how Rome evolved from a small trading post ruled by kings to a city-state of self-rule.
   - ☐ d. inform you that the appointed members of the Roman Senate were generally aristocrats who owned land.

2. What is the main idea of the second paragraph?
   - ☐ a. The patricians were forced to give the plebeians some privileges because they could not get along without the plebeians.
   - ☐ b. The plebeians left Rome because they had little money or power.
   - ☐ c. The patricians did not want to give the plebeians any power because they were frightened of them.
   - ☐ d. Eventually, the plebeians were able to attain some high positions in the government.

3. Rome became the most important city in Italy because of its
   - [ ] a. trade routes.
   - [ ] b. many banks.
   - [ ] c. military victories.
   - [ ] d. Greek slaves.

4. The major goal of the Roman Empire was to
   - [ ] a. better educate Roman children.
   - [ ] b. acquire power and wealth.
   - [ ] c. provide security for its citizens.
   - [ ] d. live in peace with its neighbors.

5. The Romans set up a city-state governed by a senate because
   - [ ] a. the common people wanted more power.
   - [ ] b. they were tired of the domination of kings.
   - [ ] c. they traded with Greek city-states.
   - [ ] d. they wanted Rome to become a big trading port.

6. Which of these events happened last?
   - [ ] a. The Punic Wars were fought.
   - [ ] b. Carthage helped the Romans drive the Greeks out of Italy.
   - [ ] c. Rome took possession of land around the city of Rome.
   - [ ] d. Carthage took possession of Sicily.

7. One way that Rome and Carthage were alike was that they both
   - [ ] a. had citizen armies.
   - [ ] b. had the same form of government.
   - [ ] c. were interested in becoming strong friends and allies.
   - [ ] d. had large numbers of slaves.

8. Which of the following does *not* fit with the other three?
   - [ ] a. Romans
   - [ ] b. Carthaginians
   - [ ] c. patricians
   - [ ] d. plebeians

9. Rome and Carthage fought each other because
   - [ ] a. Rome was governed by merchants.
   - [ ] b. the people loved luxury too much.
   - [ ] c. each wanted to become the most powerful city.
   - [ ] d. they both wanted Greek slaves to teach their children.

10. Why did the rich Romans pay so little attention to laws limiting luxury?
    - [ ] a. They wanted to live better.
    - [ ] b. They were not interested in spending money.
    - [ ] c. They had no respect for the law.
    - [ ] d. They wanted to show how much they could buy.

_____ **Number of correct answers**
Enter this number on the Critical Thinking graph on page 166.

Vocabulary

Each numbered sentence contains an underlined word from the selection. Following are four definitions. Put an **X** in the box next to the best meaning of the word as it is used in the sentence.

1. The merchants of Rome began to resent the domination of kings.
   - [ ] a. cruel method
   - [ ] b. firm attitude
   - [ ] c. complete control
   - [ ] d. unfair wage system

2. The merchants preferred to set up a city-state, as the Greeks had done, governed by a senate of influential people.
   - [ ] a. those exercising power
   - [ ] b. those most wealthy
   - [ ] c. those most intelligent
   - [ ] d. those properly elected

3. They could be bought and sold, punished or <u>liberated</u>.
   - [ ] a. tortured
   - [ ] b. released
   - [ ] c. killed
   - [ ] d. confined

4. As Rome grew, the patricians became richer and often <u>exploited</u> the plebeians.
   - [ ] a. treated kindly
   - [ ] b. oppressed with fear
   - [ ] c. treated with vengeance
   - [ ] d. used for profit

5. Its only important <u>rival</u> at that point was Carthage.
   - [ ] a. partner
   - [ ] b. friend
   - [ ] c. opponent
   - [ ] d. foreigner

6. Both cities were too powerful for peaceful <u>coexistence</u>.
   - [ ] a. living side by side
   - [ ] b. competing fairly
   - [ ] c. developing equally
   - [ ] d. ignoring competition

7. These three wars were spread out over more than 100 years, with <u>intervals</u> of peace in between.
   - [ ] a. large areas
   - [ ] b. treaties
   - [ ] c. meetings
   - [ ] d. pauses

8. They accomplished this by <u>imposing</u> taxes and taking advantage of all they could get.
   - [ ] a. offering
   - [ ] b. putting on
   - [ ] c. threatening with
   - [ ] d. indicating

9. Greek literature was <u>translated</u>, theaters were built, books were copied.
   - [ ] a. expressed in another language
   - [ ] b. performed on stage
   - [ ] c. read in public
   - [ ] d. given the definitions

10. Laws were passed to <u>restrain</u> expensive habits, such as wearing showy jewelry and using carriages.
    - [ ] a. encourage
    - [ ] b. explain
    - [ ] c. prevent
    - [ ] d. obtain

✎ _____ **Number of correct answers**
Enter this number on the Vocabulary graph on page 167.

Personal Response

I would like (or not like) to have lived in Rome during the time of the ancient Roman Empire because

_____

_____

If you had lived during the days of the ancient Roman Empire, would you rather have been a patrician or a plebeian? Explain your answer.

_____

_____

20 | Mind Games

by Henry and Melissa Billings

Hypnosis—a practice once thought by many to be just a trick or kind of game—has begun to gain acceptance in the medical community as an alternative treatment for some medical conditions.

"**Y**our eyes are getting heavy . . . you are becoming sleepy. . . ." The calm, soothing voice drones on and on. "Concentrate hard on the beam of light. Your eyes are becoming very heavy. . . . You are getting sleepy, *very* sleepy."

Hypnotists use these or similar words to induce a trance called hypnosis. For a long time, hypnosis was considered a trick, a kind of parlor game. A few enthusiasts believed it could be used to heal the sick, but most doctors scoffed at such notions. They had no faith in what they called "mind games." Now, however, times have changed. Doctors understand the importance of the mind–body connection and are willing to take a second look at hypnosis.

Just what is hypnosis? Most reference books define it as an altered state of consciousness. Some people believe that definition is accurate. Others say it is all wrong. Doctor Robert Baker of the University of Kentucky has been practicing hypnosis for more than 20 years, but he doesn't believe it produces an altered state. "It's nonsensical to argue that hypnosis involves some sort of special state," Baker says, "when we can't find it no matter how long we look." Indeed, researchers have found no evidence that the brain changes during hypnosis. People like Baker think that the hypnotized mind plays a trick on itself. Hypnosis, they say, occurs when one part of the brain shuts down and another part remains highly focused.

Other people define hypnosis as a state of repose. The body relaxes, the mind is more open and attentive, and breathing becomes more regular. Doctor Robert Fisher, a psychiatrist, says hypnosis is like going to the movies. You are aware of everything when you enter the theater. You can hear the crackle of candy wrappers. You notice the head of the person in front of you. You feel the spilled popcorn under your feet. But, says Fisher, "Once the screen fills with images, you gradually become absorbed and you're in a state of focused concentration."

Most people don't care whether or not hypnosis is an altered state of consciousness. They are not looking for the perfect definition. They only ask: Will it work for me? Will hypnosis help me stop smoking or lose weight? Will it allow me to overcome phobias such as a fear of flying? Can hypnosis ease the pain of giving birth or getting a tooth extracted? Can it help me to retrieve lost memories?

On this practical level, there is lots of evidence that hypnosis works. There is proof that it can change certain behaviors. Cigarette smoking is one example. Psychotherapist Laura Foster Collins uses hypnosis to help her clients kick the habit. Ina Josephson had been puffing away on two packs of cigarettes a day for 18 years. She had tried to quit smoking several times but had always failed. At last, she asked Collins to hypnotize her.

First, Collins made sure Josephson really wanted to quit. Without that motivation, says Collins, hypnosis will never work. Then while hypnotized, Josephson was asked to see herself as a nonsmoker. She envisioned a situation in which she would normally reach for a cigarette. But under hypnosis she could say, "No, thanks. I don't smoke."

The hypnosis worked. Josephson gave up smoking completely and even lost the urge to smoke. Still, only about one smoker in five quits for good as a result of hypnosis. Anyone who has ever smoked knows how difficult it is to break the habit. Hypnosis can help, but it must be combined with a strong desire to quit.

Helping a person give up a bad habit is one thing, but can hypnosis be used to block pain during surgery? Most experts agree that it can at least minimize such pain. A few surgeons have used it during operations to help reduce their patients' pain. Some dentists have also reported some success. In about 10 to 20 percent of cases, hypnosis can eliminate the sensation of pain completely. When that happens, the results can be pretty spectacular.

Take the case of Victor Rausch, a young Canadian. Rausch needed to have his gallbladder removed. But he decided to skip the anesthetic and rely solely on hypnosis. He even refused to take an aspirin. Just before the surgeon sliced open his abdomen, Rausch hypnotized himself. In his mind, he heard his favorite piano music and envisioned peaceful scenes. His pulse rate and blood pressure remained steady throughout the procedure. From time to time Rausch even talked and joked with the surgeon. The entire operation lasted 75 minutes. When it was over, Rausch got up off the table and walked away. He swore he felt no pain, just a little tugging.

Self-hypnosis can also help in other situations. Patients can use it to ward off asthma attacks or epileptic seizures. In 1996 the National Institutes of Health reported that hypnosis can ease headaches. It can also reduce the pain caused by cancer.

Self-hypnosis can be a wonderful healing tool for those skilled enough to practice it. It can be performed anywhere and at any time. It has no side effects and doesn't cost a thing. And most important, hypnosis gives the patient a sense of control over what is happening to his or her body. Hypnosis has also been used to jog lost or suppressed memories. The police have often used it to solve violent crimes. Eyewitnesses or victims of crimes might be badly traumatized. These people might be too fearful to speak about what they saw or to identify the criminal. But under hypnosis, people can often overcome such fears. They can then relate what happened.

How accurate are these memories? Can the testimony of a hypnotized eyewitness or victim be trusted? In recent years, more and more state courts have said no. In 1983, for instance, the New York Supreme Court ruled that hypnosis created a "mixture of accurate recall [and] fantasy." And it was impossible to tell one from the other.

Hypnosis is not for everyone. Some people are naturally better subjects than others. Who is the ideal subject? There are no barriers based on intelligence, age, or sex. Dr. Herbert Spiegel says, "Artists and writers often make good subjects because they are comfortable with fantasy and new things." Still, all good subjects should be motivated. And most of all, they must have an open mind and a willingness to concentrate. ■

✔ Enter your reading time below. Then look up your reading speed on the Words-per-Minute table on page 163.

Reading Time _____

Reading Speed _____

Enter your reading speed on the Reading Speed graph on page 164.

Comprehension

Put an **X** in the box next to the correct answer for each question or statement. Do not look back at the selection.

1. Today, doctors believe that hypnosis is a
   - ☐ a. trick.
   - ☐ b. mind game.
   - ☐ c. technique worth taking a look at.
   - ☐ d. parlor game.

2. Most reference books define hypnosis as
   - ☐ a. a state of repose.
   - ☐ b. the mind playing a trick on itself.
   - ☐ c. an altered state of consciousness.
   - ☐ d. a condition in which the brain becomes highly focused.

3. Doctor Robert Fisher, a psychiatrist, compares the state of hypnosis to
   - ☐ a. going to the movies.
   - ☐ b. having a dream.
   - ☐ c. being in a deep sleep.
   - ☐ d. floating through air.

4. People who want to use hypnosis to quit smoking must
   - ☐ a. be able to hypnotize themselves.
   - ☐ b. promise that they won't smoke after being hypnotized.
   - ☐ c. listen to music while under hypnosis.
   - ☐ d. be motivated to give up the habit.

5. What is the success rate when hypnosis is used to get smokers to quit their habit for good?
   - ☐ a. Almost all smokers quit.
   - ☐ b. One in every two quits.
   - ☐ c. One in every five quits.
   - ☐ d. One in every ten quits.

6. Most experts agree that hypnotism
   - ☐ a. has no effect on surgical pain.
   - ☐ b. can at least minimize surgical pain.
   - ☐ c. can completely block surgical pain.
   - ☐ d. should never be used in surgical procedures.

7. Before having surgery, Victor Rausch, a Canadian, was hypnotized by
   - ☐ a. himself.
   - ☐ b. Dr. Herbert Spiegel.
   - ☐ c. Dr. Robert Baker.
   - ☐ d. psychotherapist Laura Foster Collins.

8. Hypnosis is a wonderful healing tool, particularly because
   - ☐ a. it gives the patient a sense of control over what is happening to his or her body.
   - ☐ b. it provides an altered state of consciousness.
   - ☐ c. it makes the patient feel as if he or she is going to the movies.
   - ☐ d. there are no barriers to its use based on intelligence, age, or sex.

9. Under hypnosis, eyewitnesses or victims of crime
   - ☐ a. may become badly traumatized.
   - ☐ b. may be too fearful to speak about what they saw.
   - ☐ c. can sometimes overcome their fear and relate what happened.
   - ☐ d. are often not trusted to accurately recall what they saw.

10. Who are the ideal subjects for hypnotism?
   - ☐ a. artists and writers
   - ☐ b. motivated people with open minds and a willingness to concentrate
   - ☐ c. people who are open to suggestions while they are asleep
   - ☐ d. heavy smokers

✐ _____ Number of correct answers
Enter this number on the Comprehension graph on page 165.

Critical Thinking

Put an ✗ in the box next to the best answer for each question or statement. You may look back at the selection if you'd like.

1. The authors' main purpose in writing this selection was to inform you about the
   - ☐ a. many applications of hypnosis.
   - ☐ b. dangers of hypnosis.
   - ☐ c. limitations of hypnosis.
   - ☐ d. correct definition of hypnosis.

2. The authors explain this subject mainly by
   - ☐ a. retelling personal experiences.
   - ☐ b. telling different stories about the same topic.
   - ☐ c. using their creativity.
   - ☐ d. comparing different topics.

3. Which of the following statements best expresses the main idea of the selection?

☐ a. There is great disagreement as to what hypnosis is.

☐ b. Most people don't care how hypnosis is defined; they only want to know if it works.

☐ c. Hypnosis demonstrates the mind–body connection.

☐ d. Hypnosis can be an effective and inexpensive tool for changing behavior, blocking pain, and jogging memories.

4. Based on information in this selection, you can conclude that

☐ a. hypnosis is almost completely successful in helping people to quit smoking.

☐ b. many doctors will soon use hypnosis instead of anesthesia during surgery.

☐ c. more and more people are using hypnosis to help them with many different kinds of problems.

☐ d. the testimony of a hypnotized crime victim would be admissible in most courts.

5. In 1983 the New York Supreme Court ruled not to allow the testimony of hypnotized witnesses because

☐ a. most doctors scoffed at its use.

☐ b. hypnosis was considered a trick.

☐ c. no one could agree just what hypnosis was.

☐ d. the testimony of hypnotized witnesses could not be trusted.

6. Which of the following does *not* fit with the other three?

☐ a. Herbert Spiegel

☐ b. Victor Rausch

☐ c. Laura Foster Collins

☐ d. Robert Baker

7. Which of the following is a statement of opinion rather than fact?

☐ a. "Hypnosis is like going to the movies."

☐ b. Dr. Robert Baker of the University of Kentucky has been practicing hypnosis for more than 20 years.

☐ c. Doctors understand the importance of the mind–body connection and are willing to take a second look at hypnosis.

☐ d. A few surgeons have used hypnosis during operations to help reduce their patients' pain.

8. What do the authors imply by saying, "And most important, hypnosis gives the patient a sense of control over what is happening to his or her body"?

☐ a. Hypnosis allows patients to cure themselves without relying on doctors.

☐ b. Very often, patients don't feel they have any control over what is happening to them.

☐ c. The patient should determine the course of action doctors take while treating him or her.

☐ d. The patient, not the doctors, should be in control during a surgical procedure.

9. Based on what you read, you can predict that hypnosis will probably

☐ a. be ruled illegal by all courts in the United States.

☐ b. be banned by doctors from use in any medical procedures.

☐ c. continue to grow in use and number of supporters.

☐ d. gradually fall out of favor and cease to be practiced.

10. Choose the best one-sentence paraphrase for the following sentence from the selection: "Hypnosis they say, occurs when one part of the brain shuts down and another part remains highly focused."

☐ a. Hypnosis occurs when the brain completely goes to sleep.

☐ b. Hypnosis occurs when a part of the brain sleeps while another concentrates intensely.

☐ c. Hypnosis occurs when the brain shuts down completely and is then able to become highly focused.

☐ d. Hypnosis occurs when the brain becomes highly focused on sleep.

✎ _____ **Number of correct answers**
Enter this number on the Critical Thinking graph on page 166.

Vocabulary

Each numbered sentence contains an underlined word or phrase from the selection. Following are four definitions. Put an ✖ in the box next to the best meaning of the word or phrase as it is used in the sentence.

1. Hypnotists use these or similar words to induce a trance called hypnosis.

☐ a. quiet mood
☐ b. skeptical attitude
☐ c. alert condition
☐ d. dreamlike state

2. A few enthusiasts believed it could be used to heal the sick, but most doctors scoffed at such notions.

☐ a. supporters
☐ b. opponents
☐ c. dentists
☐ d. patients

3. Most reference books define it [hypnosis] as an altered state of consciousness.

☐ a. more alert
☐ b. confused
☐ c. changed
☐ d. reduced

4. Other people define hypnosis as a state of repose.

☐ a. forgetfulness
☐ b. restlessness
☐ c. amusement
☐ d. peacefulness

5. "Once the screen fills with images, you gradually become absorbed and you're in a state of focused concentration."

☐ a. very sleepy
☐ b. restless
☐ c. very interested
☐ d. bored

6. Most experts agree that it [hypnosis] can at least minimize such pain.

☐ a. increase
☐ b. greatly lessen
☐ c. cause
☐ d. endure

7. In about 10 to 20 percent of cases, hypnosis can eliminate the sensation of pain completely.

☐ a. get rid of
☐ b. prolong
☐ c. ease
☐ d. imitate

8. Patients can use it [hypnosis] to ward off asthma attacks or epileptic seizures.

☐ a. anticipate
☐ b. warn of
☐ c. prevent
☐ d. cure

9. Hypnosis has also been used to <u>jog</u> lost or suppressed memories.
   - ☐ a. hold in
   - ☐ b. stir up
   - ☐ c. erase
   - ☐ d. run slowly

10. Eyewitnesses or victims of crimes might be badly <u>traumatized</u>.
   - ☐ a. mistreated
   - ☐ b. frightened
   - ☐ c. misunderstood
   - ☐ d. harmed in the mind

✎ _____ **Number of correct answers**
Enter this number on the Vocabulary graph on page 167.

Personal Response

What new question do you have about hypnosis?

_____

_____

_____

_____

What did you learn about hypnosis in this selection that surprised you?

_____

_____

_____

_____

✔ **Check Your Progress**
Study the graphs you completed for lessons 11–20 and answer the How Am I Doing? questions on page 169.

21 | Days of Valor

by Joanna L. Stratton

In 1975 Joanna Stratton made a remarkable discovery in the attic of her grandmother's house in Kansas. She found a set of priceless autobiographical manuscripts written by 800 pioneer women. They had been collected by Ms. Stratton's great-grandmother, Lila Day Monroe, who intended to edit them into a book. Three generations later, Ms. Stratton finished her great-grandmother's project. Following is an excerpt from her book *Pioneer Women*.

"Imagine, if you can," wrote Lizzie Anthony Opdyke, "these pioneer women so suddenly transplanted from homes of comforts in eastern states to these bare, treeless, windswept, sun-scorched prairies with no comforts, not even a familiar face." For settlers like the Opdykes, Kansas was a harsh and formidable environment. Settling miles apart from one another, the emigrants faced the starkness of the wilderness alone. Deprivation and isolation were facts of everyday life for men and women alike.

To the pioneer woman, the day-to-day uncertainties of wilderness life proved especially harrowing. During the day, her husband was frequently too far out of range to respond to any call for assistance. Furthermore, circumstances often required him to leave his family for days or weeks at a time.

Nightfall, blanketing the prairie in a dense, boundless blackness, brought an even keener sense of solitude to the pioneer home. The deep silence was broken only by the occasional chirr of a cricket or the gentle swish of the tall praire grass—or by the call of the wild. For it was during the black nights that the howl of the coyote and the wolf spread terror throughout every homestead.

"In the summers of 1872 and 1873," recalled S. N. Hoisington, "the gray wolves and coyotes were very numerous. It was not safe to go out across the prairies without a weapon of some kind. My mother was a nurse and doctor combined. In early girlhood she used to help her brother mix his medicines, and after she came to Kansas people came for miles for her to doctor their families.

"A man by the name of Johnson had filed on a claim just west of us, and had built a sod house. He and his wife lived there two years, when he went to Salina to secure work. He was gone two or three months, and wrote home once or twice, but his wife grew very homesick for her folks in the east, and would come over to our house to visit mother.

"Mother tried to cheer her up, but she continued to worry until she got bedfast with the fever. At night she was frightened because the wolves would scratch on the door, on the sod, and on the windows, so my mother and I started to sit up nights with her. I would bring my revolver and ammunition and axe, and some good-sized clubs

"The odor from the sick woman seemed to attract the wolves, and they grew bolder and bolder. I would step out, fire off the revolver and they would settle back for a while, when they would start a new attack. . . .

"Finally the woman died and mother laid her out. Father took some wide boards that we had in our loft and made a coffin for her. Mother made a pillow and trimmed it with black cloth, and we also painted the coffin black.

"After that the wolves were more determined than ever to get in. One got its head in between the door casing and as it was trying to wriggle through, mother struck it in the head with an axe and killed it. I shot one coming through the window. After that they quieted down for about half an hour, when they came back again. . . . Their howling was awful. We fought these wolves five nights in succession, during which time we killed and wounded four gray wolves and two coyotes.

"When Mr. Johnson arrived home and found his wife dead and his house badly torn down by wolves he fainted away. . . . After the funeral he sold out and moved away."

To apprehensive settlers, the coyote was not the only terror of the night. Prairie fires, sweeping furiously across the plains, were a constant worry to families isolated on homesteads. From late summer through the autumn, the endless miles of tall prairie grass became a vast tinderbox, dry and brown from the scorching summer weather. It took only a quick spark from an untended campfire or a passing train engine, or a stroke of lightning, to set the countryside ablaze.

Lillian Smith well remembered the many nights spent fighting fires which threatened her family's farm. "Many a time my mother stayed up all night watching the red glare of the prairie fires in more than one direction, in fear and trembling that they might come swooping down upon us asleep in our little log cabin. However, she was always prepared. As soon as she would see the fire getting close, away we would go with our buckets of water and rags tied to hoes, rakes, and sticks, wet them and set a back fire to meet the monster coming, so when it reached our line we would stand still and wait until we knew it had passed us by for that time."

Harriet Walter also had vivid memories of the fires which threatened her family's farm in Lincoln. "One day in May I was gathering wildflowers on a hill opposite our house when I discovered fire creeping along the roadside and almost to a meadow which was in front of our house. The grass there was very tall and rank, and I knew, child that I was, that if the fire ever got in there our home was doomed. What would you have done? Well, I took off my petticoat and beat till I was exhausted but every spark was out."

In 1877, Anna and Jacob Ruppenthal brought their five children to a homestead ten miles north of Wilson, Kansas. As J. C. Ruppenthal later explained, prairie fires were a constant source of worry. "The last act at night, after seeing that the children were all asleep, and all quiet among the livestock in sheds, pens and corrals, was to sweep the entire horizon for signs of flame.

"Many times, on awakening in the dead of night, the room was light with reflection from the sky shining thru uncurtained windows from some fire ten or twenty or fifty miles away. Often in the small hours Mother watched from window to window to see if the light died away. . . . Despite the fear inspired by a prairie fire, there was a fascination to watch a fire by night, advancing, brightening, showing masses of solid flame or myriads of tiny jets that flickered and went out, to flash again farther along." ■

✔ Enter your reading time below. Then look up your reading speed on the Words-per-Minute table on page 163.

Reading Time _____

Reading Speed _____

Enter your reading speed on the Reading Speed graph on page 164.

Comprehension

Put an X in the box next to the correct answer for each question or statement. Do not look back at the selection.

1. The accounts in this selection tell about pioneers who lived in the prairie wilderness in the
   ☐ a. late 1700s.
   ☐ b. early 1800s.
   ☐ c. late 1800s.
   ☐ d. early 1900s.

2. The pioneer women told about in this selection generally came from
   ☐ a. southern states.
   ☐ b. eastern states.
   ☐ c. western states.
   ☐ d. northern states.

3. During the night, what would cause terror throughout every homestead?
   - ☐ a. prairie dust storms
   - ☐ b. signs of a tornado
   - ☐ c. howls of coyotes and wolves
   - ☐ d. sounds of Indian drums

4. S. N. Hoisington recalled that in the summers of 1872 and 1873,
   - ☐ a. gray wolves and coyotes were very numerous.
   - ☐ b. there were many severe thunderstorms.
   - ☐ c. lack of rain caused a drought.
   - ☐ d. there were numerous prairie fires.

5. The pioneer families told about in this selection had settled on the prairie lands of
   - ☐ a. Oklahoma.
   - ☐ b. the eastern states.
   - ☐ c. Nebraska.
   - ☐ d. Kansas.

6. When Mr. Johnson returned from Salina to find his wife dead and his house badly torn down by wolves, he
   - ☐ a. got his gun and killed several wolves.
   - ☐ b. rebuilt his house and stayed.
   - ☐ c. sold out and moved away.
   - ☐ d. died of a broken heart.

7. What caused the prairie fires?
   - ☐ a. the drying of the prairie grass by scorching summer weather
   - ☐ b. a quick spark from a passing train engine
   - ☐ c. a stroke of lightning
   - ☐ d. all of the above

8. Harriet Walter performed a brave act when she
   - ☐ a. helped her father set a backfire to stop an approaching prairie fire.
   - ☐ b. beat out a fire that threatened her family's farm.
   - ☐ c. killed a wolf that tried to get into her family's cabin.
   - ☐ d. saw a distant fire on the horizon and warned her family.

9. In 1877, Anna and Jacob Ruppenthal moved to a homestead 10 miles north of
   - ☐ a. Salina, Kansas.
   - ☐ b. Lincoln, Kansas.
   - ☐ c. Kansas City, Kansas.
   - ☐ d. Wilson, Kansas.

10. J. C. Ruppenthal said that the last act he performed each night was to
    - ☐ a. sweep the horizon for any signs of flame.
    - ☐ b. make sure all the children were asleep.
    - ☐ c. see that all was quiet among the livestock.
    - ☐ d. lock all the doors.

✎ _____ Number of correct answers
Enter this number on the Comprehension graph on page 165.

Critical Thinking

Put an ✗ in the box next to the best answer for each question or statement. You may look back at the selection if you'd like.

1. What is the mood created in each of these accounts of pioneer life?
   - ☐ a. suspense
   - ☐ b. triumph
   - ☐ c. fear
   - ☐ d. sadness

2. In these accounts, the general tone of several of the authors is
   - ☐ a. defiant.
   - ☐ b. resentful.
   - ☐ c. despairing.
   - ☐ d. confident.

3. Which of the following best describes this selection?
   - ☐ a. accounts of real persons' lives written by those persons
   - ☐ b. accounts of real persons' lives written by someone else
   - ☐ c. accounts made up by the author using her own imagination and creativity
   - ☐ d. accounts made up by the author based in part on historical facts

4. Based on these accounts, you can conclude that
   - ☐ a. nearly all the pioneer families stayed and lived peaceful lives.
   - ☐ b. many pioneer families became discouraged and went back east.
   - ☐ c. pioneer women preferred the beauty and solitude of the wilderness to their former homes in the crowded eastern states.
   - ☐ d. most of the pioneer women went back east while their men stayed to build homes and start farms.

5. It was necessary to carry a weapon when crossing the prairie because
   - ☐ a. rattlesnakes were numerous there.
   - ☐ b. hostile Indians were a danger.
   - ☐ c. wolves and coyotes might attack.
   - ☐ d. herds of buffalo were a threat.

6. Which of the following is a statement of opinion rather than fact?
   - ☐ a. Deprivation and isolation were facts of life for men and women alike.
   - ☐ b. Prairie fires, sweeping furiously across the plains, were a constant worry to families isolated on homesteads.
   - ☐ c. In 1877, Anna and Jacob Ruppenthal brought their five children to a homestead 10 miles north of Wilson, Kansas.
   - ☐ d. The open prairie land was probably the most dangerous place for pioneer families to settle on.

7. What made the threat of prairie fires a constant worry?
   - ☐ a. They could be started so easily in many different ways.
   - ☐ b. They moved with great speed.
   - ☐ c. They were difficult to keep from spreading.
   - ☐ d. all of the above

8. What word do you think most pioneer women would have used to describe their lives on the prairie wilderness?
   - ☐ a. boring
   - ☐ b. lonely
   - ☐ c. exciting
   - ☐ d. happy

9. Which of the following does *not* fit with the other three?
   - ☐ a. Joanna L. Stratton
   - ☐ b. Lizzie Anthony Opdyke
   - ☐ c. Lillian Smith
   - ☐ d. Harriet Walter

10. What was the most dangerous time of the year for settlers who lived on the prairie?
    - ☐ a. late summer through fall
    - ☐ b. winter
    - ☐ c. early spring to early summer
    - ☐ d. summer

✎ _____ Number of correct answers
Enter this number on the Critical Thinking graph on page 166.

Vocabulary

Each numbered sentence contains an underlined word from the selection. Following are four definitions. Put an **X** in the box next to the best meaning of the word as it is used in the sentence.

1. For settlers like the Opdykes, Kansas was a harsh and underline{formidable} environment.
   - ☐ a. rugged
   - ☐ b. hard to deal with
   - ☐ c. inviting
   - ☐ d. uncomfortable

2. To the pioneer women, the day to day uncertainties of wilderness life proved especially <u>harrowing</u>.
   - ☐ a. stimulating
   - ☐ b. challenging
   - ☐ c. distressing
   - ☐ d. revealing

3. <u>Circumstances</u> often required him to leave his family for days or weeks at a time.
   - ☐ a. job opportunities
   - ☐ b. homesickness
   - ☐ c. prospecting
   - ☐ d. existing conditions

4. Nightfall brought an even keener sense of <u>solitude</u> to the pioneer home.
   - ☐ a. loneliness
   - ☐ b. closeness
   - ☐ c. gloom
   - ☐ d. sorrow

5. The odor from the sick woman seemed to <u>attract</u> the wolves, and they grew bolder.
   - ☐ a. drive away
   - ☐ b. annoy
   - ☐ c. draw
   - ☐ d. confuse

6. To <u>apprehensive</u> settlers, the coyote was not the only terror of the night.
   - ☐ a. cautious
   - ☐ b. amazed
   - ☐ c. doubtful
   - ☐ d. fearful

7. Prairie fires were a constant worry to families <u>isolated</u> on homesteads.
   - ☐ a. settled
   - ☐ b. alone
   - ☐ c. confined
   - ☐ d. gathered

8. The endless miles of tall prairie grass became a vast tinderbox, dry and brown from the <u>scorching</u> summer weather.
   - ☐ a. burning
   - ☐ b. humid
   - ☐ c. warm
   - ☐ d. steaming

9. Harriet Walter also had <u>vivid</u> memories of the fire which threatened her family's farm.
   - ☐ a. vague
   - ☐ b. sad
   - ☐ c. frightening
   - ☐ d. clear

10. Despite the fear, there was a <u>fascination</u> to watch a fire by night.
    - ☐ a. terrible fear
    - ☐ b. irresistible attraction
    - ☐ c. need
    - ☐ d. determination

✎ _____ **Number of correct answers**
Enter this number on the Vocabulary graph on page 167.

Personal Response

What was most surprising or interesting to you about this selection?

_____

_____

22 | The Pigman

by Paul Zindel

Paul Zindel wrote his best-selling novel in 1968. The book continues to be popular today, appearing on the suggested reading lists of many high schools. This selection from the novel introduces one of the two narrators and begins the tale of two high-school misfits and their friendship with an odd old man.

Now, I don't like school, which you might say is one of the factors that got us involved with this old guy we nicknamed the Pigman. Actually, I hate school, but then again most of the time I hate everything.

I used to really hate school when I first started at Franklin High. I hated it so much the first year they called me the Bathroom Bomber. They called me that because I used to set off bombs in the bathroom. I set off 23 bombs before I didn't feel like doing it anymore.

The reason I never got caught was because I used to take a tin can (that's a firecracker, as if you didn't know) and mold a piece of clay around it so it'd hold a candle attached to the fuse. One of those skinny little birthday candles. Then I'd light the thing, and it'd take about eight minutes before the fuse got lit. I always put the bombs in the first-floor boys' john right behind one of the porcelain unmentionables where nobody could see it. Then I'd go off to my next class. No matter where I was in the building I could hear the blast.

If I got all involved, I'd forget I had lit the bomb, and then even I'd be surprised when it went off. Of course, I was never as surprised as the poor guys who were in the boys' john on the first floor sneaking a cigarette, because the boys' john is right next to the Dean's office and a whole flock of gestapo would race in there and blame them. Sure they didn't do it, but it's pretty hard to say you're innocent when you're caught with a lungful of rich, mellow tobacco smoke. When the Dean catches you smoking, it really may be hazardous to your health.

After my bomb avocation, I became the organizer of the supercolossal fruit roll. You could only do this on Wednesdays because that was the only day they sold old apples in the cafeteria. Sick, undernourished, antique apples. They sold old oranges on Fridays, but they weren't as good because they don't make much noise when you roll them. But on Wednesdays when I knew there was going to be a substitute teaching one of the classes, I'd pass the word at lunch and all the kids in that class would buy these scrawny apples. Then we'd take them to class and wait for the right moment—like when the substitute was writing on the blackboard. You couldn't depend on a substitute to write on the blackboard though, because usually they just told you to take a study period so they didn't have to do any work and could just sit at the desk reading. But you could depend on the substitute to be mildly retarded, so I'd pick out the right moment and clear my throat quite loudly—which was the signal for everyone to get the apples out. Then I gave this phony sneeze that meant to hold them down near the floor. When I whistled, that was the signal to roll 'em. Did you ever hear a buffalo stampeding? Thirty-four scrawny, undernourished apples rolling up the aisles sound just like a herd of buffalo stampeding.

Every one of the fruit rolls was successful, except for the time we had a retired postman for General Science 1H5. We were supposed to study incandescent lamps, but he spent the period telling us about commemorative stamps. He was so enthusiastic about the old days at the P.O. I just didn't have the heart to give the signals, and the kids were a little put out because they all got stuck with old apples.

But I gave up all that kid stuff now that I'm a sophomore. The only thing I do now that is faintly criminal is write on desks. Like right this minute I feel like writing something on the nice polished table here, and since the Cricket is down at the other end of the library showing some four-eyed dimwit how to use the encyclopedias, I'm going to do it.

Now that I've artistically expressed myself, we might as well get this cursing thing over with too.

I was a little annoyed at first since I was the one who suggested writing this thing because I couldn't stand the miserable look on Lorraine's face ever since the Pigman died. She looked a little bit like a Saint Bernard that just lost its keg, but since she agreed to work on this, she's gotten a little livelier and more opinionated. One of her opinions is that I shouldn't curse.

"Not in a memorial epic!"

"Let's face it," I said, "everyone curses."

She finally said I could curse if it was excruciatingly necessary by going like this @#$%. Now that isn't too bad an idea because @#$% leaves it to the imagination and most people have a worse imagination than I have. So I figure I'll go like @#$% if it's a mild curse—like the kind you hear in the movies when everyone makes believe they're morally violated but have really gotten the thrill of a lifetime. If it's going to be a revolting curse, I'll just put a three in front of it—like 3@#$%—and then you'll know it's the raunchiest curse you can think of.

Just now I'd better explain why we call Miss Reillen the Cricket. Like I told you, she's the librarian at Franklin and is letting us type this thing on her quiet typewriter, which isn't quiet at all.

Miss Reillen is a little on the fat side, but that doesn't stop her from wearing these tight skirts which make her nylon stockings rub together when she walks so she makes this scraaaaaaatchy sound. That's why the kids call her the Cricket.

Lorraine is panting to get at the typewriter now, so I'm going to let her before she has a heart attack. ■

✔ Enter your reading time below. Then look up your reading speed on the Words-per-Minute table on page 163.

Reading Time   _____

Reading Speed   _____

Enter your reading speed on the Reading Speed graph on page 164.

Comprehension

Put an ✗ in the box next to the correct answer for each question or statement. Do not look back at the selection.

1. As a freshman, the narrator was
   - ☐ a. caught smoking in the boy's room.
   - ☐ b. elected class president.
   - ☐ c. a cafeteria assistant.
   - ☐ d. called the Bathroom Bomber.

2. Who were the most surprised persons when the bombs went off?
   - ☐ a. people in the Dean's office
   - ☐ b. students in class
   - ☐ c. guys smoking in the boys' bathroom
   - ☐ d. substitute teachers

3. Who did the people from the Dean's office blame for setting off the bombs?
   - ☐ a. the smokers in the boys' bathroom
   - ☐ b. the narrator
   - ☐ c. the janitor
   - ☐ d. the boys in General Science

4. The fruit roll could only be done on
   - ☐ a. Mondays.
   - ☐ b. Tuesdays.
   - ☐ c. Wednesdays.
   - ☐ d. Fridays.

5. Apples were used for the supercolossal fruit roll because they
   - ☐ a. could be eaten later by students.
   - ☐ b. made the best noise when rolled.
   - ☐ c. were cheaper than oranges.
   - ☐ d. weren't as sticky as oranges when they broke.

6. The narrator would pull the supercolossal fruit roll prank on
   - ☐ a. the Dean.
   - ☐ b. the gym teacher.
   - ☐ c. Miss Reillen.
   - ☐ d. a substitute teacher.

7. The rolling apples were compared with
   - ☐ a. buffalo stampeding.
   - ☐ b. bowling balls.
   - ☐ c. firecrackers exploding.
   - ☐ d. the gestapo.

8. The narrator is in which year of high school?
   - ☐ a. freshman
   - ☐ b. junior
   - ☐ c. sophomore
   - ☐ d. senior

9. Lorraine had a miserable look on her face ever since the
   - ☐ a. narrator became a sophomore.
   - ☐ b. bombing incident in the boy's bathroom.
   - ☐ c. supercolossal fruit roll prank.
   - ☐ d. Pigman died.

10. Who was given the nickname "Cricket"?
    - ☐ a. Miss Reillen
    - ☐ b. Lorraine
    - ☐ c. the Dean
    - ☐ d. the narrator

✎ _____ Number of correct answers
Enter this number on the Comprehension graph on page 165.

Critical Thinking

Put an ✖ in the box next to the best answer for each question or statement. You may look back at the selection if you'd like.

1. The author's main purpose in writing this selection was to
   - ☐ a. describe life in a typical high school.
   - ☐ b. criticize the behavior of high-school misfits.
   - ☐ c. entertain you with a good story.
   - ☐ d. suggest ways to help high-school misfits.

2. The author tells this part of the story mainly by
   - ☐ a. retelling personal experiences.
   - ☐ b. telling it from two different points of view.
   - ☐ c. using his imagination and creativity.
   - ☐ d. comparing different topics.

3. In this story, the author's tone is
   - ☐ a. secretive.
   - ☐ b. humorous.
   - ☐ c. sad.
   - ☐ d. serious.

4. The narrator shows that he cares about others' feelings when he
   - ☐ a. doesn't interrupt the retired postman's talk about stamps.
   - ☐ b. shows some students how to use the encyclopedia.
   - ☐ c. encourages the students to buy apples instead of oranges.
   - ☐ d. writes on the desk about the science teacher.

5. According to the story, smoking is dangerous to your health because
   - ☐ a. you will miss a class by smoking a cigarette.
   - ☐ b. the smoke could set off a fire alarm.
   - ☐ c. it could cause cancer.
   - ☐ d. the Dean will blame you for the bombs in the boys' bathroom.

6. Which of the following is a statement of opinion rather than fact?
   - ☐ a. I set off 23 bombs before I didn't feel like doing it anymore.
   - ☐ b. She looked a little bit like a Saint Bernard that just lost its keg.
   - ☐ c. I used to really hate school when I first started at Franklin High.
   - ☐ d. You could only do this on Wednesdays because that was the only day they sold apples in the cafeteria.

7. Which word best describes the narrator?
   - ☐ a. mischevious
   - ☐ b. self-conscious
   - ☐ c. reliable
   - ☐ d. studious

8. Compared to his freshman year at Franklin High, the narrator is now
   - ☐ a. more serious.
   - ☐ b. more destructive.
   - ☐ c. less happy.
   - ☐ d. less confident.

9. Which of the following does *not* fit with the other three?
   - ☐ a. the postman
   - ☐ b. Miss Reillen
   - ☐ c. the Dean
   - ☐ d. Lorraine

10. Based on this selection, you can predict that the narrator will probably
   - ☐ a. quit school.
   - ☐ b. be a model student.
   - ☐ c. be expelled from school.
   - ☐ d. become even more serious.

✎ _____ Number of correct answers
Enter this number on the Critical Thinking graph on page 166.

Vocabulary

Each numbered sentence contains an underlined word from the selection. Following are four definitions. Put an ✗ in the box next to the best meaning of the word as it is used in the sentence.

1. When the Dean catches you smoking, it really may be hazardous to your health.
   - ☐ a. dangerous
   - ☐ b. forceful
   - ☐ c. useful
   - ☐ d. compared

2. After my bomb avocation, I became the organizer of the supercolossal fruit roll.
   - ☐ a. explosion
   - ☐ b. skill
   - ☐ c. vacation
   - ☐ d. hobby

3. Sick, undernourished, antique apples.
   - ☐ a. hard and green
   - ☐ b. soft and brown
   - ☐ c. poorly fed
   - ☐ d. poorly polished

4. All the kids in that class would buy these scrawny apples.
   - ☐ a. skinny
   - ☐ b. crisp
   - ☐ c. delicious
   - ☐ d. juicy

5. Did you ever hear a herd of buffalo stampeding?
   - ☐ a. calling loudly
   - ☐ b. eating voraciously
   - ☐ c. sneezing suddenly
   - ☐ d. rushing wildly

6. He spent the period telling us about commemorative stamps.
   - ☐ a. priceless
   - ☐ b. in memory of
   - ☐ c. used but valuable
   - ☐ d. canceled

7. "Not in a memorial epic!"
   - ☐ a. monument
   - ☐ b. period of time
   - ☐ c. heroic tale
   - ☐ d. ceremony

8. She finally said I could curse if it was excruciatingly necessary.
   - ☐ a. painfully
   - ☐ b. convincingly
   - ☐ c. doubtfully
   - ☐ d. supposedly

9. Everyone makes believe they're morally violated.
   - ☐ a. satisfied
   - ☐ b. oriented
   - ☐ c. injured
   - ☐ d. bewildered

10. I'll just put a three in front of it—like 3@#$%—and then you'll know it's the raunchiest curse you can think of.
    - ☐ a. pleasantest
    - ☐ b. funniest
    - ☐ c. strangest
    - ☐ d. dirtiest

✎ _____ **Number of correct answers**
Enter this number on the Vocabulary graph on page 167.

Personal Response

Based on what you've read about the narrator, can you think of any good qualities he has? Explain.

_____

_____

_____

Does the narrator have any qualities you consider undesirable? Explain.

_____

_____

_____

23 | Life Among the Aztecs

An often-forgotten fact of history is that the Europeans did not bring civilization to the New World. The Spanish came to North America centuries ago and conquered a people who already had an advanced civilization in place.

Long before Europeans migrated to this continent, American Indians were making history. One of the most important groups of Indians in North America was the Aztecs, who lived in the high valley where Mexico City now stands. The Aztecs had developed a standard of living equal to that of many Europeans of that time.

The Aztecs left records of various kinds. Some of their history is carved in stone, while some is written on long sheets of paper made from cactus plants or the bark of certain trees. The Aztecs built solidly constructed temples and houses. They were skilled in astronomy, law, and government. And, in many ways, they were kind and gentle.

The Aztecs rose to power because of their military abilities. Wars were often fought in order to capture enemies who could be sacrificed to the Aztec war god. Although such human sacrifice was shocking to the Europeans, it was the result of a civilization that combined religion and warfare. When the Spanish finally vanquished the Aztecs, the conquerors had to fight vigorously to stop the practice of human sacrifice.

According to tradition, in 1325—167 years before Columbus first landed on American shores—the Aztecs started to build their capital city, Tenochtitlán. This city was destroyed by Spanish conquerors, who eventually built a new city on the site.

Tenochtitlán was built on an island in a large lake. The city was connected to the mainland by causeways, which contained well-guarded bridges. Since these bridges could be removed in case of danger, it was very difficult to attack Tenochtitlán from the edge of the lake.

When the Aztecs first settled in the Mexican valley, they did not have much land of their own.

They gradually obtained land for farming by building islands in the lake. They also supported themselves by fishing and by trading with nearby tribes. The Aztecs learned a good deal from their more advanced neighbors. And, as their military power grew, they used the lands they conquered to start more farms.

By the end of the 15th century the Aztecs were the leaders of a united group of surrounding tribes. They received tributes from other tribes they had conquered. Many of these tribes were frequently at the point of rebellion. Cortés, the Spanish conqueror, took advantage of this situation and allied his troops with those tribes who hated the Aztecs.

The Aztecs achieved great power by building upon the wealth of the tribes they conquered. Their capital was a great center of commerce, wealth, and culture. Skilled architects and stonemasons, aided by slave labor, built great temples and palaces, as well as comfortable houses. The Aztecs even had botanical gardens, which were unknown in Europe at that time.

To aid irrigation and travel throughout the city, the Aztecs built an elaborate canal system. They grew cotton and made fine clothes, which were often ornamented with gold, rare furs, and the bright feathers of tropical birds.

The Aztecs had no alphabet, but they kept records of their history by means of picture writing. They had a system of education that was run by their priests and priestesses. Their schools were open only to the upper classes.

The Aztecs had hospitals and doctors and surgeons who were probably quite as good as the 15th-century European medical facilities and staffs. The Aztecs' study of astronomy was so advanced that they were able to make a very accurate calendar and to predict eclipses. Their calendar stone is a famous relic of their civilization. It is a round, flat stone, 3 feet thick and about 12 feet in diameter, with signs and pictures representing the days and months of the year.

An Aztec legend prophesied that one day a white god would come to them from the east and rule over them. Hernando Cortés, the Spanish captain, took advantage of this belief, which helped him greatly in his conquest of the Aztecs.

In 1519 the beautiful Aztec city of Tenochtitlán, with its gleaming white temples and palaces, dazzled the eyes of the invading Spaniards. It was built in a most attractive natural setting, and the Spaniards saw it first from the high peaks that surrounded the valley of Mexico.

What the Spanish soldiers found in the Aztec city surpassed their wildest dreams. There were shady parks and gardens, containing rare plants from all parts of Mexico. There were strange animals in the zoo. And there were many large, busy markets, where the Spaniards found articles of food, clothing, and handicrafts that they had never seen before. When Cortés arrived at Tenochtitlán with his 450 Spanish soldiers and his Indian allies, the Aztec emperor Montezuma received them and gave them quarters in the city. Cortés realized that he was in a dangerous position. He invited Montezuma to the Spanish camp, where Montezuma was held prisoner until he died.

After the death of their emperor, the Aztecs revolted against the Spaniards. It was only after fierce fighting that the Aztecs were defeated and Spanish rule was established.

The Aztec country became an important part of the Spanish empire. It was called New Spain, and Spanish priests came to establish Christianity in the new possession of the Spanish king. Mule trains, carrying the Aztecs' treasures, were sent down the hills to the coast. From there, the treasures were shipped to Spain.

Today, more than four centuries after the Spanish conquest, there are still many Indians living in Mexico who speak the language of the Aztecs. Modern Mexicans are proud of their Aztec ancestry. Many of the Aztec customs have been preserved, and Mexican ways of living and eating show strong Aztec influence. Aztec designs are found in the pottery and painting of today. Many words of the Aztec language have been added to the Spanish spoken in the country. And some of the words (such as *chocolate, tomato, ocelot, coyote,* and *avocado*) have even become part of the English language. ■

✔ Enter your reading time below. Then look up your reading speed on the Words-per-Minute table on page 163.

Reading Time   _____

Reading Speed   _____

Enter your reading speed on the Reading Speed graph on page 164.

Comprehension

Put an **X** in the box next to the correct answer for each question or statement. Do not look back at the selection.

1. The Aztecs lived in a land that is now
   - ☐ a. Spain.
   - ☐ b. Europe.
   - ☐ c. the United States.
   - ☐ d. Mexico.

2. The Aztecs became powerful because of their
   - ☐ a. government.
   - ☐ b. knowledge of astronomy.
   - ☐ c. military ability.
   - ☐ d. ability in farming and weaving.

3. How long before Columbus discovered America was the capital city of Tenochtitlán built?
   - ☐ a. 300 years
   - ☐ b. 193 years
   - ☐ c. 167 years
   - ☐ d. 120 years

4. The Aztec capital was first built
   - ☐ a. on the shores of a lake.
   - ☐ b. on a mountain.
   - ☐ c. in a swamp.
   - ☐ d. on an island.

5. What did the Aztecs do to aid irrigation?
   - ☐ a. constructed canals
   - ☐ b. built reservoirs
   - ☐ c. used rainwater
   - ☐ d. drained mountain streams

6. Did the Aztecs use slave labor?
   - ☐ a. no
   - ☐ b. yes
   - ☐ c. not often
   - ☐ d. The selection does not say.

7. The Aztecs kept records by using
   - ☐ a. their alphabet.
   - ☐ b. picture writing.
   - ☐ c. religious sculpture.
   - ☐ d. special round stones.

8. The Aztecs' schools were open only to the
   - ☐ a. priests and priestesses.
   - ☐ b. architects and astronomers.
   - ☐ c. upper classes.
   - ☐ d. middle classes.

9. The Aztecs were defeated by the Spanish conqueror
   - ☐ a. Cortés.
   - ☐ b. Columbus.
   - ☐ c. Montezuma.
   - ☐ d. DeSoto.

10. What was the Aztec country called when it became part of the Spanish empire?
   - ☐ a. Mexico
   - ☐ b. New Mexico
   - ☐ c. New Spain
   - ☐ d. España

✎ _____ Number of correct answers
Enter this number on the Comprehension graph on page 165.

Critical Thinking

Put an ✗ in the box next to the best answer for each question or statement. You may look back at the selection if you'd like.

1. The main purpose of the first paragraph of the selection is to
   - ☐ a. inform you where the Aztec Indians live.
   - ☐ b. inform you that the Aztec Indians had a high standard of living.
   - ☐ c. express an opinion about the importance of the Aztec Indians.
   - ☐ d. introduce you to the topic of the selection.

2. Which of the following statements best expresses the main idea of the selection?
   - ☐ a. The Aztecs built solidly constructed temples and houses and were skilled in astronomy, law, and government.
   - ☐ b. The Aztecs rose to power because of their military abilities, and yet, in many ways, they were kind and gentle.
   - ☐ c. The Spanish conquered the Aztecs by allying themselves with surrounding tribes who hated the Aztecs.
   - ☐ d. The Aztecs developed an advanced civilization equal to that of many Europeans of that time and were one of the most important groups of Indians in North America.

3. The Aztecs seemed interested primarily in
   - ☐ a. useful, practical things.
   - ☐ b. beauty and utility.
   - ☐ c. luxury and furs.
   - ☐ d. beauty and ornaments.

4. Cortés's behavior toward the Aztecs could best be described as
   - ☐ a. unwise.
   - ☐ b. cruel.
   - ☐ c. treacherous.
   - ☐ d. cunning.

5. The Aztec practice of human sacrifice was the result of a civilization that
   - a. was warlike as well as religious.
   - b. often appeared shocking to Spanish conquerors.
   - c. developed outside the European traditions.
   - d. depended upon conquest to build wealth.

6. Which of the following is a statement of opinion rather than fact?
   - a. The Aztec country became an important part of the Spanish empire.
   - b. The Aztecs had hospitals and doctors and surgeons who were probably quite as good as the 15th-century European medical facilities and staff.
   - c. The Aztecs achieved great power by building upon the wealth of the tribes they conquered.
   - d. To aid irrigation and travel throughout the city, the Aztecs built an elaborate canal system.

7. Why was it difficult to attack the capital city, Tenochtitlán?
   - a. The Aztecs maintained a powerful army.
   - b. The surrounding tribes were hostile.
   - c. Ambushes could be set up on the mountains.
   - d. The bridges to the city could be removed.

8. Which event happened first?
   - a. The Aztecs started to build their capital city, Tenochtitlán.
   - b. Columbus discovered America.
   - c. The Aztecs revolted against the Spaniards.
   - d. The Aztec emperor, Montezuma, died.

9. Which of the following does *not* fit with the other three?
   - a. Europe
   - b. Aztec country
   - c. New Spain
   - d. Mexico

10. In which of the following ways were the Aztec Indians different from their Spanish conquerors?
    - a. They had good hospitals, doctors, and surgeons.
    - b. They engaged in human sacrifices.
    - c. They used military conquest to gain power.
    - d. They had a system of education with good schools.

_____ Number of correct answers
Enter this number on the Critical Thinking graph on page 166.

Vocabulary

Each numbered sentence contains an underlined word from the selection. Following are four definitions. Put an **X** in the box next to the best meaning of the word as it is used in the sentence.

1. When the Spanish finally underlined vanquished the Aztecs, the conquerors had to fight vigorously to stop the practice of human sacrifice.
   - a. defeated
   - b. frightened
   - c. sent running
   - d. abused

2. The Aztecs learned a good deal from their more advanced neighbors.
   - a. available
   - b. upgraded
   - c. promoted
   - d. progressive

3. They received <u>tributes</u> from other tribes that they had conquered.
   - [ ] a. words of gratitude
   - [ ] b. violent arguments
   - [ ] c. taxes and land
   - [ ] d. gifts in appreciation

4. Many of these tribes were frequently on the point of <u>rebellion</u>.
   - [ ] a. an uprising against authority
   - [ ] b. an organization of resisters
   - [ ] c. a feeling of insubordination
   - [ ] d. a carelessly formed group

5. Their capital was a great center of <u>commerce</u>, wealth, and culture.
   - [ ] a. entertainment
   - [ ] b. business and trade
   - [ ] c. travel
   - [ ] d. adventure and risk

6. To aid irrigation and travel throughout the city, the Aztecs built an <u>elaborate</u> canal system.
   - [ ] a. too complicated
   - [ ] b. carefully detailed
   - [ ] c. up to date
   - [ ] d. simple but effective

7. They were able to make a very accurate calendar and to <u>predict</u> eclipses.
   - [ ] a. produce
   - [ ] b. foretell
   - [ ] c. study about
   - [ ] d. keep a record of

8. An Aztec legend <u>prophesied</u> that one day a white god would come to them from the east and rule over them.
   - [ ] a. uttered statements
   - [ ] b. spoke with feeling
   - [ ] c. acted suddenly
   - [ ] d. indicated beforehand

9. What the Spanish soldiers found in the Aztec city <u>surpassed</u> their wildest dreams.
   - [ ] a. contributed to
   - [ ] b. satisfied
   - [ ] c. went beyond
   - [ ] d. fulfilled

10. Montezuma received them and gave them <u>quarters</u> in the city.
    - [ ] a. a place to stay
    - [ ] b. a separate section of land
    - [ ] c. a piece of money
    - [ ] d. a rich estate

✎ _____ Number of correct answers
Enter this number on the Vocabulary graph on page 167.

Personal Response

What information in this selection surprised or interested you the most?

_____

_____

How do you feel about the way Hernando Cortés treated the Aztec emperor, Montezuma?

_____

_____

_____

24 | The Wall

by Scott C. Ingram

On the black walls of the Vietnam Veterans Memorial are inscribed the names of all those Americans who died in the Vietnam War. America has tried to forget that war, but this memorial has assured that the men and women who lost their lives in that conflict will not be forgotten.

For most Americans old enough to remember the Vietnam War (1959–75), recalling what happened brings back feelings of pain, confusion, and anger. What began as an attempt to aid South Vietnam in a struggle with North Vietnam became the longest and costliest conflict in our history. More than 58,000 Americans lost their lives in a land far away from their homes and families.

Like other wars, the Vietnam War had its full share of horrors and grief. Many areas of Vietnam were devastated. Families were torn apart. Civilians, many of them women and children, suffered terribly from forces beyond their control.

Though the war was fought across the Pacific in Southeast Asia, many of its scenes appeared on the nightly news in American homes. Day after day, year after year, people across the United States watched as bombings, firefights, burning villages, and wounded soldiers flickered on their TV screens.

As the war dragged on, it became the focus of angry arguments and violent protests. To some, the fight was necessary; to others, it was needless. Some said that true patriots supported the war; others answered that true patriots opposed the conflict. In the end the Vietnam War became one that many Americans simply wanted to forget. For those Americans who fought in and returned from "'Nam," the memories were especially troubling. There were nightmares of war—ambushes in dark, steaming jungles; cries of fear; curses and screams of agony; friends returning home in body bags.

In Vietnam death could happen anytime, anywhere. One moment, a friend might be walking beside you on patrol; the next, he could be cut down by a sniper's bullet or blown apart by a mine. Vietnamese who greeted you with friendly smiles by day might set a booby trap to kill you at night.

For many veterans, there were also bitter memories of the return home. Unlike soldiers returning from other wars, those who fought in Vietnam were not greeted by cheering crowds or stirring parades. Sometimes they were greeted by indifference; often they were branded as "losers," "drug addicts," or "baby killers." Some were spit upon simply for wearing a uniform.

By the late '70s, images of the war had faded from TV screens—and from many memories. Most Americans seemed eager to forget Vietnam, to put it behind them. But in the rush to forget the war, those who had fought were also forgotten.

In 1979 one Vietnam vet, Jan Scruggs, conceived the idea of a memorial to those who had given their lives in America's most unpopular war. By 1980, Scruggs had secured two acres in Washington, D.C., for the memorial and had received nearly 7 million dollars in private donations. All that remained was a competition for the design of the memorial.

Maya Ying Lin, a college architecture student, won the competition with a simple but elegant design. It consisted of two walls of black granite, 250 feet long, sloping into the ground to a depth of 10 feet. The names of all who had died would be arranged in the order of their death from 1959 to 1975. For some, the design was not traditional enough. As a result, a lifelike sculpture of three soldiers was erected near the wall.

The Vietnam Veterans Memorial was dedicated on Veterans Day in 1982 and was immediately recognized for its great dignity and immense power. As veterans and bereaved families flocked to Washington, the wall became almost a sacred place.

Since its dedication, the wall has drawn millions of visitors each year. It has served to draw Americans together—whatever their feelings about the war—to assure that the men and women who gave their lives will not be forgotten.

I was in Washington, D.C., in the spring of 1985 on business. Washington was at its most scenic, and it was packed with tourists. After I had completed my work, I had a few hours before I had to leave. I decided to go to the Vietnam Wall, since I had read and heard a great deal about it. No words, however, had prepared me for the experience I would have.

At first I couldn't see the wall because it was hidden in a grove of dogwood trees in full bloom. Then I approached the sculpture of the three soldiers. I followed their gaze and there it was—a stark, black V cut into a gentle slope.

At each end of the wall, the granite sections were no more than a foot above the ground. Each of the first few sections was inscribed with three or four names. I looked at them briefly as I moved along the walkway. At each new section, the wall grew higher, and the number of names grew by the dozens.

At the center of the wall, the mirrorlike granite towered over my head. I looked at my reflection and saw that it was broken by the names of the dead—so many names, thousands upon thousands. I felt surrounded by death.

Suddenly an overwhelming sense of sorrow pulled tears from deep within me. Two of my friends had lost their lives in Vietnam. But my tears were not for them alone; they were for the many lives cut short, for the many dreams unfulfilled, for the sadness and waste of war. I felt as alone as I have ever felt—perhaps, I thought, as alone as soldiers at their moment of death. I was alive, though, and I wasn't alone. There was a steady stream of people filing slowly past the names.

I looked away and saw a pot of bright yellow flowers on the ground. A note was tied to the stem of one flower.

Dear Michael,

Your name is here, but you are not. I made a rubbing of it, thinking that if I rubbed hard enough, I would rub your name off the wall. Then you would be alive and come back to me. I miss you so much. ■

✔ Enter your reading time below. Then look up your reading speed on the Words-per-Minute table on page 163.

Reading Time _____

Reading Speed _____

Enter your reading speed on the Reading Speed graph on page 164.

Comprehension

Put an **X** in the box next to the correct answer for each question or statement. Do not look back at the selection.

1. The number of Americans who died in Vietnam totaled over
   - ☐ a. 50,000.
   - ☐ b. 100,000.
   - ☐ c. 500,000.
   - ☐ d. one million.

2. In what year did the Vietnam War end?
   - ☐ a. 1959
   - ☐ b. 1965
   - ☐ c. 1975
   - ☐ d. 1982

3. Vietnam is located in
   - ☐ a. South Africa.
   - ☐ b. Southeast Asia.
   - ☐ c. southern Europe.
   - ☐ d. Central America.

4. The Vietnam War
   - ☐ a. was supported by all Americans.
   - ☐ b. was opposed by all Americans.
   - ☐ c. caused controversy among many Americans.
   - ☐ d. was ignored by most Americans.

5. In the end, the Vietnam War become one that many Americans
   - ☐ a. wanted to forget.
   - ☐ b. were proud Americans fought in.
   - ☐ c. wanted America to continue fighting.
   - ☐ d. were not affected by at all.

6. Maya Ying Lin, who designed the wall, was a
   - ☐ a. Vietnam veteran.
   - ☐ b. Vietnamese soldier.
   - ☐ c. Vietnamese refugee.
   - ☐ d. college student.

7. Where is the Vietnam Veterans Memorial?
   - ☐ a. South Vietnam
   - ☐ b. Philadelphia
   - ☐ c. Washington, D.C.
   - ☐ d. North Vietnam

8. The Memorial was dedicated on
   - ☐ a. Veterans Day in 1982.
   - ☐ b. Veterans Day in 1979.
   - ☐ c. Memorial Day in 1980.
   - ☐ d. the 4th of July in 1975.

9. What is the wall of the Memorial made of?
   - ☐ a. marble
   - ☐ b. granite
   - ☐ c. wood
   - ☐ d. bricks

10. Since the Memorial was completed, it has
   - ☐ a. helped Americans forget the war.
   - ☐ b. been avoided by everyone.
   - ☐ c. raised seven million dollars.
   - ☐ d. had millions of visitors every year.

✎ _____ **Number of correct answers**
Enter this number on the Comprehension graph on page 165.

Critical Thinking

Put an ✗ in the box next to the best answer for each question or statement. You may look back at the selection if you'd like.

1. The author's main purpose in writing this selection was to
   - ☐ a. express an opinion about the necessity of America's fighting in the Vietnam War.
   - ☐ b. inform you how the Vietnam Veterans Memorial came into being.
   - ☐ c. persuade you that America should not have become involved in the war.
   - ☐ d. describe his personal experience in visiting the Vietnam Veterans Memorial and the emotions he felt there.

2. Which of the following best expresses the main idea of the selection?
   - ☐ a. Many Americans forgot the Vietnam War and the veterans who fought there.
   - ☐ b. The Vietnam War caused a lot of controversy in America.
   - ☐ c. The Vietnam Veterans Memorial has assured that the men and women who gave their lives in that war will not be forgotten.
   - ☐ d. Vietnam veterans, unlike soldiers returning from other wars, were greeted at home by scorn and indifference.

3. If so many people tried to forget the war, why was the Memorial built?
   - ☐ a. to draw Americans together
   - ☐ b. to honor the people who died
   - ☐ c. to show how many people died in Vietnam
   - ☐ d. all of the above

4. Which word best describes the author's feelings when visiting the Memorial?
   ☐ a. sorrow
   ☐ b. love
   ☐ c. hate
   ☐ d. indifference

5. What caused the author to feel alone at the wall of the Memorial?
   ☐ a. No one else was there.
   ☐ b. People wouldn't speak to him.
   ☐ c. He was surrounded by the names of the dead.
   ☐ d. It was the middle of winter.

6. Why was a sculpture of three soldiers erected near the wall?
   ☐ a. Some people felt the original design was not traditional enough.
   ☐ b. Some people felt the original design was not impressive enough.
   ☐ c. Some people felt there would be too much open space without it.
   ☐ d. Some people felt a war memorial should include statues of soldiers.

7. Which of these people was the first to become involved with the building of the Vietnam Veterans Memorial?
   ☐ a. the president of the United States
   ☐ b. Maya Ying Lin
   ☐ c. the author
   ☐ d. Jan Scruggs

8. Compared to other wars America has fought in, the Vietnam War was the
   ☐ a. most popular.
   ☐ b. most remembered.
   ☐ c. longest and costliest.
   ☐ d. shortest and least costly.

9. What did the author mean when he said "I felt surrounded by death"?
   ☐ a. A veteran's cemetery encircled the site of the Memorial.
   ☐ b. He was surrounded by thousands of names of the dead.
   ☐ c. He felt as if he would die from grief.
   ☐ d. The thought of death frightened him.

10. Choose the best one-sentence paraphrase for the following sentences from the selection: "As the war dragged on, it became the focus of angry arguments and violent protests. To some, the fight was necessary; to others, it was needless."
    ☐ a. The war became the subject of much discussion.
    ☐ b. The war caused great controversy, with widespread disagreement about its necessity.
    ☐ c. To some, it was not necessary to drag the war on for so long.
    ☐ d. Some believed the war should continue because the fight was necessary.

✎ _____ Number of correct answers
Enter this number on the Critical Thinking graph on page 166.

Vocabulary

Each numbered sentence contains an underlined word from the selection. Following are four definitions. Put an ✗ in the box next to the best meaning of the word as it is used in the sentence.

1. Many areas of Vietnam were devastated.
   ☐ a. built up
   ☐ b. overrun
   ☐ c. ruined
   ☐ d. developed

2. To some, the fight was necessary; to others, it was needless.
   ☐ a. purposeful
   ☐ b. unnecessary
   ☐ c. important
   ☐ d. evil

3. Those who fought in Vietnam were not greeted by cheering crowds or stirring parades. Sometimes they were greeted by <u>indifference</u>.
   - ☐ a. eagerness
   - ☐ b. hate
   - ☐ c. interest
   - ☐ d. unconcern

4. One Vietnam vet, Jan Scruggs, <u>conceived</u> the idea of a memorial to those who had given their lives.
   - ☐ a. discovered
   - ☐ b. created
   - ☐ c. supported
   - ☐ d. bought

5. Maya Ying Lin, a college architecture student, won the competition with a simple but <u>elegant</u> design.
   - ☐ a. refined
   - ☐ b. costly
   - ☐ c. plain
   - ☐ d. old-fashioned

6. The Vietnam Veterans Memorial was immediately recognized for its great <u>dignity</u> and immense power.
   - ☐ a. length
   - ☐ b. popularity
   - ☐ c. expense
   - ☐ d. excellence

7. It has served to <u>assure</u> that the men and women who gave their lives will not be forgotten.
   - ☐ a. find
   - ☐ b. forget
   - ☐ c. assume
   - ☐ d. make certain

8. Each of the first few sections was <u>inscribed</u> with three or four names.
   - ☐ a. engraved
   - ☐ b. plastered
   - ☐ c. covered
   - ☐ d. recorded

9. Suddenly an <u>overwhelming</u> sense of sorrow pulled tears from deep within me.
   - ☐ a. surprising
   - ☐ b. uplifting
   - ☐ c. overpowering
   - ☐ d. annoying

10. My tears were for the many lives cut short, for the many dreams <u>unfulfilled</u>, for the sadness and waste of war.
    - ☐ a. not dreamed
    - ☐ b. not realized
    - ☐ c. not forgotten
    - ☐ d. not remembered

✎ _____ **Number of correct answers**
Enter this number on the Vocabulary graph on page 167.

Personal Response

How do you think Vietnam War veterans felt when they came home to indifference or protests?

_____

_____

I can understand how the author felt when he visited the wall because

_____

_____

_____

25 | Univeristy Days

by James Thurber

James Thurber was one of the most famous American humorists. Most of his stories involve shy, bumbling men who have great difficulty coping with life. This passage suggests where some of Thurber's ideas may have come from.

I passed all the other courses that I took at my university, but I could never pass botany. This was because all botany students had to spend several hours a week in a laboratory looking through a microscope at plant cells, and I could never see through a microscope. I never once saw a cell through a microscope. This used to enrage my instructor. He would wander around the laboratory pleased with the progress all the students were making in drawing the involved and, so I am told, interesting structure of flower cells, until he came to me. I would just be standing there. "I can't see anything," I would say. He would begin patiently enough, explaining how anybody can see through a microscope, but he would always end up in a fury, claiming that I could *too* see through a microscope but just pretended that I couldn't. "Try it just once again," he'd say, and I would put my eye to the microscope and see nothing at all, except now and again a nebulous milky substance—a phenomenon of maladjustment. "I see what looks like a lot of milk," I would tell him. This, he claimed, was the result of my not having adjusted the microscope properly, so he would readjust it for me, or rather, for himself. And I would look again and see milk.

I finally took a deferred pass, as they call it, and waited a year and tried again. The professor had come back from vacation as brown as a berry, bright-eyed, and eager to explain cell structure again to his classes. "Well," he said to me, cheerily, when we met in the first laboratory hour of the semester, "we're going to see cells this time, aren't we?" "Yes, sir," I said. Students to the right of me and to the left of me and in front of me were seeing cells; what's more, they were quietly drawing pictures of them in their notebooks. Of course, I didn't see anything.

"We'll try it," the professor said to me, grimly, "with every adjustment to the microscope known to man. As God is my witness, I'll arrange this glass so that you see cells through it or I'll give up teaching. In 22 years of botany, I—" He cut off abruptly for he was beginning to quiver all over, like Lionel Barrymore, and he genuinely wished to hold onto his temper; his scenes with me had taken a great deal out of him.

So we tried it with every adjustment of the microscope known to man. With only one of them did I see anything but blackness or the familiar lacteal opacity, and that time I saw to my pleasure and amazement, a variegated constellation of flecks, specks, and dots. These I hastily drew. The instructor, noting my activity, came back from an adjoining desk, a smile on his lips and his eyebrows high in hope. He looked at my cell drawing. "What's that?" he demanded, with a hint of a squeal in his voice. "That's what I saw," I said. "You didn't, you didn't, you *didn't!*" he screamed, losing control of his temper instantly, and he bent over and squinted into the microscope. His head snapped up. "That's your eye!" he shouted. "You've fixed the lens so that it reflects! You've drawn your eye!"

Another course that I didn't like, but somehow managed to pass, was economics. I went to that class straight from the botany class, which didn't help me any in understanding either subject. I used to get them mixed up. But not as mixed up as another student in my economics class who came there directly from a physics laboratory. He was a tackle on the football team, named Bolenciecwcz. At that time Ohio State University had one of the best football teams in the country, and Bolenciecwcz was one of its outstanding stars. In order to be eligible to play it

131

was necessary for him to keep up in his studies, a very difficult matter, for while he was not dumber than an ox he was not any smarter. Most of his professors were lenient and helped him along. None gave him more hints in answering questions or asked him simpler ones than the economics professor, a thin, timid man named Bassum. One day when we were on the subject of transportation and distribution, it came to Bolenciecwz's turn to answer a question. "Name one means of transportation," the professor said to him. No light came into the big tackle's eyes. "Just any means of transportation," said the professor. Bolenciecwcz sat staring at him. "That is," pursued the professor, "any medium, agency, or method of going from one place to another." Bolenciecwcz had the look of a man who is being led into a trap. "You may choose among steam, horsedrawn, or electrically propelled vehicles," said the instructor. "I might suggest the one which we commonly take in making long journeys across land." There was a profound silence in which everybody stirred uneasily, including Bolenciecwcz and Mr. Bassum. Mr. Bassum abruptly broke this silence in an amazing manner. "Choo-choo-choo," he said, in a low voice, and turned instantly scarlet. He glanced appealingly around the room. All of us, of course, shared Mr. Bassum's desire that Bolenciecwcz should stay abreast of the class in economics, for the Illinois game, one of the hardest and most important of the season, was only a week off. "Toot, toot, too-toooooooot!" some student with a deep voice moaned, and we all looked encouragingly at Bolenciecwcz. Somebody else gave a fine imitation of a locomotive letting off steam. Mr. Bassum himself rounded off the little show. "Ding, dong, ding, dong," he said, hopefully. Bolenciecwcz was staring at the floor now, trying to think, his great brow furrowed, his huge hands rubbing together, his face red.

"How did you come to college this year, Mr. Bolenciecwcz? asked the professor. "*Chuffa* chuffa, *chuffa* chuffa."

"M'father sent me," said the football player.

"What on?" asked Bassum.

"I git an 'lowance," said the tackle, in a low, husky voice, obviously embarrassed.

"No, no," said Bassum. "Name a means of transportation. What did you *ride* here on?"

"Train," said Bolenciecwcz.

"Quite right," said the professor, "Now Mr. Nugent, will you tell us—" ∎

✔ Enter your reading time below. Then look up your reading speed on the Words-per-Minute table on page 163.

Reading Time   _____

Reading Speed   _____

Enter your reading speed on the Reading Speed graph on page 164.

Comprehension

Put an **X** in the box next to the correct answer for each question or statement. Do not look back at the selection.

1. The author had difficulty with botany because
   - ☐ a. his instructor would ignore him.
   - ☐ b. he never went to class.
   - ☐ c. he couldn't see through the microscope.
   - ☐ d. his friends wouldn't help him.

2. How many times did the author take botany?
   - ☐ a. once
   - ☐ b. twice
   - ☐ c. three times
   - ☐ d. half a dozen times

3. How long had the instructor taught botany?
   - ☐ a. 10 years
   - ☐ b. 12 years
   - ☐ c. 18 years
   - ☐ d. 22 years

4. Based on what he saw in the microscope, the author drew a picture of
   - ☐ a. flower cells.
   - ☐ b. his eye.
   - ☐ c. his thumb.
   - ☐ d. black dots.

5. The author also didn't like
   - ☐ a. physics.
   - ☐ b. economics.
   - ☐ c. football.
   - ☐ d. mathematics.

6. In his economics class, the author
   - ☐ a. confused economics with botany.
   - ☐ b. annoyed the professor.
   - ☐ c. helped other students.
   - ☐ d. studied hard.

7. What school was the author attending?
   - ☐ a. Michigan State University
   - ☐ b. Penn State University
   - ☐ c. Ohio State University
   - ☐ d. Florida State University

8. Bolenciecwcz was a member of the school's
   - ☐ a. football team.
   - ☐ b. wrestling team.
   - ☐ c. basketball team.
   - ☐ d. baseball team.

9. Who was Mr. Bassum?
   - ☐ a. an economics professor
   - ☐ b. a botany instructor
   - ☐ c. the wrestling coach
   - ☐ d. another student

10. Bolenciecwcz had trouble answering a question when the class was on the subject of
    - ☐ a. investing.
    - ☐ b. banking.
    - ☐ c. real estate.
    - ☐ d. transportation.

✎ _____ **Number of correct answers**
Enter this number on the Comprehension graph on page 165.

Critical Thinking

Put an ✗ in the box next to the best answer for each question or statement. You may look back at the selection if you'd like.

1. The author's main purpose in writing this selection was to
   - ☐ a. entertain you with a good story.
   - ☐ b. teach you about botany.
   - ☐ c. express an opinion about dumb football players.
   - ☐ d. make fun of college classes.

2. The author tells this story mainly by
   - ☐ a. using his imagination and creativity.
   - ☐ b. telling different stories about the same incident.
   - ☐ c. comparing several different incidents.
   - ☐ d. retelling personal experiences.

3. In this story, the author's tone is
   - ☐ a. impatient.
   - ☐ b. humorous.
   - ☐ c. critical.
   - ☐ d. somber.

4. Why did everyone try to help Bolenciecwcz?
   - ☐ a. They felt sorry for him.
   - ☐ b. They wanted him to get an A.
   - ☐ c. They wanted him to stay on the football team.
   - ☐ d. They liked his attitude during class.

5. Why did the author draw a picture of his own eye?
   - ☐ a. He wanted to get out of class.
   - ☐ b. It was the only thing he knew how to draw.
   - ☐ c. He wanted to make the professor angry.
   - ☐ d. It was the only thing he saw when he looked in the microscope.

6. Which of the following is a statement of opinion rather than fact?
   - ☐ a. Bolenciecwcz had the look of a man who is being led into a trap.
   - ☐ b. I passed all the other courses that I took at my university, but I could never pass botany.
   - ☐ c. "You've fixed the lens so that it reflects! You've drawn your eye!"
   - ☐ d. At that time Ohio State University had one of the best football teams in the country, and Bolenciecwcz was one of its outstanding stars.

7. Which word best describes the emotion the economics professor must have felt by the end of the story?
   - ☐ a. relief
   - ☐ b. love
   - ☐ c. anger
   - ☐ d. envy

8. Compared to his botany professor, the author's economics professor
   - ☐ a. had more interest in flowers.
   - ☐ b. was more easily upset.
   - ☐ c. was more patient.
   - ☐ d. had less sense of humor.

9. Which of the following does *not* fit with the other three?
   - ☐ a. botany
   - ☐ b. football
   - ☐ c. economics
   - ☐ d. physics

10. Based on this selection, you can predict that Bolenciecwz will probably become a
    - ☐ a. stock broker.
    - ☐ b. high school science teacher.
    - ☐ c. computer analyst.
    - ☐ d. professional football player.

✎ _____ **Number of correct answers**
Enter this number on the Critical Thinking graph on page 166.

Vocabulary

Each numbered sentence contains an underlined word from the selection. Following are four definitions. Put an ✗ in the box next to the best meaning of the word as it is used in the sentence.

1. I would put my eye to the microscope and see nothing at all, except now and again a <u>nebulous</u> milky substance—a phenomenon of maladjustment.
   - ☐ a. starry
   - ☐ b. black
   - ☐ c. vague
   - ☐ d. slow

2. I finally took a <u>deferred</u> pass, as they call it, and waited a year and tried again.
   - ☐ a. speeded up
   - ☐ b. doubtful
   - ☐ c. requested
   - ☐ d. delayed

3. He cut off <u>abruptly</u> for he was beginning to quiver all over.
   - ☐ a. suddenly
   - ☐ b. shakily
   - ☐ c. slowly
   - ☐ d. coldly

4. With only one of them did I see anything but blackness or the familiar lacteal <u>opacity</u>.
   - ☐ a. murkiness
   - ☐ b. transparency
   - ☐ c. clarity
   - ☐ d. variety

5. I saw, to my pleasure and amazement, a variegated constellation of flecks, specks, and dots. These I <u>hastily</u> drew.
   - ☐ a. neatly
   - ☐ b. quickly
   - ☐ c. reluctantly
   - ☐ d. ornately

6. Most of his professors were <u>lenient</u> and helped him along.
   - ☐ a. cowardly
   - ☐ b. biased
   - ☐ c. upset
   - ☐ d. tolerant

7. "You may choose among steam, horsedrawn, or electrically <u>propelled</u> vehicles."
   - ☐ a. pulled
   - ☐ b. powered
   - ☐ c. designed
   - ☐ d. none of the above

8. He glanced <u>appealingly</u> around the room.
   - ☐ a. sweetly
   - ☐ b. repulsively
   - ☐ c. sickenly
   - ☐ d. pleadingly

9. Bolenciecwcz should stay <u>abreast</u> of the class in economics.
   - ☐ a. at the head of
   - ☐ b. out of date with
   - ☐ c. up to date with
   - ☐ d. out of line with

10. "I git an 'lowance," said the tackle, in a low, <u>husky</u> voice, obviously embarrassed.
    - ☐ a. hoarse
    - ☐ b. dog-like
    - ☐ c. tiny
    - ☐ d. quivering

✎ _____ Number of correct answers
Enter this number on the Vocabulary graph on page 167.

Personal Response

I know how the author felt in his botany class because

_____

_____

_____

Do you think the author is unfairly stereotyping football players in this story? Explain your answer.

_____

_____

_____

26 | My Family and Other Animals

by Gerald Durrell

This selection describes the author's unusual adventures as an English boy living on a Greek island with his family and a large collection of animals. In this passage from the book, the boy, his sister, and their mother unexpectedly get to meet a saint under the most unusual circumstances.

The next morning Spiro drove Mother, Margo, and myself into the town to buy furniture. We noticed that the town was more crowded, more boisterous, than usual, but it never occurred to us that anything special was happening until we had finished bargaining with the dealer and made our way out of his shop into the narrow, twisted streets. We were jostled and pushed as we struggled to get back to the place where we had left the car. The crowd grew thicker and thicker, and the people were so tightly wedged together that we were carried forward against our will.

"I think there must be something going on," said Margo observantly. "Maybe it's a fiesta or something interesting."

"I don't care *what* it is, as long as we get back to the car," said Mother.

But we were swept along, in the opposite direction to the car, and eventually pushed out to join a vast crowd assembled in the main square of the town. I asked an elderly peasant woman near me what was happening, and she turned to me, her face lit up with pride.

"It is Saint Spiridion, my dear," she explained. "Today we may enter the church and kiss his feet."

Saint Spiridion was the patron saint of the island. His mummified body was enshrined in a silver coffin in the church, and once a year he was carried in procession round the town. He was very powerful, and could grant requests, cure illness, and do a number of other wonderful things for you if he happened to be in the right mood when asked. Today was a special day; apparently they would open the coffin and allow the faithful to kiss the slippered feet of the mummy, and make any request they cared to. The composition of the crowd showed how well-loved the saint was by the Corfiots: there were elderly peasant women in their best black clothes, and their husbands, hunched as olive-trees, with sweeping white mustaches; there were fishermen, bronzed and muscular, with the dark stains of octopus ink on their shirts; there were the sick too, the mentally defective, the consumptive, the crippled, old people who could hardly walk, and babies wrapped and bound like cocoons, their pale, waxy little faces crumpled up as they coughed and coughed. There were even a few tall, wild-looking Albanian shepherds, mustached and with shaven heads, wearing great sheepskin cloaks. This dark multi-colored wedge of humanity moved slowly toward the dark door of the church, and we were swept along with it, wedged like pebbles in a lava-flow. I was caught firmly between five fat peasant women, who pressed on me like cushions and exuded sweat and garlic, while Mother was hopelessly entangled between two of the enormous Albanian shepherds. Steadily, firmly, we were pushed up the steps and into the church.

Inside, it was dark as a well, lit only by a bed of candles that bloomed like yellow crocuses along one wall. A bearded, tall-hatted priest clad in black robes flapped like a crow in the gloom, making the crowd form into a single line that filed down the church, past the great silver coffin, and out through another door into the street. The coffin was standing upright, looking like a silver chrysalis, and at its lower end a portion had been removed so that the saint's feet, clad in the richly-embroidered slippers, peeped out. As each person reached the coffin he bent, kissed the feet, and murmured a prayer, while at the top of the sarcophagus the saint's black and withered face peered out of a glass panel with an expression of acute distaste. I looked back and saw Mother making frantic efforts to get to my side, but the Albanian bodyguard would not give an inch, and she struggled ineffectually. Presently she caught my eye and started to grimace and point at the coffin, shaking her head vigorously. I was greatly puzzled by this, and so were the two Albanians, who were watching her with undisguised suspicion. At last, in desperation, she threw caution to the winds and hissed at me over the heads of the crowd: "Tell Margo . . . *not* to kiss . . . kiss the air . . . kiss the *air*."

I turned to deliver Mother's message to Margo, but it was too late; there she was, crouched over the slippered feet, kissing them with an enthusiasm that enchanted and greatly surprised the crowd. When it came to my turn I obeyed Mother's instructions, kissing loudly and with a considerable show of reverence a point some six inches above the mummy's left foot. Then I was pushed along and disgorged through the church door and out into the street, where the crowd was breaking up into little groups, laughing and chattering. Margo was waiting on the steps, looking extremely self-satisfied. The next moment Mother appeared, shot from the door by the brawny shoulders of her shepherds.

"Those *shepherds*," she exclaimed faintly. "So ill-mannered—the smell nearly killed me—a mixture of incense and garlic—How do they manage to smell like that?"

"Oh, well," said Margo cheerfully. "It'll have been worth it if Saint Spiridion answers my request."

"A most *insanitary* procedure," said Mother, "more likely to spread disease than cure it. I dread to think what we would have caught if we'd *really* kissed his feet."

"But I kissed his feet."

"Margo! You didn't!"

"Well, everyone else was doing it."

"And after I expressly told you *not* to."

"You never told me not to . . ."

I interrupted and explained that I had been too late with Mother's warning.

"After all those people have been slobbering over those slippers you have to go and kiss them. I can't think what on earth possessed you to *do* such a thing."

"Well, I thought he might cure my acne."

The next day Margo went down with a severe attack of influenza, and Saint Spiridion's prestige with Mother reached rock bottom. ∎

✔ Enter your reading time below. Then look up your reading speed on the Words-per-Minute table on page 163.

Reading Time _____

Reading Speed _____

Enter your reading speed on the Reading Speed graph on page 164.

Comprehension

Put an **X** in the box next to the correct answer for each question or statement. Do not look back at the selection.

1. The Durrell family had come into town to
   - ☐ a. go to church.
   - ☐ b. buy furniture.
   - ☐ c. go to lunch.
   - ☐ d. shop for clothes.

2. Why did the family go into the church?
   - ☐ a. It was time for Sunday mass.
   - ☐ b. They were invited in by the priest.
   - ☐ c. They wanted to see Saint Spiridion.
   - ☐ d. They got caught up in the crowd.

3. How often did the ceremony honoring Saint Spiridion occur?
   - ☐ a. every Sunday
   - ☐ b. once a month
   - ☐ c. once a year
   - ☐ d. once every five years

4. Why did the townspeople kiss Saint Spiridion's feet?
   - ☐ a. They wanted Saint Spiridion to grant them favors.
   - ☐ b. It made the priest happy.
   - ☐ c. It was the law of the church.
   - ☐ d. The pope asked them to.

5. Mother didn't want her children to kiss the saint's feet because
   - ☐ a. the crowd was watching.
   - ☐ b. he wasn't a real saint.
   - ☐ c. they might catch a disease.
   - ☐ d. it would bring bad luck.

6. When Margo's turn came, she
   - ☐ a. kissed the air above the saint's feet.
   - ☐ b. kissed the saint's feet.
   - ☐ c. hid behind the shepherds.
   - ☐ d. got sick at the thought of kissing his feet.

7. The crowd was happy with what Margo did because they
   - ☐ a. appreciated the respect she had shown.
   - ☐ b. knew her so well.
   - ☐ c. wanted to cure her acne.
   - ☐ d. liked her.

8. Margo kissed the saint's feet even though her mother didn't want her to because she
   - ☐ a. was afraid the crowd would be angry if she didn't.
   - ☐ b. wanted to do it before her brother did.
   - ☐ c. got Mother's message too late.
   - ☐ d. was stubborn and decided to disobey her mother.

9. Mother was critical of the behavior of
   - ☐ a. the Albanian shepherds.
   - ☐ b. the elderly peasant woman.
   - ☐ c. the fishermen.
   - ☐ d. Spiro.

10. What happened the day after Margo kissed the saint's feet?
    - ☐ a. She got influenza.
    - ☐ b. Her acne was cured.
    - ☐ c. The family left the island.
    - ☐ d. The priest thanked her for her gesture in the church.

✎ _____ Number of correct answers
Enter this number on the Comprehension graph on page 165.

Critical Thinking

Put an **X** in the box next to the best answer for each question or statement. You may look back at the selection if you'd like.

1. The author's main purpose in writing this selection was to
   - ☐ a. describe life on a small Greek island.
   - ☐ b. entertain you with an interesting story.
   - ☐ c. inform you about Saint Spiridion.
   - ☐ d. express an opinion about an ancient religious custom.

2. Who is the narrator of this story?
   - ☐ a. the sister
   - ☐ b. the mother
   - ☐ c. the boy
   - ☐ d. an outside observer

3. In this selection the author's tone is
   - ☐ a. serious.
   - ☐ b. angry.
   - ☐ c. humorous.
   - ☐ d. depressing.

4. You can conclude that the Durrell family
   - ☐ a. was not native to the village.
   - ☐ b. attended the church regularly.
   - ☐ c. disliked the townspeople.
   - ☐ d. wanted to live in the village.

5. What caused Saint Spiridion's prestige to decline with Mother?
   - ☐ a. Margo didn't get her wish.
   - ☐ b. She had a bad experience in the church.
   - ☐ c. Margo got influenza.
   - ☐ d. She didn't believe he was a saint.

6. Based on the selection, you can predict that probably
   - ☐ a. the practice of kissing Saint Spiridion's feet will be discontinued.
   - ☐ b. the Durrell family will not come to town next year on Saint Spiridion's Day.
   - ☐ c. next year Mother will request that Saint Spiridion grant her a wish.
   - ☐ d. the Durrell family will attend the church regularly.

7. Which of the following does *not* fit with the other three?
   - ☐ a. Spiro
   - ☐ b. Margo
   - ☐ c. the boy
   - ☐ d. Mother

8. Compared to her brother, Margo was
   - ☐ a. cautious.
   - ☐ b. timid.
   - ☐ c. disrespectful.
   - ☐ d. bolder.

9. Why did Margo look "extremely self-satisfied" after the episode?
   - ☐ a. She was the first person out of the church.
   - ☐ b. Her mother didn't catch her kissing Saint Spiridion's feet.
   - ☐ c. She had done something her brother did not do.
   - ☐ d. She was sure her wish would be granted.

10. What word best describes Margo's reason for doing what she did?
    - ☐ a. love
    - ☐ b. envy
    - ☐ c. disgust
    - ☐ d. hope

✎ _____ Number of correct answers
Enter this number on the Critical Thinking graph on page 166.

Vocabulary

Each numbered sentence contains an underlined word from the selection. Following are four definitions. Put an ✗ in the box next to the best meaning of the word as it is used in the sentence.

1. We were <u>jostled</u> and pushed as we struggled to get back to the place where we had left the car.
   - ☐ a. mugged
   - ☐ b. frisked
   - ☐ c. shoved
   - ☐ d. thrilled

2. His <u>mummified</u> body was enshrined in a silver coffin in the church.
   - ☐ a. preserved
   - ☐ b. wrinkled
   - ☐ c. blackened
   - ☐ d. holy

3. The <u>composition</u> of the crowd showed how well-loved the saint was by the Corfiots.
   - ☐ a. noise
   - ☐ b. makeup
   - ☐ c. flavor
   - ☐ d. heat

4. There were the sick too, the mentally defective, the <u>consumptive</u>, the crippled, old people who could hardly walk.
   - ☐ a. hungry
   - ☐ b. wasted
   - ☐ c. fat
   - ☐ d. ordinary

5. I was caught firmly between five fat peasant women, who pressed on me like cushions and <u>exuded</u> sweat and garlic.
   - ☐ a. displayed
   - ☐ b. made
   - ☐ c. dissolved
   - ☐ d. oozed

6. At the top of the <u>sarcophagus</u> the saint's black and withered face peered out of a glass panel.
   - ☐ a. coffin
   - ☐ b. altar
   - ☐ c. room
   - ☐ d. church

7. The saint's black and withered face peered out of a glass panel with an expression of <u>acute</u> distaste.
   - ☐ a. attractive
   - ☐ b. weird
   - ☐ c. intense
   - ☐ d. obvious

8. I looked back and saw Mother making <u>frantic</u> efforts to get to my side.
   - ☐ a. few
   - ☐ b. frenzied
   - ☐ c. many
   - ☐ d. calm

9. Then I was pushed along and <u>disgorged</u> through the church door.
   - ☐ a. squeezed
   - ☐ b. helped
   - ☐ c. ejected
   - ☐ d. danced

10. Saint Spiridion's <u>prestige</u> with Mother reached rock bottom.
   - ☐ a. good luck
   - ☐ b. disease
   - ☐ c. comfort
   - ☐ d. reputation

✎ _____ **Number of correct answers**
Enter this number on the Vocabulary graph on page 167.

Personal Response

What would you have done in the church if you were Margo? Explain.

_____

_____

_____

What do you think of Mother's behavior in the church?

_____

_____

_____

27 | Going Up

For centuries, human beings have wanted to be able to fly like the birds of the sky. But our first successful venture into the air was not on wings—it was by balloon.

During the Middle Ages, thinkers outlined ideas for building machines that could travel in the air. However, no such machines were ever built at that time. In the 17th century, an Italian priest designed a flying machine composed of a wicker basket attached to four thin metal balls. He thought that if all the air were taken out of the balls the machine would be light enough to float in the air. We now realize, however, that these empty balls would have been crushed by atmospheric pressure. In the 18th century, a Scottish professor suggested that animal bladders filled with hydrogen might float in the air. However, this idea, too, remained untried.

In 1783 the Montgolfier brothers, in France, built a balloon that successfully carried a man into the air. The brothers had noticed that smoke rises and floats in the air, and so they tried filling paper bags with smoke. When this proved successful, they tried the same experiment with cloth bags. They soon discovered that smoke rises when the air around it is cooler. However, as soon as the smoke cools, it stops rising. Consequently, they made a little fire of charcoal on a pan underneath the bag. This arrangement kept the air under the bag warm for some time.

After three months of experimentation, the Montgolfier brothers sent some animals up in a balloon. For this occasion, King Louis XVI came to the town of Annonay where the Montgolfiers lived. The brothers put a duck, a rooster, and a sheep in a basket attached to the bag. Then they sent the whole thing into the air. The bag stayed up for eight minutes, and landed safely. Plans were quickly made for a man to go up.

The king was willing to provide for the experiment a criminal who had been sentenced to death. However, the king's historian said that he would be honored to go himself. A month later the balloon was ready. Under the balloon they erected a platform large enough for a man, a fire pan, and damp straw that could burn slowly to provide the necessary heat and smoke.

The new experiment worked. The king's historian stayed about 80 feet up in the air for four and a half minutes. A month later, the same historian and a colleague went up 500 feet and stayed there 25 minutes, floating over Paris. Not long after, a bigger balloon carried seven passengers 3,000 feet over Lyons.

Despite their apparent success, these balloons had certain disadvantages. For one thing, the fire was always a possible source of danger because it might ignite the balloon.

Some physicists, realizing this, found a way of making hydrogen-filled balloons. First, they varnished fine silk so that no hydrogen could pass through it. Then they had to obtain enough hydrogen to fill the silk balloon. When the first hydrogen balloon was finally completed and sent up, it rose to 3,000 feet above Paris. It stayed in view for an hour and came down in a field 15 miles away. There it was promptly torn into pieces by peasants who were afraid of it. Some peasants thought it was an evil spirit. Others thought that it was the moon, which had fallen down to crush the earth. To quell these misapprehensions, the king issued a proclamation describing balloons, telling people not to be afraid of them, and ordering everyone not to damage them.

In December 1783 two French scientists went up in a hydrogen balloon. They traveled a distance of 25 miles and stayed up almost two hours. When the balloon landed, one of the men stepped out and the other man quickly shot up in the balloon to a height of 9,000 feet! He found the air up there very cold and very thin. He did, however, return safely to earth.

An American doctor, in 1784, made the first scientific records of air pressure at high altitudes. Soon after that, two Frenchmen flew across the English Channel in a hydrogen balloon. It took them two hours to cross from Dover to Calais. However, the balloon leaked, and some gas was lost. The men almost fell into the water, but they threw out their ballast and most of their clothes in order to make a safe landing on ground.

In 1793 President George Washington watched a balloon ascent in Philadelphia. During the next 100 years balloonists, like acrobats, were popular at fairs and celebrations. One man dropped leaflets from a balloon—copies of poems he had written about the joys of flying. Another man made a practice of letting his balloon burst, and then using it as a parachute to float slowly down to earth.

In 1870 the Prussian armies surrounded Paris. For four months the Parisians kept in touch with the outside by means of balloons and carrier pigeons. Quite a lot of mail and messages were carried by balloons. Balloons also aided over 100 people, including many political leaders, to escape from Paris.

After this war, balloon corps were established in the armies of many large countries. During the First World War, they were used for observation, especially for the spotting of submarines.

During the 20th century, balloons have been used for the exploration of the upper atmosphere and stratosphere. Before the era of rockets and spaceships, men went up in balloons to a height of 14 miles. Weather forecasters find balloons most useful in finding out what the weather is like at different places and different levels of the atmosphere. The balloons send back the recordings of the instruments they carry by way of small shortwave radios. Such observations help the forecasters predict what the weather is going to be.

Although balloons are not easy to steer and can only travel as fast as they are pushed by the wind, they have served an important function by introducing human beings to the pleasures and problems of flight. Through the use of balloons it became evident that it was indeed possible for people to travel in the air. ■

✔ Enter your reading time below. Then look up your reading speed on the Words-per-Minute table on page 163.

Reading Time _____

Reading Speed _____

Enter your reading speed on the Reading Speed graph on page 164.

Comprehension

Put an **X** in the box next to the correct answer for each question or statement. Do not look back at the selection.

1. People fitst went up in balloons in the
   - ☐ a. Middle Ages.
   - ☐ b. 1600s.
   - ☐ c. 1700s.
   - ☐ d. 1800s.

2. The first successful balloon flight took place in
   - ☐ a. France.
   - ☐ b. England.
   - ☐ c. Prussia.
   - ☐ d. Scotland.

3. The Montgolfier brothers discovered that
   - ☐ a. paper bags could not be filled with smoke.
   - ☐ b. smoke rises when the air around it is cooler.
   - ☐ c. smoke rises when the air around it is warmer.
   - ☐ d. when heated, smoke becomes hydrogen.

4. How high did the first balloon flight with a man aboard manage to go?
   - ☐ a. 80 feet
   - ☐ b. 500 feet
   - ☐ c. 1,000 feet
   - ☐ d. 3,000 feet

5. Some physicists found a way to make balloons
safer by filling them with
☐ a. smoke.
☐ b. hydrogen.
☐ c. heated air.
☐ d. oxygen.

6. When a balloon came down in a field near
Paris, the peasants were
☐ a. happy.
☐ b. curious.
☐ c. amused.
☐ d. afraid.

7. In the late 1700s, two Frenchmen flew across
the English Channel in a hydrogen balloon in
☐ a. two days.
☐ b. one day.
☐ c. five hours.
☐ d. two hours.

8. Which president of the United States saw a
balloon ascent in Philadelphia in 1793?
☐ a. Thomas Jefferson
☐ b. James Madison
☐ c. George Washington
☐ d. John Quincy Adams

9. During the First World War, balloons were
mainly used for
☐ a. carrying soldiers.
☐ b. dropping bombs.
☐ c. observation.
☐ d. carrying messages.

10. One of the most important modern uses of
balloons is for
☐ a. exploration of outer space.
☐ b. weather forecasting.
☐ c. transportation.
☐ d. amusement-park rides.

✎ _____ **Number of correct answers**
**Enter this number on the Comprehension graph
on page 165.**

Critical Thinking

Put an ✗ in the box next to the best answer for
each question or statement. You may look back at
the selection if you'd like.

1. The author's main purpose in writing this
selection was to
☐ a. describe how balloons are able to stay
up in the air.
☐ b. inform you about the history,
development, and uses of balloons.
☐ c. convince you that the balloon was the
most important development in
aviation history.
☐ d. emphasize the contribution made by
the early balloonists to the
development of manned flight.

2. Which of the following best expresses the
main idea of the selection?
☐ a. Through the use of balloons, it became
evident that it was indeed possible for
people to travel in the air.
☐ b. The use of hydrogen made it possible
to keep balloons in the air for long
periods of time and to make them
safer.
☐ c. Balloons were found to have several
important uses during wartime.
☐ d. Throughout history, human beings
have found many practical uses for
balloons.

3. In order for balloons to float in the air, they
must be filled with
☐ a. a gas lighter than air.
☐ b. a gas heavier than air.
☐ c. a gas equal in weight to air.
☐ d. smoke.

4. Which word best describes the Montgolfier brothers?
- ☐ a. confident
- ☐ b. wealthy
- ☐ c. inventive
- ☐ d. discouraged

5. When air is heated it
- ☐ a. becomes smoke.
- ☐ b. cools.
- ☐ c. falls.
- ☐ d. rises.

6. Which of the following is a statement of opinion rather than fact?
- ☐ a. Before the era of rockets and spaceships, men went up in balloons to a height of 14 miles.
- ☐ b. The first successful balloon flight is the most important event in aviation history.
- ☐ c. In 1783, the Montgolfier brothers built a balloon that successfully carried a man into the air.
- ☐ d. When the first hydrogen balloon was finally completed and sent up, it rose to 3,000 feet above Paris.

7. The most important advantage in using hydrogen in balloons was that it
- ☐ a. was easy to make.
- ☐ b. was cheap.
- ☐ c. was safer than hot air.
- ☐ d. carried the balloon higher.

8. Which of the following events happened first?
- ☐ a. President George Washington watched a balloon ascent in Philadelphia.
- ☐ b. Over 100 people escaped from Paris in a balloon while the city was surrounded by Prussian armies.
- ☐ c. An American doctor made the first scientific records of air pressure at high altitudes.
- ☐ d. Two French scientists flew across the English Channel in a hydrogen balloon.

9. Which of the following does not fit with the other three?
- ☐ a. hydrogen
- ☐ b. balloon
- ☐ c. hot air
- ☐ d. smoke

10. One important effect of the successful flights of the early balloons was that they
- ☐ a. showed that humans could fly.
- ☐ b. entertained many people.
- ☐ c. provided a means of escape during wartime.
- ☐ d. speeded up travel.

✎ _____ **Number of correct answers**
Enter this number on the Critical Thinking graph on page 166.

Vocabulary

Each numbered sentence contains an underlined word from the selection. Following are four definitions. Put an ✗ in the box next to the best meaning of the word as it is used in the sentence.

1. During the Middle Ages, thinkers <u>outlined</u> ideas for building machines that could travel in the air.
- ☐ a. ridiculed
- ☐ b. described
- ☐ c. ignored
- ☐ d. fought against

2. In the 17th century, an Italian priest designed a flying machine <u>composed</u> of a wicker basket attached to four thin metal balls.
- ☐ a. compiled in an orderly way
- ☐ b. made by uniting parts
- ☐ c. put together with difficulty
- ☐ d. attached carefully

3. <u>Consequently</u>, they made a little fire of charcoal on a pan underneath the bag.
   - ☐ a. much later in time
   - ☐ b. with great care
   - ☐ c. with regret
   - ☐ d. for this reason

4. Despite their <u>apparent</u> success, these balloons had certain disadvantages.
   - ☐ a. lack of
   - ☐ b. occasional
   - ☐ c. observable
   - ☐ d. frequent

5. For one thing, the fire was always a possible <u>source</u> of danger.
   - ☐ a. an important part
   - ☐ b. a weak condition
   - ☐ c. a total cause
   - ☐ d. a beginning point

6. The fire was always a possible source of danger because it might <u>ignite</u> the balloon.
   - ☐ a. overheat
   - ☐ b. set on fire
   - ☐ c. deflate
   - ☐ d. overinflate

7. To <u>quell</u> these misapprehensions, the king issued a proclamation describing balloons.
   - ☐ a. make important
   - ☐ b. establish firmly
   - ☐ c. put an end to
   - ☐ d. bring out into the open

8. To quell these <u>misapprehensions</u>, the king issued a proclamation describing balloons.
   - ☐ a. ignorant comments
   - ☐ b. strong feelings of disappointment
   - ☐ c. poor evaluations
   - ☐ d. incorrect ideas

9. In 1793 President George Washington watched a balloon <u>ascent</u> in Philadelphia.
   - ☐ a. rise
   - ☐ b. experiment
   - ☐ c. race
   - ☐ d. landing

10. Before the <u>era</u> of rockets and spaceships, men went up in balloons to a height of 14 miles.
    - ☐ a. a distinctive period of time
    - ☐ b. a time denoting mistakes
    - ☐ c. a short space of time
    - ☐ d. a specific date

✎ _____ **Number of correct answers**
Enter this number on the Vocabulary graph on page 167.

Personal Response

What would you like about a balloon ride?

_____

_____

_____

What would you dislike about riding in a balloon?

_____

_____

28 Points of Origin

by Michael Omert

For centuries, certain animals have been loved as pets. Some have even been worshiped. But pet animals have also been cruelly treated through the ages. In this selection, the author relates some anecdotes about two of the most popular pet animals.

Throughout the history of mankind there has always been room for those tamed animals we now consider pets. The great pet in history and legend is, of course, the cat. There was a cat cult among the Egyptians of the late dynasties, and its best-known goddess was named Bastet. The Romans had *Felis catus* to help with the mousing and to play with around the hearth. (The designation *Felis domesticus* is modern scientific notation, not a Roman one.) This pet appears in classical Roman art, in literature, and on coins. There is even a Latin word, *murmare*, meaning "to purr."

The Italian poet Petrarch is remembered by some fugitive lines in Latin attributed to his cat, who seems as beloved as his human heartthrob, Laura. The feline narrator of the verse suggests that he was rewarded by Petrarch for his fidelity even as Laura was for her grace and beauty: "She first inspired the poet's lay,/But since I drove the mice away,/His love repaid my duty."

The cat has nowhere been the subject of more fascination and respect than in Britain. Indeed, the braininess of British cats is attested by a letter to the respected journal, *Notes and Queries*, in 1868:

"We were talking about the sagacity shown by some animals, when I mentioned the story which I think Archbishop Whately tells in some of his writings, of his cat ringing the doorbell. This anecdote brought out a still better one from my neighbor, who had come in to see me for a chat. He said that when he was about 25 years of age, there was belonging to his house a certain cat which up to that time had not attracted notice for any particular sagacity. But the pantry window of the old-fashioned house was found to be repeatedly broken. Time after time the broken

square—for one only was broken at a time—was repaired. At length my friend, growing tired of mending, made up his mind to have a board nailed over the lower row of the window-panes. Not very long after this precaution had been taken, being awake one night, he heard in his bedroom, which was close by, several distinct taps, as of a stone, upon glass. Getting out of bed, and looking down from the window, he saw then and there his cat resting with her hind feet upon the window-sill, her left paw clinging to the top of the new board, and with her other paw, in which she held a pebble, she was tapping the glass, in order no doubt to break it. He shouted out, and the cat jumped down, dropping the pebble—about the size of a marble—which in the morning he picked up."

But for all the respect they have inspired, cats have also been cruelly treated in many ages. The municipal records of Colchester, England, detail the 1651 trial of William Beard, who was alleged to have cut off the tail of Tom Burgis's cat. (For their part, the Burgis family retaliated by either poisoning or bewitching their pet's tormentor.)

Medieval students are known to have gambled with cats. As a result, medieval schools usually forbade the keeping of pets of any kind, but to little apparent avail. Students at the University of Paris in the 13th century are known to have used stray cats to play dice by balancing the cubes on their paws until they flicked them off. Winning cats were fed; losers had their skins sold.

The folklore associated with dogs, like that of cats, is rich and varied. A belief in East Anglia held that if a dog turned around three times, a stranger would call. A person should never handle children's teeth that were accidentally knocked out: otherwise, he himself would grow dog's teeth. These superstitions were current in the 19th century.

The reputation for faithfulness attached to dogs gave rise to their being a symbol of fidelity and to their being selected to appear on tomb effigies with ladies and knights of great stature. In one celebrated case, a dog was buried along with the body of a 13th-century bishop. A liturgical reason for this is obvious. As the shepherd of his flock, a bishop has a fit companion in the dog.

As for the "pet" saints of the medieval Christians, their stories are as memorable as they are charming. For example, St. Dominic is symbolized by a dog (at his birth his mother dreamt she had brought forth a whelp with a torch in its mouth), and fittingly founded the religious order called the Dominicans (from the Latin, *Domini canes*, "dogs of the Lord").

Although Aristotle flatly states that fish are the only creatures that cannot be tamed, a cult of St. Anthony of Padua (1195–1231) seems to give the lie to that assertion. The legend records that, at a time when a group of heretics refused to be moved by his preaching, he turned his voice to the shore of the Adriatic and addressed the multitude of fishes, which obliged him and arranged themselves neatly according to their species. When the good saint pointed out that God had spared them alone from the destruction of the deluge, and that they were also insensible to the vicissitudes of the weather and seasons that attack the world above water, "the fish, as though they had been endowed with reason, bowed down their heads with all the marks of a profound humility and devotion, moving their bodies up and down with a kind of fondness." Such was the tale presented to Padua tourists in 1705, when the English essayist Joseph Addison recorded his travels in Italy.

A similar legend is attached to the medieval lore of St. Patrick, on whose feast day the fish were expected to rise from the sea and parade before his altar. St. Patrick might well have sent the snakes away, as every true Irishman knows,

but to my mind bringing the fish back was a much bigger feat. ■

✔ Enter your reading time below. Then look up your reading speed on the Words-per-Minute table on page 163.

Reading Time _____

Reading Speed _____

Enter your reading speed on the Reading Speed graph on page 164.

Comprehension

Put an ✗ in the box next to the correct answer for each question or statement. Do not look back at the selection.

1. The great pet in history and legend is the
   - ☐ a. dog.
   - ☐ b. pig.
   - ☐ c. cat.
   - ☐ d. rabbit.

2. The Latin word *murmare* means
   - ☐ a. to purr.
   - ☐ b. mother cat.
   - ☐ c. to scratch.
   - ☐ d. to meow.

3. The Italian poet Petrarch wrote a poem that he attributed to
   - ☐ a. Aristotle.
   - ☐ b. his love, Laura.
   - ☐ c. his cat.
   - ☐ d. his dog.

4. Which country shows special fascination and the most respect for cats?
   - ☐ a. Ireland
   - ☐ b. Italy
   - ☐ c. Scotland
   - ☐ d. Britain

5. An article published in 1868 described
   - ☐ a. a poem written by a cat.
   - ☐ b. a cat that was poisoned.
   - ☐ c. the Egyptian cat cult.
   - ☐ d. a cat who broke windows with a stone.

6. In the 1651 trial in Colchester, England, William Beard was alleged to have
   - ☐ a. stolen a horse.
   - ☐ b. cut off a cat's tail.
   - ☐ c. poisoned a cat.
   - ☐ d. starved a dog.

7. What did some medieval students do with cats?
   - ☐ a. gambled with them
   - ☐ b. used them to keep mice away
   - ☐ c. arranged for cat fights
   - ☐ d. buried them alive

8. A superstition in East Anglia held that if a dog turned around three times its owner would
   - ☐ a. grow dog's teeth.
   - ☐ b. be called on by a stranger.
   - ☐ c. have three years of bad luck.
   - ☐ d. have three years of good luck.

9. Which creature did Aristotle flatly state could not be tamed?
   - ☐ a. the cat
   - ☐ b. the dog
   - ☐ c. the fish
   - ☐ d. the bird

10. According to the selection, every true Irishman knows that Saint Patrick
   - ☐ a. sent the snakes out of Ireland.
   - ☐ b. founded the Dominican religious order.
   - ☐ c. gave Ireland its name.
   - ☐ d. is the patron saint of fishermen.

✎ _____ **Number of correct answers**
Enter this number on the Comprehension graph on page 165.

Critical Thinking

Put an ☒ in the box next to the best answer for each question or statement. You may look back at the selection if you'd like.

1. What was the author's main purpose in writing *Points of Origin?*
   - ☐ a. to entertain you with amusing animal stories
   - ☐ b. to compare how dogs and cats have been treated throughout history
   - ☐ c. to express an opinion about the treatment of cats in medieval times
   - ☐ d. to inform you of some of the history of pet animals

2. Another good title for this selection would be
   - ☐ a. "Cruelty to Animals."
   - ☐ b. "Pets of History and Legend."
   - ☐ c. "Cats."
   - ☐ d. "Saints and Their Love of Animals."

3. The "shepherd and his flock" mentioned in this selection represents
   - ☐ a. a shepherd and a flock of geese.
   - ☐ b. sheep and their young.
   - ☐ c. the saying "birds of a feather flock together."
   - ☐ d. a religious leader and his followers.

4. Which word best describes the treatment of cats by University of Paris students in the 13th century?
   - ☐ a. caring
   - ☐ b. cruel
   - ☐ c. responsible
   - ☐ d. neglectful

5. Why did medieval schools usually forbid the keeping of pets of any kind?
   - ☐ a. It cost too much to feed them.
   - ☐ b. Students had gambled with cats.
   - ☐ c. They made too much mess.
   - ☐ d. They would fight among themselves.

6. Which of the following is a statement of opinion rather than fact?
   - ☐ a. Medieval students are known to have gambled with cats.
   - ☐ b. There was a cat cult among the Egyptians of the late dynasties.
   - ☐ c. But for all the respect they have inspired, cats have also been cruelly treated in many ages.
   - ☐ d. St. Patrick might well have sent the snakes away, but to my mind bringing the fish back was a much bigger feat.

7. Which event happened last?
   - ☐ a. St. Dominic founded the religious order called the Dominicans.
   - ☐ b. Aristotle flatly stated that fish are the only creatures that cannot be tamed.
   - ☐ c. The English essayist Joseph Addison recorded his travels in Italy.
   - ☐ d. Saint Patrick sent the snakes out of Ireland.

8. The Italian poet Petrarch loved his cat because the cat was so
   - ☐ a. clever.
   - ☐ b. beautiful.
   - ☐ c. faithful.
   - ☐ d. lonely.

9. Which of the following does *not* fit with the other three?
   - ☐ a. fish
   - ☐ b. cats
   - ☐ c. dogs
   - ☐ d. horses

10. Saint Anthony of Padua is said to have preached to the fish because
    - ☐ a. the fish were arranged by species.
    - ☐ b. St. Patrick had also preached to the fish.
    - ☐ c. a group of heretics refused to listen to him.
    - ☐ d. his mother had a dream about the fish.

✎ _____ **Number of correct answers**
Enter this number on the Critical Thinking graph on page 166.

Vocabulary

Each numbered sentence contains an underlined word from the selection. Following are four definitions. Put an ✘ in the box next to the best meaning of the word as it is used in the sentence.

1. In the history of mankind there has always been room for those <u>tamed</u> animals we now consider pets.
   - ☐ a. wild
   - ☐ b. trained
   - ☐ c. tired
   - ☐ d. clever

2. There was a cat <u>cult</u> among the Egyptians of the late dynasties, and its best-known goddess was named Bastet.
   - ☐ a. infectious disease
   - ☐ b. extreme religious group
   - ☐ c. outstanding performance
   - ☐ d. unreasonable fear

3. The Italian poet Petrarch is remembered by some <u>fugitive</u> lines in Latin attributed to his cat, who seems as beloved as his human heartthrob, Laura.
   - ☐ a. figurative
   - ☐ b. beautiful and sad
   - ☐ c. descriptive
   - ☐ d. fleeting

4. "There was belonging to his house a certain cat, which up to that time had not attracted notice for any particular <u>sagacity</u>."
   - ☐ a. intelligence
   - ☐ b. stupidity
   - ☐ c. companionship
   - ☐ d. thoughtfulness

5. As a result, medieval schools usually <u>forbade</u> the keeping of pets of any kind, but to little apparent avail.
- ☐ a. forced
- ☐ b. allowed
- ☐ c. prohibited
- ☐ d. forgave

6. The reputation for faithfulness attached to dogs gave rise to their being a symbol of <u>fidelity.</u>
- ☐ a. loyalty
- ☐ b. love and partnership
- ☐ c. fierceness
- ☐ d. good behavior

7. A dog was buried with the body of a 13th-century bishop. A <u>liturgical</u> reason for this is obvious.
- ☐ a. humorous
- ☐ b. odd
- ☐ c. logical
- ☐ d. religious

8. Although Aristotle flatly states that fish are the only creatures that cannot be tamed, a cult of Saint Anthony of Padua seems to give the lie to that <u>assertion</u>.
- ☐ a. lie
- ☐ b. question
- ☐ c. statement
- ☐ d. theory

9. The good saint pointed out that God had spared them from the <u>deluge</u>, and that they were also insensible to the vicissitudes of the weather and seasons that attack the world above the water.
- ☐ a. countryside
- ☐ b. fire
- ☐ c. flood
- ☐ d. desert

10. "The fish, as though they had been endowed with reason, bowed down their heads with all the marks of a <u>profound</u> humility and devotion."
- ☐ a. perfected
- ☐ b. shallow
- ☐ c. deep
- ☐ d. narrow

✎ _____ **Number of correct answers**
Enter this number on the Vocabulary graph on page 167.

Personal Response

Have you or someone you know ever had a very "special" pet? In three or four sentences, explain what made that pet so special.

_____

_____

Three reasons why I think dogs (or cats) make better pets are

_____

_____

_____

29 | The Complete Breath

by Yogi Ramacharaka

Eastern religions and philosophies have long studied the connection between physical fitness and a healthy, productive life. Now Westerners want to learn such Oriental practices as yoga. Yoga teaches a method of breathing that is believed to be essential in acquiring good health. This method, the Yogi Complete Breath, is explained in this selection.

Perhaps the best way to teach you how to develop the Yogi Complete Breath would be to give you simple directions regarding the breath itself, and then follow up the same with general remarks concerning it. Right here we wish to say that this Complete Breath is not a forced or abnormal thing, but on the contrary is a going back to first principles—a return to Nature. The healthy adult savage and the healthy infant of civilization both breathe in this manner, but civilized man has adopted unnatural methods of living, clothing, etc., and has lost his birthright. And we wish to remind the reader that the Complete Breath does not necessarily call for the complete filling of the lungs at every inhalation. One may inhale the average amount of air, using the Complete Breathing Method and distributing the air inhaled, be the quantity large or small, to all parts of the lungs. But one should inhale a series of full Complete Breaths several times a day, whenever opportunity offers, in order to keep the system in good order and condition.

The following simple exercise will give you a clear idea of what the Complete Breath is:

(1) Stand or sit erect. Breathing through the nostrils, inhale steadily, first filling the lower part of the lungs, which is accomplished by bringing into play the diaphragm, which descending exerts a gentle pressure on the abdominal organs, pushing forward the front walls of the abdomen. Then fill the middle part of the lungs, pushing out the lower ribs, breastbone, and chest. Then fill the higher portion of the lungs, protruding the upper chest, thus lifting the chest, including the upper six or seven pairs of ribs. In the final movement, the lower part of the abdomen will be slightly drawn in, which gives the lungs a support and also helps to fill the highest parts of the lungs.

At first reading it may appear that this breath consists of three distinct movements. This, however, is not the correct idea. The inhalation is continuous, the entire chest cavity from the lower diaphragm to the highest point at the chest in the region of the collarbone, being expanded with a uniform movement. Avoid a jerky series of inhalations, and strive to attain a steady continuous action.

(2) Retain the breath a few seconds.

(3) Exhale quite slowly, holding the chest in a firm position and drawing the abdomen in a little and lifting it upward slowly as the air leaves the lungs. When the air is entirely exhaled, relax the chest and abdomen. A little practice will render this part of the exercise easy, and the movement once acquired will be afterward performed almost automatically.

It will be seen that by this method of breathing all parts of the respiratory apparatus are brought into action, and all parts of the lungs, including the most remote air cells, are exercised. The chest cavity is expanded in all directions.

At the beginning of practice, you may have more or less trouble in acquiring the Complete Breath, but when you have once acquired it you will never willingly return to the old methods.

Colds may often be prevented by practicing a little vigorous Complete Breathing whenever you feel that you are being unduly exposed. When chilled, breathe vigorously a few minutes, and you will feel a glow all over your body. Most colds can be cured by Complete Breathing and partial fasting for a day.

The stomach and other organs of nutrition suffer much from improper breathing. Not only are they ill-nourished by reason of the lack of oxygen, but as the food must absorb oxygen from the blood and become oxygenated before it can be digested and assimilated, it is readily seen how digestion and assimilation are impaired by incorrect breathing. And when assimilation is not normal, the system receives less and less nourishment, the appetite fails, bodily vigor decreases, and energy diminishes, and the man withers and declines.

Even the nervous system suffers from improper breathing, inasmuch as the brain, the spinal cord, the nerve centers, and the nerves themselves, when improperly nourished by means of the blood, become poor and inefficient instruments for generating, storing, and transmitting the nerve currents.

In the practice of the Complete Breath, during inhalation, the diaphragm contracts and exerts a gentle pressure upon the liver, stomach, and other organs, which in connection with the rhythm of the lungs acts as a gentle massage of these organs and stimulates their actions, and encourages normal functioning. Each inhalation aids in this internal exercise, and assists in causing a normal circulation to the organs of nutrition and elimination.

The Western world is paying much attention to physical culture just now. But in their enthusiasm they must not forget that the exercise of the external muscles is not everything. The internal organs also need exercise. The diaphragm is Nature's principal instrument for this internal exercise. Its motion vibrates the important organs of nutrition and elimination, and massages and kneads them at each inhalation and exhalation, forcing blood into them, and then squeezing it out, and imparting a general tone to the organs. Any organ or part of the body which is not exercised gradually atrophies and refuses to function properly, and lack of the internal exercise afforded by the diaphragmatic action leads to diseased organs. The Complete Breath gives the proper motion to the diaphragm, as well as exercising the middle and upper chest.

From the standpoint of Western physiology alone, without reference to the Oriental philosophies and science, this Yogi system of Complete Breathing is of vital importance to every man, woman, and child who wishes to acquire health and keep it. Its very simplicity keeps thousands from seriously considering it, while they spend fortunes in seeking health through complicated and expensive "systems." Health knocks at their door and they answer not. Verily the stone which the builders reject is the real cornerstone of the Temple of Health. ■

✔ Enter your reading time below. Then look up your reading speed on the Words-per-Minute table on page 163.

Reading Time   _____

Reading Speed   _____

Enter your reading speed on the Reading Speed graph on page 164.

Comprehension

Put an **X** in the box next to the correct answer for each question or statement. Do not look back at the selection.

1. The Complete Breath is a
   - ☐ a. rigorous physical exercise.
   - ☐ b. martial arts secret.
   - ☐ c. method of breathing efficiently and naturally.
   - ☐ d. way of breathing that takes years to learn.

2. How often should you inhale a series of Complete Breaths?
   - ☐ a. once a week
   - ☐ b. several times a day
   - ☐ c. every time you breathe
   - ☐ d. several times a week

3. When using the Complete Breath method, you should first fill with air the
   - ☐ a. lower part of the lungs.
   - ☐ b. upper part of the lungs.
   - ☐ c. diaphragm.
   - ☐ d. front of the abdomen.

4. The Complete Breath is performed
   - ☐ a. with no movement at all.
   - ☐ b. in three distinct movements.
   - ☐ c. in one continuous movement.
   - ☐ d. with one quick movement.

5. After retaining the breath a few seconds, you should
   - ☐ a. inhale slowly.
   - ☐ b. inhale quickly.
   - ☐ c. exhale quickly.
   - ☐ d. exhale slowly.

6. How does the Complete Breath aid digestion and assimilation?
   - ☐ a. by removing oxygen in the blood
   - ☐ b. by massaging the stomach
   - ☐ c. by causing the diaphragm to atrophy
   - ☐ d. none of the above

7. People in the Western world must not forget that
   - ☐ a. internal organs also need exercise.
   - ☐ b. the exercise of external muscles is everything.
   - ☐ c. the exercise of internal organs is not everything.
   - ☐ d. its more important to exercise internal organs than external muscles.

8. What causes any organ or part of the body to atrophy?
   - ☐ a. insufficient sleep
   - ☐ b. lack of exercise
   - ☐ c. too much exercise
   - ☐ d. overeating

9. Which of the following suffer from improper breathing?
   - ☐ a. stomach
   - ☐ b. brain
   - ☐ c. nerves
   - ☐ d. all of the above

10. Why don't more people consider learning the Complete Breath?
   - ☐ a. They don't have the time.
   - ☐ b. It's complicated and difficult to perform.
   - ☐ c. It's so simple that they don't believe it works.
   - ☐ d. They don't accept Oriental philosophies.

✎ _____ Number of correct answers
Enter this number on the Comprehension graph on page 165.

Critical Thinking

Put an ✖ in the box next to the best answer for each question or statement. You may look back at the selection if you'd like.

1. The author's main purpose in writing this selection is to
   - ☐ a. impress people with his knowledge.
   - ☐ b. teach people how to stay healthier.
   - ☐ c. force people to breathe differently.
   - ☐ d. show how other people live.

2. Which of the following statements best expresses the main idea of the selection?
   - ☐ a. To stay healthier, people need to exercise their internal organs as well as their external muscles.
   - ☐ b. The Complete Breath does not necessarily call for the complete filling of the lungs at every inhalation.
   - ☐ c. By not learning the Complete Breath method, people are endangering their health.
   - ☐ d. The Western world is paying too much attention to physical culture just now.

3. Why does the author call the Complete Breath the "real cornerstone of the Temple of Health"?
- ☐ a. It enables the body to perform and function at its best.
- ☐ b. It's an ancient concept.
- ☐ c. It can only be taught by experienced yogis.
- ☐ d. all of the above

4. Which word best describes the Complete Breath method?
- ☐ a. complicated
- ☐ b. essential
- ☐ c. dangerous
- ☐ d. natural

5. According to the author, if you don't practice the Complete Breath, you
- ☐ a. will catch many colds.
- ☐ b. will not be as healthy as you could be.
- ☐ c. may stop breathing.
- ☐ d. may often feel dizzy.

6. Which of the following is a statement of opinion rather than fact?
- ☐ a. You may have more or less trouble in acquiring the Complete Breath, but once you have acquired it, you will never willingly return to the old method.
- ☐ b. The stomach and other organs of nutrition suffer much from improper breathing.
- ☐ c. The Western world is paying much attention to physical culture now.
- ☐ d. The internal organs also need exercise.

7. A good time to practice the Complete Breath would be
- ☐ a. before hard exercise.
- ☐ b. before mealtimes.
- ☐ c. before bedtime.
- ☐ d. all of the above

8. Which of the following does *not* fit with the other three?
- ☐ a. lungs
- ☐ b. oxygen
- ☐ c. stomach
- ☐ d. heart

9. When using the Complete Breath method, what should you do next after filling your lungs with air?
- ☐ a. Slightly draw in the lower part of the abdomen.
- ☐ b. Retain the breath a few seconds.
- ☐ c. Stand or sit erect.
- ☐ d. Exhale quite slowly.

10. Choose the best one-sentence paraphrase for the following sentence from the selection: "Health knocks at their door and they answer not."
- ☐ a. They aren't home when the doctor calls.
- ☐ b. They don't hear the doctor knocking at their door.
- ☐ c. They ignore health when it is offered.
- ☐ d. They are interested in acquiring good health.

✎ _____ **Number of correct answers**
Enter this number on the Critical Thinking graph on page 166.

Vocabulary

Each numbered sentence contains an underlined word from the selection. Following are four definitions. Put an ✗ in the box next to the best meaning of the word as it is used in the sentence.

1. Inhale steadily, first filling the lower part of the lungs, which is accomplished by bringing into play the <u>diaphragm</u>.
- ☐ a. a bone
- ☐ b. a mechanical device
- ☐ c. an air tube
- ☐ d. a muscle

2. Then fill the higher portion of the lungs, <u>protruding</u> the upper chest.
   - ☐ a. breaking into
   - ☐ b. pulling in
   - ☐ c. pushing out
   - ☐ d. twisting down

3. It will be seen that by this method of breathing all parts of the <u>respiratory</u> apparatus are brought into action.
   - ☐ a. breathing
   - ☐ b. circulation
   - ☐ c. absorption
   - ☐ d. expulsion

4. The chest <u>cavity</u> is expanded in all directions.
   - ☐ a. a lump
   - ☐ b. a patch of skin
   - ☐ c. a hollow area
   - ☐ d. none of the above

5. When chilled, breathe <u>vigorously</u> for a few minutes, and you will feel a glow all over.
   - ☐ a. shallowly
   - ☐ b. energetically
   - ☐ c. slowly
   - ☐ d. coarsely

6. The food must absorb oxygen from the blood and become oxygenated before it can be digested and <u>assimilated</u>.
   - ☐ a. rejected
   - ☐ b. absorbed
   - ☐ c. exhaled
   - ☐ d. circulated

7. The diaphragm contracts and <u>exerts</u> a gentle pressure upon the liver, stomach, and other organs.
   - ☐ a. removes
   - ☐ b. deposits
   - ☐ c. remains
   - ☐ d. pushes

8. But in their <u>enthusiasm</u> they must not forget that the exercise of the external muscles is not everything.
   - ☐ a. excitement
   - ☐ b. boredom
   - ☐ c. busyness
   - ☐ d. repetition

9. Any organ or part of the body that is not exercised gradually <u>atrophies</u>.
   - ☐ a. wastes away
   - ☐ b. grows stronger
   - ☐ c. gets larger
   - ☐ d. disappears

10. Complete Breathing is vital to every man, woman, and child who wishes to <u>acquire</u> health and keep it.
    - ☐ a. get rid of
    - ☐ b. discover
    - ☐ c. obtain
    - ☐ d. win

✎ _____ **Number of correct answers**
Enter this number on the Vocabulary graph on page 167.

Personal Response

In thinking about the Complete Breath, I wonder why

_____

_____

Would you recommend this selection to others? Explain why or why not.

_____

_____

30 | The World of the Gods

by Michael Gibson

The myth and the legend, or hero tale, had their origins in Greece. Greek literature began with stories about gods and heroes. In the beginning, these tales were not written down, but were recited or sung from memory.

Greece is a land of many contrasts. It has flat plains, foothills, and mountain ranges. In places along its jagged coastline are high cliffs, and the surrounding seas are sprinkled with islands both large and small, some inhabited and some not. The lower-lying lands are fertile, and on the slopes are vineyards. In spring in the wilder places the ground is ablaze with wildflowers, which grow for some way up the mountains; contrasting with the grey-green leaves of the herbs which also flourish there. However, the brilliant colors last only for a short while before the heat of the summer sun makes the flowers vanish as quickly as they came. Then the only vegetation outside the more sheltered valleys consists of clumps of small, stunted pines and scrub. In winter there is snow on the mountain peaks.

In ancient times, particularly on the higher ground, the country was much more wooded and less barren than it is today. Many centuries of close cropping by the herds of long-eared goats and sheep kept by peasant farmers have destroyed sapling trees and young shrubs. Without these, there were no long roots to help bind the soil together when it dried out in the burning summer sun, and over the years it became thin and powdery and was blown away. The rocks, never far below the surface, were exposed and in the scanty soil left in the cracks only the toughest grasses and the herbs which grow best in these poor conditions could survive. At the time of the legends, however, none of this had happened and woods and forests were plentiful.

The coast is probably much the same as it was in the old days. As was perhaps to be expected in a land with so many natural harbors, the ancient Greeks were excellent sailors. Their influence spread well beyond the mainland of Greece and its surrounding islands to many of the other Mediterranean countries, particularly the eastern ones. This is reflected in the legends, many of which mention voyages to other lands. Greece itself, though one country overall, was divided into many city-states, each with its own king and queen and ruling families. The city-states sometimes combined in a common cause, as many did in the war against Troy, and in the long siege of the city. At other times there was often intense rivalry between different states or, at the very least, a great sense of independence. Many states were separated from their neighbors by high mountain ranges, which made communication far from easy.

The isolation of one state from another was one reason why the stories the people told of the gods and mortals varied from place to place. They were not written down until long afterwards, but were passed from one generation to another by word of mouth. Each storyteller gave his own version, perhaps elaborating on it if he had the imagination to do so. Gradually one part of the country would accept a particular account, but it might differ greatly from the story established in another place. Few people traveled far enough around the country to compare the different versions. It was not until between 600 and 700 years before the birth of Christ, and about 400 years after Troy had fallen, that the poet Homer and a few other Greek writers collected the stories together. Homer wrote two great narrative poems about the old heroes, the *Iliad*, which tells the story of the siege of Troy, and the *Odyssey*, which is the story of Odysseus's journey home after the war.

In the folk legends of most countries there is some element of truth, and this is probably true of Greece also. Archaeologists have unearthed many objects that seem to have a link with some of the tales. Perhaps the most famous example of this occurred in the case of the German businessman Heinrich Schliemann. As a boy, his favorite stories were the old legends of Greece. He believed very strongly that many of them were based on fact. When he grew up he went into business so that he could make enough money to realize the dream that had always been at the forefront of his mind—to find the ancient city of Troy. He was middle-aged by the time he actually started excavating at what he believed to be the right place, but he had spent the years studying the texts of the stories in great detail. By following every clue he could find in them he did indeed find the site of Troy—much to the amazement of the professional archaeologists of the time, who had ridiculed his theories. In fact, through lack of training and skilled help, he dug right through the Troy described in the works of Homer and found underneath the remains of an even older city. Later, among other discoveries, he unearthed the old city of Mycenae, home of the Greek king Agamemnon, following clues from the legends in the same way.

Like many early peoples, the Greeks did not believe in only one god. They had many gods and goddesses, some of which they associated with the great forces of nature or with human emotions. Thus Poseidon was the god of the sea and Aphrodite the goddess of love. Before a battle the Greeks would ask Ares, god of war, for his help. Other gods and goddesses were chosen to represent practical and leisure activities: Hestia was the goddess of the home, Demeter the goddess of harvests, Apollo the god of music and Athene the goddess of the arts, especially spinning and weaving, and of wisdom. Some gods were given a number of attributes: Apollo, for instance, was responsible not only for music, but for archery, medicine, and prophecy. Oracles, special shrines where priests and priestesses interpreted the messages of the gods, were found in many places, the most famous being the oracle of Apollo at Delphi. Both gods and goddesses

were adopted as patrons of a particular city or state, as Athene was for Athens. Over all the gods ruled Zeus and his wife Hera, who watched everything that happened from the heights of Mount Olympus—a mountain in northern Greece.

In time, perhaps because the ancient Greeks wished to feel that the gods they worshiped were not too remote from themselves, the gods were described in the legends as mixing freely with mortals in their adventures. However, there were strict rules as to what mortals might or might not do. For example, they could never be allowed to challenge a god's supremacy; the few who tried to do so usually regretted it, for the gods were jealous and vengeful. ∎

✔ Enter your reading time below. Then look up your reading speed on the Words-per-Minute table on page 163.
Reading Time _____
Reading Speed _____
Enter your reading speed on the Reading Speed graph on page 164.

Comprehension

Put an **X** in the box next to the correct answer for each question or statement. Do not look back at the selection.

1. The ancient Greeks were excellent
   - ☐ a. farmers.
   - ☐ b. sailors.
   - ☐ c. archaeologists.
   - ☐ d. gladiators.

2. The country of Greece was divided into
   - ☐ a. several small empires.
   - ☐ b. different time zones.
   - ☐ c. many city-states.
   - ☐ d. different geographical regions.

3. Greek writers did not begin to collect and write down the stories people told about the gods and mortals until
   - [ ] a. 400 years before the fall of Troy.
   - [ ] b. 400 to 500 years before the birth of Christ.
   - [ ] c. 500 to 600 years before the birth of Christ.
   - [ ] d. 600 to 700 years before the birth of Christ.

4. Why was communication so difficult between the Greek peoples in different parts of Greece?
   - [ ] a. They did not have a common language.
   - [ ] b. High mountain ranges separated them.
   - [ ] c. Bitter rivalries kept them apart.
   - [ ] d. They had no desire to communicate with each other.

5. Who is the author of the great narrative poems the *Iliad* and the *Odyssey*?
   - [ ] a. Odysseus
   - [ ] b. Demeter
   - [ ] c. Oracles
   - [ ] d. Homer

6. The *Iliad* tells the story of
   - [ ] a. the discovery of the ancient city of Mycenae.
   - [ ] b. the siege of the city of Troy.
   - [ ] c. Odysseus's journey home from Troy.
   - [ ] d. the reign of the Greek king Agamemnon.

7. What dream had always been in the forefront of Heinrich Schliemann's mind?
   - [ ] a. to find the ancient city of Troy
   - [ ] b. to find the ancient city of Mycenae
   - [ ] c. to find the tomb of King Agamemnon
   - [ ] d. to collect and then publish a book of his favorite Greek legends

8. Heinrich Schliemann was
   - [ ] a. Greek.
   - [ ] b. Italian.
   - [ ] c. German.
   - [ ] d. Trojan.

9. Who ruled over of all the gods and goddesses?
   - [ ] a. Ares and Hera
   - [ ] b. Zeus and Athene
   - [ ] c. Zeus and Hera
   - [ ] d. Apollo and Aphrodite

10. From where did the rulers of all the gods and goddesses watch over everything?
   - [ ] a. Delphi
   - [ ] b. Mt. Olympus
   - [ ] c. Athens
   - [ ] d. Mycenae

✎ _____ **Number of correct answers**
Enter this number on the Comprehension graph on page 165.

Critical Thinking

Put an **X** in the box next to the best answer for each question or statement. You may look back at the selection if you'd like.

1. The author's main purpose in writing this selection was to
   - [ ] a. compare the Greece of today with ancient Greece.
   - [ ] b. inform you how the division of Greece into city-states influenced its history.
   - [ ] c. explain how the land, culture, and historical circumstances of Greece combined to shape the Greek folk legends.
   - [ ] d. inform you that Heinrich Schliemann made some of the most important finds in archaeological history despite not having any training as an archaeologist.

2. Which of the following best describes what folk legends are?
- [ ] a. made-up stories that teach a useful lesson
- [ ] b. made-up stories about heroes, based in some part on truth
- [ ] c. made-up stories, often involving gods and goddesses, and usually explaining some happening of nature
- [ ] d. made-up stories so full of exaggerations no one could believe them

3. Based on the information in this selection, you can conclude that the ancient Greeks were
- [ ] a. religious.
- [ ] b. uneducated.
- [ ] c. peaceful.
- [ ] d. landlocked.

4. Which of the following events happened first?
- [ ] a. Homer wrote the great narrative poems the *Iliad* and the *Odyssey*.
- [ ] b. Christ was born.
- [ ] c. Heinrich Schliemann found the remains of the city of Mycenae.
- [ ] d. The city of Troy was defeated.

5. The stories told by the Greeks of their gods and mortals varied from one city-state to another. This was mainly caused by
- [ ] a. a lack of communication between the states.
- [ ] b. jealousy between the states.
- [ ] c. a desire by each state to have its own version.
- [ ] d. continual wars between the states.

6. Which of the following is a statement of opinion rather than fact?
- [ ] a. In ancient times, particularly on the higher ground, the country was much more wooded and less barren than it is today.
- [ ] b. In the folk legends of most countries there is some element of truth, and this is probably true of Greece also.
- [ ] c. Like many early peoples, the Greeks did not believe in only one god.
- [ ] d. Later, amongst other discoveries, he [Heinrich Schliemann] unearthed the old city of Mycenae.

7. How were the Greeks able to spread their influence beyond the mainland of Greece?
- [ ] a. The Greeks were excellent sailors who often sailed to faraway places.
- [ ] b. Greek armies conquered many distant lands.
- [ ] c. People from distant lands came to Greece to be educated.
- [ ] d. The Greeks sent missionaries to foreign lands.

8. Before Heinrich Schliemann made his famous discoveries, professional archaeologists of the time ridiculed his theories because
- [ ] a. he did not seek their advice.
- [ ] b. they resented his interference in their field of study.
- [ ] c. he had no formal training as an archaeologist.
- [ ] d. he was not a Greek.

9. Which of the following does *not* fit with the other three?
- [ ] a. Ares
- [ ] b. Poseidon
- [ ] c. Homer
- [ ] d. Apollo

10. In which of the following ways was ancient Greece different from the Greece of today?
- ☐ a. It had many natural harbors.
- ☐ b. It had mountain ranges.
- ☐ c. It had high cliffs along its jagged coastline.
- ☐ d. It had plentiful woods and forests.

✎ _____ Number of correct answers
Enter this number on the Critical Thinking graph on page 166.

Vocabulary

Each numbered sentence contains an underlined word from the selection. Following are four definitions. Put an ✗ in the box next to the best meaning of the word as it is used in the sentence.

1. Greece is a land of many contrasts.
- ☐ a. similarities
- ☐ b. unusual features
- ☐ c. great differences
- ☐ d. changes

2. The rocks, never far below the surface, were exposed and in the scanty soil left in the cracks only the toughest grasses could survive.
- ☐ a. insufficient
- ☐ b. plentiful
- ☐ c. rich
- ☐ d. poor

3. The city-states sometimes combined in a common cause, as many did in the war against Troy, and in the long siege of the city.
- ☐ a. period of peace
- ☐ b. period of hardship
- ☐ c. arguments
- ☐ d. long-continued attack

4. Each storyteller gave his own version, perhaps elaborating on it if he had the imagination to do so.
- ☐ a. commenting
- ☐ b. pausing
- ☐ c. adding details
- ☐ d. shortening up

5. In the folk legends of most countries there is some element of truth.
- ☐ a. claim
- ☐ b. part
- ☐ c. denial
- ☐ d. admission

6. He did indeed find the site of Troy—much to the amazement of the professional archaeologists of the time who had ridiculed his theories.
- ☐ a. remembered
- ☐ b. disagreed with
- ☐ c. made fun of
- ☐ d. misunderstood

7. Some gods were given a number of attributes: Apollo for instance, was responsible not only for music, but for archery, medicine, and prophecy.
- ☐ a. things appropriate to
- ☐ b. things to choose from
- ☐ c. characteristics
- ☐ d. opportunities

8. Oracles, special shrines where priests and priestesses interpreted the messages of gods, were found in many places.
- ☐ a. responded to
- ☐ b. listened to
- ☐ c. explained the meaning of
- ☐ d. wrote down

9. Both gods and goddesses were adopted as <u>patrons</u> of a particular city or state.
   - ☐ a. rulers
   - ☐ b. citizens
   - ☐ c. protectors
   - ☐ d. customers

10. The ancient Greeks wished to feel that the gods they worshiped were not too <u>remote</u> from themselves.
    - ☐ a. unreal
    - ☐ b. distant
    - ☐ c. unknown
    - ☐ d. close

✎ _____ Number of correct answers
Enter this number on the Vocabulary graph on page 167.

Personal Response

The most interesting part of the selection was

_____

_____

_____

One question that I have about this selection is

_____

_____

✔ Check Your Progress
Study the graphs you completed for lessons 21–30 and answer the How Am I Doing? questions on page 170.

Words per Minute: Lessons 1–15

Lesson	Sample	1	2	3	4	5	6	7	8	9	10	11	12	13	14	15
No. of Words	950	1005	725	1045	1025	1050	1050	1050	1110	1035	1150	1071	1060	1050	1060	975
1:30	633	670	483	697	683	700	700	700	740	690	767	714	707	700	707	650
1:40	493	603	435	627	615	630	630	630	666	621	690	643	636	630	636	585
1:50	448	548	395	570	559	573	573	573	605	565	627	584	578	573	578	532
2:00	411	503	363	523	513	525	525	525	555	518	575	536	530	525	530	488
2:10	379	464	335	482	473	485	485	485	512	478	531	494	489	485	489	450
2:20	352	431	311	448	439	450	450	450	476	444	493	459	454	450	454	418
2:30	328	402	290	418	410	420	420	420	444	414	460	428	424	420	424	390
2:40	308	377	272	392	384	394	394	394	416	388	431	402	398	394	398	366
2:50	290	355	256	369	362	371	371	371	392	365	406	378	374	371	374	344
3:00	274	335	242	348	342	350	350	350	370	345	383	357	353	350	353	325
3:10	259	317	229	330	324	332	332	332	351	327	363	338	335	332	335	308
3:20	246	302	218	314	308	315	315	315	333	311	345	321	318	315	318	293
3:30	235	287	207	299	293	300	300	300	317	296	329	306	303	300	303	279
3:40	224	274	198	285	280	286	286	286	303	282	314	292	289	286	289	266
3:50	214	262	189	273	267	274	274	274	290	270	300	279	277	274	277	254
4:00	205	251	181	261	256	263	263	263	278	259	288	268	265	263	265	244
4:10	197	241	174	251	246	252	252	252	266	248	276	257	254	252	254	234
4:20	189	232	167	241	237	242	242	242	256	239	265	247	245	242	245	225
4:30	182	223	161	232	228	233	233	233	247	230	256	238	236	233	236	217
4:40	176	215	155	224	220	225	225	225	238	222	246	230	227	225	227	209
4:50	170	208	150	216	212	217	217	217	230	214	238	222	219	217	219	202
5:00	164	201	145	209	205	210	210	210	222	207	230	214	212	210	212	195
5:10	159	195	140	202	198	203	203	203	215	200	223	207	205	203	205	189
5:20	154	188	136	196	192	197	197	197	208	194	216	201	199	197	199	183
5:30	149	183	132	190	186	191	191	191	202	188	209	195	193	191	193	177
5:40	145	177	128	184	181	185	185	185	196	183	203	189	187	185	187	172
5:50	141	172	124	179	176	180	180	180	190	177	197	184	182	180	182	167
6:00	137	168	121	174	171	175	175	175	185	173	192	179	177	175	177	163
6:10	133	163	118	169	166	170	170	170	180	168	186	174	172	170	172	158
6:20	130	159	114	165	162	166	166	166	175	163	182	169	167	166	167	154
6:30	126	155	112	161	158	162	162	162	171	159	177	165	163	162	163	150
6:40	123	151	109	157	154	158	158	158	167	155	173	161	159	158	159	146
6:50	120	147	106	153	150	154	154	154	162	151	168	157	155	154	155	143
7:00	117	144	104	149	146	150	150	150	159	148	164	153	151	150	151	139
7:10	115	140	101	146	143	147	147	147	155	144	160	149	148	147	148	136
7:20	112	137	99	143	140	143	143	143	151	141	157	146	145	143	145	133
7:30	109	134	97	139	137	140	140	140	148	138	153	143	141	140	141	130
7:40	107	131	95	136	134	137	137	137	145	135	150	140	138	137	138	127
7:50	105	128	93	133	131	134	134	134	142	132	147	137	135	134	135	124
8:00	103	126	91	131	128	131	131	131	139	129	144	134	133	131	133	122

Minutes and Seconds

Words per Minute: Lessons 16—30

Lesson	16	17	18	19	20	21	22	23	24	25	26	27	28	29	30
No. of Words	960	1220	990	1045	1105	1140	1080	1025	1050	1090	1055	1040	1040	1050	1150
1:30	640	813	660	697	737	760	720	683	700	727	703	693	693	700	767
1:40	576	732	594	627	663	684	648	615	630	654	633	624	624	630	690
1:50	524	665	540	570	603	622	589	559	573	595	575	567	567	573	627
2:00	480	610	495	523	553	570	540	513	525	545	528	520	520	525	575
2:10	443	563	457	482	510	526	498	473	485	503	487	480	480	485	531
2:20	411	523	424	448	474	489	463	439	450	467	452	446	446	450	493
2:30	384	488	396	418	442	456	432	410	420	436	422	416	416	420	460
2:40	360	458	371	392	414	428	405	384	394	409	396	390	390	394	431
2:50	339	431	349	369	390	402	381	362	371	385	372	367	367	371	406
3:00	320	407	330	348	368	380	360	342	350	363	352	347	347	350	383
3:10	303	385	313	330	349	360	341	324	332	344	333	328	328	332	363
3:20	288	366	297	314	332	342	324	308	315	327	317	312	312	315	345
3:30	274	349	283	299	316	326	309	293	300	311	301	297	297	300	329
3:40	262	333	270	285	301	311	295	280	286	297	288	284	284	286	314
3:50	250	318	258	273	288	297	282	267	274	284	275	271	271	274	300
4:00	240	305	248	261	276	285	270	256	263	273	264	260	260	263	288
4:10	230	293	238	251	265	274	259	246	252	262	253	250	250	252	276
4:20	222	282	228	241	255	263	249	237	242	252	243	240	240	242	265
4:30	213	271	220	232	246	253	240	228	233	242	234	231	231	233	256
4:40	206	261	212	224	237	244	231	220	225	234	226	223	223	225	246
4:50	199	252	205	216	229	236	223	212	217	226	218	215	215	217	238
5:00	192	244	198	209	221	228	216	205	210	218	211	208	208	210	230
5:10	186	236	192	202	214	221	209	198	203	211	204	201	201	203	223
5:20	180	229	186	196	207	214	203	192	197	204	198	195	195	197	216
5:30	175	222	180	190	201	207	196	186	191	198	192	189	189	191	209
5:40	169	215	175	184	195	201	191	181	185	192	186	184	184	185	203
5:50	165	209	170	179	189	195	185	176	180	187	181	178	178	180	197
6:00	160	203	165	174	184	190	180	171	175	182	176	173	173	175	192
6:10	156	198	161	169	179	185	175	166	170	177	171	169	169	170	186
6:20	152	193	156	165	174	180	171	162	166	172	167	164	164	166	182
6:30	148	188	152	161	170	175	166	158	162	168	162	160	160	162	177
6:40	144	183	149	157	166	171	162	154	158	164	158	156	156	158	173
6:50	140	179	145	153	162	167	158	150	154	160	154	152	152	154	168
7:00	137	174	141	149	158	163	154	146	150	156	151	149	149	150	164
7:10	134	170	138	146	154	159	151	143	147	152	147	145	145	147	160
7:20	131	166	135	143	151	155	147	140	143	149	144	142	142	143	157
7:30	128	163	132	139	147	152	144	137	140	145	141	139	139	140	153
7:40	125	159	129	136	144	149	141	134	137	142	138	136	136	134	150
7:50	123	156	126	133	141	146	138	131	134	139	135	133	133	134	147
8:00	120	153	124	131	138	143	135	128	131	136	132	130	130	131	144

Minutes and Seconds

164

Reading Speed

Directions. Use the graph below to show your reading speed improvement.

First, along the top of the graph, find the lesson number of the selection you just read. Then put a small X on the line directly below the number of the lesson and across from the number of words per minute you read.

As you mark your speed for each lesson, graph your progress by drawing a line to connect the X's. This will help you see right away if your reading speed is going up as it should be. If the line connecting the X's is not going up, see your teacher for advice.

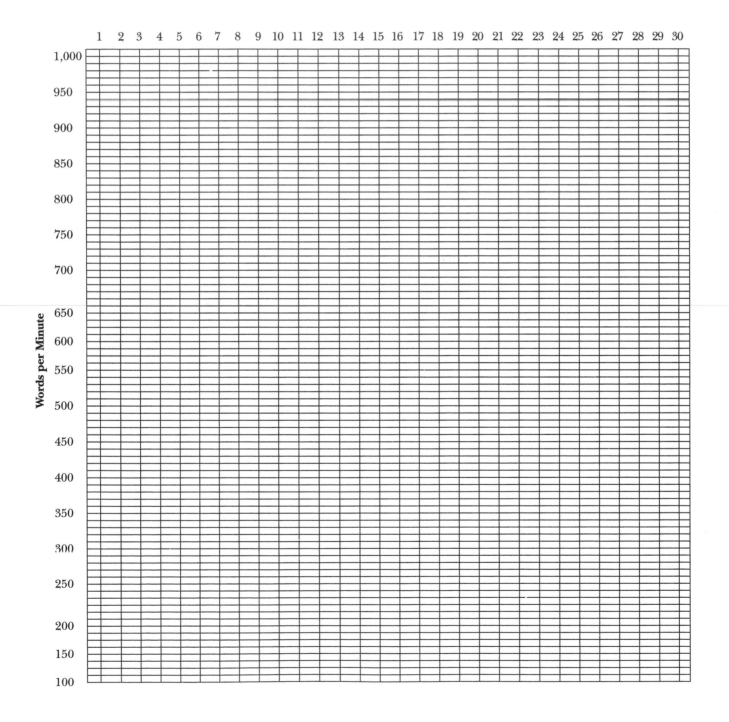

Comprehension

Directions. Use the graph below to show your comprehension scores.

First, along the top of the graph, find the lesson number of the selection you just read. Then put a small X on the line directly below the number of the lesson and across from the score you earned.

As you mark your score for each lesson, graph your progress by drawing a line to connect the X's. This will help you see right away if your comprehension scores are going up or down. If your scores are below 75%, or if they are going down, see your teacher. Try to keep your scores at 75% or above while you continue to build your reading speed.

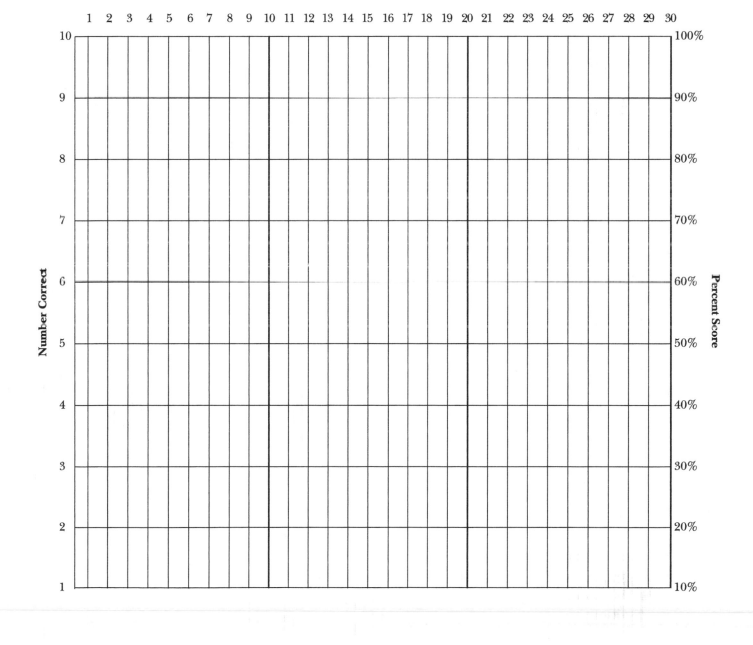

Critical Thinking

Directions. Use the graph below to show your critical thinking scores.

First, along the top of the graph, find the lesson number of the selection you just read. Then put a small X on the line directly below the number of the lesson and across from the score you earned.

As you mark your score for each lesson, graph your progress by drawing a line to connect the X's. This will help you see right away if your critical thinking scores are going up or down. If your scores are below 75%, or if they are going down, see your teacher. Try to keep your scores at 75% or above as you continue to build your reading speed.

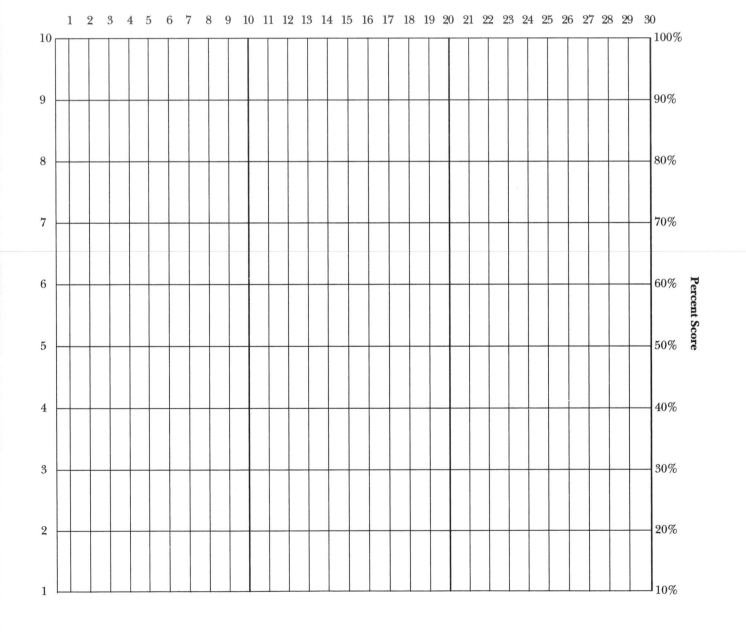

Vocabulary

Directions. Use the graph below to show your vocabulary scores.

First, along the top of the graph, find the lesson number of the selection you just read. Then put a small X on the line directly below the number of the lesson and across from the score you earned.

As you mark your score for each lesson, graph your progress by drawing a line to connect the X's. This will help you see right away if your vocabulary scores are going up or down. If your scores are not going up, see your teacher for advice. Vocabulary scores of 75% are good, but try to earn scores of 88% and 100% when you can.

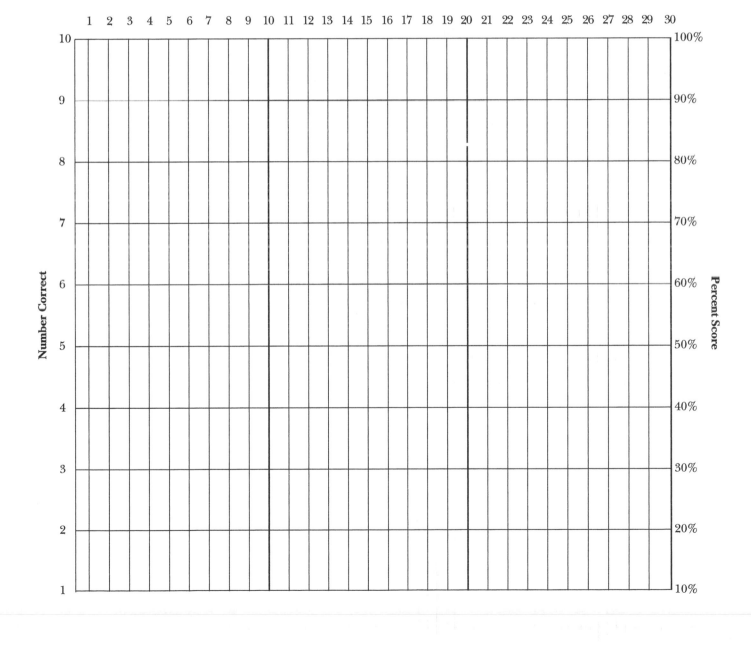

How Am I Doing?

Lessons 1–10

1. Which lesson did you do best on and why?

_____

_____

_____

_____

2. Which lesson was most confusing and why?

_____

_____

_____

_____

3. What skills or strategies will you use to improve your reading comprehension scores in the following lessons?

_____

_____

_____

_____

4. How can you improve your reading speed in the following lessons?

_____

_____

_____

5. Overall, which exercises were the most difficult for you? What can you do to improve your scores on those exercises in lessons 11–20?

_____

_____

_____

How Am I Doing?

Lessons 11—20

1. How does your reading speed for nonfiction selections compare with your reading speed for fiction? Explain.

   _____

   _____

   _____

   _____

2. When you read faster, do your comprehension scores go up or down? What do you think may be happening?

   _____

   _____

   _____

   _____

3. What do you find most difficult about the vocabulary exercises? What is easiest?

   _____

   _____

   _____

   _____

4. Which type of exercises are still difficult for you—comprehension, critical thinking, or vocabulary? Why?

   _____

   _____

   _____

5. What have you improved upon the most at this point in the lessons?

   _____

   _____

   _____

How Am I Doing?

Lessons 21—36

1. Did your reading speed increase as you completed the lessons in this book? Explain why you think it did or did not.

_____

_____

_____

_____

2. Can you think of ways you can transfer what you have learned in this book about reading comprehension and speed to your everyday reading? Explain.

_____

_____

_____

_____

3. Overall, what was most difficult about the lessons in this book? What was easiest? Explain both answers.

_____

_____

_____

_____

_____

4. In which area—reading, speed, comprehension, critical thinking, or vocabulary—do you feel most confident? Explain.

_____

_____

_____

_____

_____